Social Science Research and Decision-Making

SOCIAL SCIENCE RESEARCH
and
DECISION-MAKING

Carol H. Weiss

with

Michael J. Bucuvalas

Columbia University Press
New York   1980

Library of Congress Cataloging in Publication Data

Weiss, Carol H
Social science research and decision-making.

Bibliography: p.
Includes index.
1. Social science research.   2. Policy
sciences.   3. Public administration—Decision
making.   I. Bucuvalas, Michael J., joint author.
II. Title.
H62.W3965   300′.7′2   80-12840
ISBN 0-231-04676-8

Columbia University Press
New York   Guildford, Surrey

For Janet A. Weiss,
colleague and friend

CONTENTS

TABLES AND FIGURES

PREFACE

THIS IS A BOOK about the usefulness of social science research to people in positions of authority. It grapples with questions about the kinds of social science research studies that are attended to, who finds them useful, and how they are used. Most of the book reports the results of a study conducted with federal, state, and local officials in mental health agencies, and with social science researchers and members of research review committees in the mental health field. Through the views of holders of these different strategic positions, we come to understand much about the use and usefulness of social science research for decision-making.

Chapter 1 reviews the literature on the relationship between research and policy. Although we do not take for granted that the major issue in this area is how to *increase* the use of research, much of the discussion has heretofore revolved around problems and obstacles to use, and this chapter sets forth a series of explanations that observers have offered about the reasons why research has had little observable effect on policy and program. Chapter 2 presents a framework for empirical study of the issues. It describes why we designed the study we did, how and why we chose the site, the variables we decided to focus on and how we operationalized them, and the choice we made to ground the inquiry in concrete research studies. Chapter 3 describes the conduct of the investigation in some detail. For those readers who are neither interested in field work nor concerned with replicating or adapting our research strategy, this chapter is a good candidate for skimming.

Chapter 4 describes the theoretical orientation with which we began the study and our specific hypotheses. It then presents an analysis of the factors that respondents used to describe the social science studies that we gave them to assess—factors that were congruent with some of the original hypotheses but that led to revision of others.

Chapter 5 is the meat of the analysis. It presents the characteristics of social science research studies that were related to decision makers' judgments of the usefulness of studies. Some of the results were sufficiently unexpected to make us recast our understanding of the situation, and we take you along on that intellectual hegira. We present a formulation of "truth tests" and "utility tests" that sums up decision makers' responses to the research studies that they assessed.

Chapter 6 presents respondents' reports of who the most appropriate users for the studies would be. Chapter 7 looks at characteristics of decision makers and how they affect the ratings of research usefulness. It aims to specify the characteristics of the "user" that are important. Statistically the most technical of the chapters, it is summarized in the last few pages. The subject of chapter 8 is the phases of the decision-making cycle that are served by social science research.

Chapter 9 discusses how decision makers have used research in the past. This chapter, based on respondents' narrative reports, calls for dramatic reformulation of the concept of "using" research. It not only leads to new understandings of how research permeates arenas of action; it also raises serious questions about the models of decision-making in common use.

Chapter 10 compares respondents' reports of their criteria for useful research with the criteria they actually used in judging the usefulness of particular studies. It contrasts espoused criteria with criteria-in-action. Chapter 11 presents the perceptions of social science researchers about their own research—the extent to which they intend to make it useful and what they do. It also gives their views of decision makers' responses to social science research. Chapter 12 is a report on members of mental health research review committees—their criteria and their committees' criteria for approving research proposals. They, too, indicate their perceptions of how decision makers react to research studies. Chapter 13 presents opinion data from decision makers, researchers, and review committee members about obstacles to the use of social science research in decision-making.

Chapter 14 is a summary of the major conclusions of the investigation. It ends with a set of suggestions for further research, in effect staking out a new subfield of inquiry.

A number of people made important contributions to the study and to the intellectual odyssey it represents. Laurie Bauman was in at the beginning while I was struggling to cast the issues in researchable terms, and she discussed, argued, and thought with me throughout the development of the research plan. Once the study began, she took charge of the fieldwork with her usual thoroughness and skill and contributed importantly to the coding, processing, and interpretation of the data. Michael Bucuvalas, who came on the project as data analyst, brought a high level of statistical skill to the study. He found creative ways to analyze the data, and the analysis presented here is largely his doing. His participation in all phases of the study was critical to the understandings we arrived at. Thelma Anderson, who assisted with interviewer training, also handled the difficult tasks of interviewer assignment and reassignment without losing either her good humor or the respondent count. Sara Tollstrup was much more than project secretary. Beyond the chores of typing, filing, and bibliographic search, she became an expert in data coding and helped to identify significant themes in respondents' accounts. Janet Weiss, who worked with all of us in developing and pretesting the interview during the first summer of the investigation, went off to other things, but she maintained contact with the unfolding ideas of the project throughout the successive drafts of the book. Her insightful comments added significantly to its ideas and to the clarity of their presentation. Allen Barton was a continuing source of valuable advice. Many people—Amitai Etzioni, W. Phillips Davison, Jack Elinson, John Colombotos, Irving Lukoff, Harold Watts, David K. Cohen, Howard Davis, Nathan Caplan, Eleanor Singer, and others—said things that stirred us to further thought. Gail Keeley typed the final manuscript and conscientiously organized, checked, and updated the bibliography.

For support of the research reported here, I would also like to thank the National Institute of Mental Health, the Mental Health Services Research Review Committee, and the NIMH project officers, Howard Davis and Susan Salasin. Whatever complaints other people may have about research review committees and research program managers (see chapter 13), my experience has been uniformly excellent.

All of us who participated in the investigation learned much from it. Subjecting what seem like logical and cogent ideas to the crucible of empirical test is—whatever else—a bracing experience. Perhaps the most important lesson we learned, one we try to communicate in this book, is that most earlier discussions of "the utilization of research in decision-making" founder on conceptual ambiguities in all three terms—utilization, research, and decision-making. Each of the concepts is more complex than most of us imagine. Until we forgo the easy terminology (and the simplistic imagery that underlies it) and develop a realistic conceptual vocabulary to capture the multifaceted reality these concepts encompass, we will make little headway in understanding when and how research affects the development of policy. It is toward the achievement of that understanding that we dedicate the book. We hope that it contributes to the enterprise of making sense of the obscure and knotty relationships between social science and public policy.

Cambridge, Massachusetts   Carol H. Weiss
August 1979

Social Science Research and Decision-Making

Chapter One
DEFINITIONS
OF THE PROBLEM

THE SUBJECT OF THIS BOOK is the relationship of social science research to the choices and decisions of government officials and agency managers. Our aim is to understand decision makers' responses to research studies on topics relevant to their work, the conditions under which they find research useful, and if, when, and how they apply the lessons from research to the work they do.

Much of the prior discussion about "research utilization" has been conducted at the normative level. The significant questions were assumed to revolve around ways of *increasing* the use of social science research in governmental bodies. Our intent is empirical. We want to understand when and how research has an influence. Nor do we assume that *more* use of research is necessarily better. Reliance on research can have many consequences, good and bad. For example, one effect can be to increase the centralization of power at the levels where research is used (Straussman 1978); another may be to divert attention away from key issues in a policy debate with which research can not cope, and toward peripheral issues with which it can (Aaron 1978:32). Even more detrimental would be the grounding of policy in social science research that turns out to be inadequate, incomplete, or wrong. We try to make no assumptions about the virtue of attending to the results of research (although it is difficult to excise all biases). We concentrate on learning what the conditions are that foster or inhibit attention to social science research by occupants of decision-making positions.

Most of the book is devoted to the report of a study that we conducted with decision makers and social scientists in the field

1

of mental health. There are both "applied" and "basic" themes in this inquiry. From an applied perspective, we aimed to find out how decision makers perceive the work of social scientists and what criteria they use in assessing its usefulness. If they know the factors that govern officials' acceptance of research, investigators who want to increase the influence of their studies can fashion them in ways calculated to meet prevailing expectations. Even basic research, undertaken on purely disciplinary grounds, may influence official thought and action, and an understanding of the conditions under which research is heeded can help social scientists recognize the potential scope and inherent limits of its influence.

But there are grounds for investigating the intersection of social science research and decision-making as a subject in its own right. Information is a key input into the making of policy, and social science has become a major supplier of information. Discovering the extent to which the evidence and analyses it supplies compete successfully with other sources of information and contribute to the shaping of policy will enable us to know more about the bases on which policy is made. And social science supplies more than data, it also supplies perspectives on events, generalizations about cause and effect, theories about the ways in which people and institutions interact, constructions of the nature of social, political, and economic systems. To the extent that these permeate the understanding and underlie the choices of those in positions of authority, they can substantially influence not only discrete decisions but the whole framework within which issues are defined and policy responses considered. On the other hand, if decision makers reject most of what social science has to offer, there may be grounds for analyzing the world in which social science functions—its organization, its norms, the way it chooses its research problems and communicates its results—whatever factors interfere with its influence on practical affairs.

Many social scientists consciously reject the role of "technician for the state" and choose to be social critics, "unattached intellectuals" without commitments to any group or social stratum, or advocates for underrepresented groups in the society. They do not look upon government as their natural audience but choose to stand outside and raise fundamental questions about the assumptions and operations of the current order. Nevertheless, even the most wide-ranging critics expect their work to have some influence on human events (Rule 1979), and it is a matter of no little interest whether—and through what channels—such influence is exerted.

Other social scientists who lay equal claim to the role of critic look upon government agencies as potential allies. They do not necessarily accept the constraints of existing policy and practice as the parameters for their research, but they expect that even basically critical research can influence officials—at least some officials—who are committed to effective social action. In human service fields particularly, they see the people who manage the programs and staff the services as potentially receptive to research results that suggest more effective ways to accomplish their missions of human betterment.

Whether and to what extent such expectations are justified is the subject of our inquiry. Past experience suggests that social science and public decision-making are distinctly different systems, governed by different structures of incentive and reward. At best they seem to achieve an uneasy fit. Systematic study can help to illumine the factors that shape them and the dynamics of their interaction. When we understand the forces to which they respond, we can reach a clearer and more realistic view of the circumstances under which social science research contributes to the making of policy.[1] Our inquiry marks a modest start toward that end.

The Current Enigma

Our starting point is the general contention that social science research is largely ignored by government officials as a basis for decisions. Observers in government and out find few instances in which research conclusions visibly affect the course of policy. In fact, there is a sizable literature that, with minor differences in shading and emotional overtone, echoes the words of a disillusioned participant in the enterprise of conveying social science research to government decision makers:

The first and most important observation I derive from these experiences is that only rarely have I witnessed serious governmental attention being given to serious social science research. (Wilson 1978:82)

Yet at the same time governments, particularly the federal government of the United States, spend substantial sums of money to support social science research. The federal government not only provides funding for basic research, but it also actively solicits and supports a wide range of social science studies that are expected to help improve government activities. There is an avowed and explicit intent to use research results to inform action. Thus, for example, the Elementary and Secondary Education Act of 1965 authorized cooperative research in education specifically to enable the Office of Education more effectively to accomplish the purposes and perform the duties for which it was originally established (PL 89-10, sec. 401). With the few exceptions in which advancement of basic social science knowledge is itself the stated objective, government support of social science research is predicated on the assumption that research will aid in improving policy and advancing the achievement of agency missions.

The discontinuity between government commitment to social science research, as evidenced by the expenditure of money and the surrounding rhetoric, and its neglect of the results that social science research produces, presents a paradox. This chapter reviews the record of commitment and neglect in an effort to establish the parameters of the problem. Next it summarizes an array of factors that have been offered as explanations for government inattention to research, factors that involve the nature of research, the nature of agency decision-making, and the frail communications that link the two. Finally, it outlines an emergent field of study, "the sociology of knowledge application," that would address the issues that arise at the intersection of social science and agency action. It is to this field of inquiry that our study belongs.

Purported Commitment and
Alleged Neglect

According to the latest and most thorough effort to determine the extent of federal funding for social science research (NAS 1978), the government spent $1.2 billion dollars in 1976 for knowledge production on social problems and another $600 million for dissemination and research application. The figure for knowledge production includes what the National Academy classifies as basic, applied, and policy research, policy formulation demonstrations (e.g., social experiments), program evaluation, and general purpose statistics. Over \$650 million was for research alone, with the Department of Health, Education, and Welfare (HEW) accounting for almost \$250 million of the research total. By including agencies and activities that the annual survey of federal research support by the National Science Foundation (NSF) omits, the National Academy reported expenditures considerably higher than the approximately \$500 million for research and development in the social sciences and psychology reported by NSF (NSF 1978). The resulting figure is a tidy sum. If we were to add in the amounts spent by state and local governments, especially if the costs of internal data collection and analysis were included, it would be tidier still.

Furthermore, the Congress is increasingly writing requirements for research and evaluation into programmatic legislation and allocating money for their support. Percentages of program funds are set aside for systematic data collection and analysis, as in the Health Revenue Sharing and Health Services Act of 1975 which mandates that at least 2 percent of the federal operating grants to Community Mental Health Centers shall be used for evaluations of their programs. The intent is not only to help the Centers improve their programs but also to "provide recommendations on improving services to HEW and to Congress" (U.S. House of Representatives 1975).

Yet with all the money going out and the high hopes expressed for improvement in policy and program, dissatisfaction abounds. The limited impact of social science research on government decisions and agency practice has been attested to by a series of blue-ribbon commissions (NRC 1968; NRC 1969; NSF 1969; NRC 1971; NRC 1976) and at extensive hearings on "the use of social research in federal domestic programs" held by the Committee on Government Operations of the House of Representatives (U.S. Congress 1967). Other observers have added to the steady stream of discontent about what Lyons (1969) called "the uneasy partnership" between social science and government (for example, Orlans 1968, 1973; Cowhig 1971; Horowitz 1971; Williams 1971; Chinitz 1972; Roberts 1974). Lynn's (1978b) title betokens no progress; it terms the link between knowledge and policy "the uncertain connection."

Neither the topic nor the posture of concern is new. Since

at least the Progressive Era, American reformers have had faith in the power of social science research to further their causes, and there have been intermittent episodes of disillusionment whenever it failed to move public bodies to action. Triggered by the Great Depression and the international crises of the 1930s, sociologist Robert S. Lynd published the classic *Knowledge for What?* in 1939, urging his colleagues to become more responsive to social needs. There has been much similar advice to social scientists before and since, and much counsel to government officials to heed the wisdom that social scientists can offer.[2]

The level of current dissatisfaction with the social science-government nexus is not only high, it has a special poignancy. In the early and middle 1960s, at the time of the Great Society programs, it seemed for a time that the partnership had become easy, the connection certain, and the effect synergistic. Not only was government support leading to advances in the social sciences, but social science was contributing to the development and enactment of government programs—Medicare, federal aid to education, equal employment opportunity, Head Start, community organization, urban aid through the Model Cities program, legal services for the poor, community mental health centers, and a host of other programs that were redressing the wrongs of generations' standing. Important program developments were being based on social science research, or at least on social science concepts and values.[3] It appeared that just as economics was taming the business cycle and bringing full employment without inflation, so sociology and psychology were leading to solutions for the nation's social problems.

Then, just about the time that the economic bubble burst and economists were seen to be fallible creatures, news began coming in that many of the vaunted social programs created through social science collaboration were falling far short of expectations. The messengers of bad news were themselves members of the social science community—evaluation researchers. Employed to systematically examine the effectiveness of programs (however underfinanced or overpromised the programs might be), they brought in reports of small victories and major failures.

A certain ambivalence now prevails in Washington agencies about the contributions of social science to programming. Although most agencies retain formal allegiance to support of social science research, to use of social science techniques of policy analysis and program evaluation, and to belief that social science research can aid in controlling local program efforts and making programs accountable, there seems to be a consensus that social science research is not fulfilling the larger expectations held for it.

That government officials give high endorsement to the potentials of social science research is shown repeatedly. Caplan and his colleagues at the University of Michigan Institute for Social Research found that 85 percent of the upper-level federal officials whom they interviewed agreed that "social science knowledge can contribute to the improvement of government policies," and 87 percent believed that "government should make the fullest possible use of social science" (Caplan, Morrison, and Stambaugh 1975:24). At the same time, federal officials often echo the testimony for the House Committee on Government Operations: "The extent to which existing knowledge is utilized in shaping . . . welfare programs leaves a good deal to be desired" (U.S. Congress 1967:265, testimony by Margaret S. Gordon); ". . . total neglect by the Congress of even social research directly called for by the Congress itself" (U.S. Congress 1967:265, testimony by Thomas F. Pettigrew); "existing economic, social, and psychological data is rarely utilized in shaping national and local health programs" (U.S. Congress 1967:402, testimony by Harold M. Visotsky).

More recent citations bring the story up to date:

Social science findings in the past have not been totally unrelated to public issues. But the help they offer is slight in comparison with the magnitude of perceived problems such as poverty, welfare, racial antagonism, and urban deterioration. No systematic social theory and research currently illuminate key national issues on a continuing basis. (Goodwin 1975:vii–viii)

Rich examined uses of the Continuous National Survey, a repeated survey planned by the National Opinion Research Center in close collaboration with federal agencies to meet articulated government information needs. He concludes that it received relatively little use (Rich 1975). Similarly, Caplan and Barton studied uses of *Social Indicators '73* (SI '73), a compendium of up-to-date social indicator data prepared by the Office of Management and Budget (OMB) and extensively circulated to federal officials. Their conclusion is: almost uniform neglect (Caplan and Barton 1976). Despite the fasionability and hoopla attending the "social indicator movement,"

Upper level government officials rarely used SI '73. No more than four per cent of our sample made use of it in connection with their work. . . . The few uses made of SI '73 mainly involved the application of information in ancillary roles, such as for speech writing and background reference purposes. (Caplan and Barton 1976:27)

In 1977, the General Accounting Office (GAO) released a report to the Congress entitled *Social Research and Development of Limited Use to National Policymakers*. The cover page carries a summary, which begins:

Federal social research and development generates information to improve the formulation of social policy and to enhance the effectiveness of agencies' programs. The results of social research and development, however, are generally of limited use to national policymakers. . . . (U.S. General Accounting Office 1977a:cover page)

The report goes on to criticize methods of planning social research and poor dissemination for making research use in policy-making so uncommon.

Nor is the neglect of social research limited to domestic agencies. Of the extensive social research supported by the Department of Defense on actions of governments and revolutionary movements in foreign nations, a close observer writes, "On the whole, for all it taught those involved, the impact of the research on the most important affairs of state was, with few exceptions, nil" (Deitchman 1976:390).

Not all observers are convinced of the nullity of effects. Some of them find evidence that social science research does indeed influence policy, but not always in the direction intended. There are reports that research and evaluation sometimes has perverse consequences.

Even though these evaluation efforts failed to meet the expectations of reformers, they had uses, often indirect and unexpected, within the policy system. Ironically, the impact and function of Title I [of the Elementary and Secondary Education Act] evaluations have been antithetical to the anticipation of reformers. . . . [Evaluations] have been used selectively to support policy positions suggested by political or economic constraints, not by new information. (McLaughlin 1975:ix)

Lampman made a similar point about "the evaluations and cost-effectiveness studies and experiments" of the poverty program and President Nixon's use of them "to support his decision to cut back on certain parts of the poverty program" (Lampman 1974: 74). Others argued that a consequence of increasing reliance on social science research and policy analysis has been "the centralization of power within the executive branch. . . . In short, the politics of knowledge and information use has reinforced the subservience of experts to the president and his White House staff" (Straussman 1978:138).

Aaron's extensive and insightful review of the effects of research in the areas of poverty and discrimination, education and jobs, and unemployment and inflation indicates that research has influenced but not driven the development of policy. He finds striking parallels between

development of social science and the views of scholars, on the one hand, and developments of public policy during this period, on the other. . . . But in many cases, the findings of social science seemed to come after, rather than before, changes in policy, which suggests that political events may influence scholars more than research influences policy. (Aaron 1978:9)

He concludes that both research and policy rest largely on preconceptions and faiths that are beyond the purview of either.

So even among those who perceived that social science research was neither irrelevant nor impotent in the policy arena, satisfaction has been small. The potential of social science research for informing the processes of government, it is widely believed, has not been realized.

Bases for Disappointment: Definition of Use

Before accepting this rush to judgment about the unproductiveness of social science research, we might do well to examine the bases for the assessments. There are two sets of assumptions that appear to enter into these disenchanted judgments, one about the form that research use should take and one about the felicitous outcomes that would result if only research were well and wisely used. Let us look at both these implicit assumptions.

The imagery of research use that undergirds the disillusionment of observers appears to be the direct and immediate application of the results of a social science research study to a particular decision. The expectation is that specific findings point to a specific answer and that responsible policy makers proceed to implement that answer in policy or practice. Research makes a difference, in this formulation, only if it changes a decision from what it would have been had there been no research to one fully in accord with what the research results imply should be done. The "use of research" is thus discernible, clear to the naked eye. Observers are disappointed, and occasionally vitriolic, because they see few phenomena that meet these specifications.

But the switching of a specific decision from one track to another because of the cogency of one research study (or a handful of related studies) is a very restrictive definition of research use. Even observable influence on a decision in the direction of research findings, without the expectation that the research prevail completely over competing positions, calls for extraordinary power. Such definitions identify what program directors in the applied research offices at NSF used to call "nuggets," those occasional gems of direct application that they mined and cherished for their value in proving the utility of their research programs to a hostile Congress. Uses of this type are relatively rare, because they require an unusual concatenation of circumstances. Among the requisite conditions appear to be: research directly relevant to an issue up for decision, available before the time of decision, that addresses the issue within the parameters of feasible action, that comes out with clear and unambiguous results, that is known to decision makers, who understand its concepts and findings and are willing to listen, that does not run athwart of entrenched interests or powerful blocs, and that is implementable within the limits of existing resources. *And* that is different from what decision makers had planned to do. Many of these conditions appear to be necessary if research use is to be visible in the instrumental sense.

The direct application imagery is a traditional one in the sociological literature (Valdes and Dean 1965; Shostak 1966;

Lazarsfeld, Sewell, and Wilensky 1967; Evans 1975; Goodwin 1975). But it makes demands that are generally unreasonable, particularly for social science research that is done outside of government.

There are many other kinds of research use. Even within the context of one concrete decision, we can think of uses of research to reinforce officials' commitment to a decision, reduce their uncertainties, persuade or neutralize critics, bolster supporters, shift responsibility to the (sometimes) politically acceptable shoulders of "scientific research," legitimate decisions already made on other grounds. Sometimes decision makers misuse research for such purposes, for example by ripping research conclusions out of context and brandishing only those that conform with predetermined positions or by oversimplifying findings and dispensing with the essential qualifications. But often research is used responsibly in these ways. Although the research may not change the decision discernibly from what it would otherwise have been, it can give decision makers confidence and strengthen the case that the research itself supports. Its partisans are ready-made, but the research has influence. At the margin, such uses may have significant effect in ensuring adoption of a contested course of action.

Other definitions of research use go beyond the results of a single research study or small set of parallel studies. Research can be used to bring social scientific perspectives into the making of a policy decision. For example, a social scientist may be brought into the policy-making process as a consultant. With his stock of knowledge of research, he participates in the give-and-take of policy development. Donnison describes this interactive mode of research use as it was practiced in developing British legislation for town planning and rent regulation. He says that members of four fields—politics, technology, practice, and research—participated in the development of the bills:

Research workers could not present authoritative findings for others to apply; neither could others commission them to find the "correct" solution to policy problems: they were not that kind of problem. Those in the four fields from which experience had to be brought to bear contributed on equal terms. Each was expert in a few things, ignorant about most things, offered what he could, and generally learnt more than he could teach. (Donnison 1972:526–27)

Researchers bring not so much discrete findings as their whole theoretical, conceptual, and empirical fund of knowledge into the decision-making process. What they contribute becomes one input into the policy decision. The "use" of social science research in this mode is part of a complicated set of interchanges that also "uses" practical experience, political insight, social technologies, and judgment.

Thus far, we have limited definitions of research use to the case of a single decision, but there can be broader and more diffuse uses. Social science research can affect the premises of policy argument. It can provide concepts, sensitivities, models, paradigms, theories. Such conceptual derivatives from research can influence which issues are placed on the policy agenda and which kinds of policy options are considered. They can enter into decision makers' orientation toward priorities, the manner in which they formulate problems, the range of solutions they canvas, the criteria of choice they apply. Since the process by which decision makers absorb understandings of this sort are subtle and indirect, they may not be able to identify specific social science studies that influenced them—nor are observers likely to recognize them.

Caplan and his colleagues surveyed decision makers in a large number of federal agencies and asked them to report social science studies that had affected their decisions. Many of the responses they received referred to what the authors call "soft knowledge," i.e., "non-research based, qualitative, and couched in lay language" (Caplan, Morrison, and Stambaugh 1975:18). The assimilation of "soft" social science concepts into their perspectives on problems, say the authors, was "the modal type of social science knowledge use" among the federal executives whom they studied (Caplan, Morrison, and Stambaugh 1975:19). Both the respondents and the researchers believed that such use had real effects.

If "nuggets" are rare happenstances, other types of research use appear to be more common. They lack the crispness of the straightforward decision-switch, but in the long run, they may be no less significant. Yet observers who look only for quick, direct, instrumental applications of research results to concrete decisions become disillusioned and cynical when they fail to find them.

Bases for Disappointment:
Expectations of Benefit

There is another set of assumptions that observers bring to bear on their discussions of the failures in the research-policy nexus. These have to do with the outcomes that would ensue if only decision makers took research seriously. Implicit in most of the writings on the subject, but rarely articulated, are articles of faith about the capability of social science research to improve the wisdom of decisions. It is part of a tradition that goes back to the Enlightenment—the faith that, just as the natural sciences lead to technology that makes society wealthy, the social sciences can lead to practices that will make society happy, healthy, and wise.

One example, not the most optimistic but one of the most reputable:

Our society cannot delay dealing with its major social problems. We cannot consume our resources and pollute our environment and then hope to replenish and restore them. We cannot permit international relations to deteriorate to the point of resorting to nuclear weapons. Social unrest, a result of rising expectations and frustrated hopes, will eventually reach a point of no return.

The social sciences will provide no easy solutions in the near future, but they are our best hope, in the long run, for understanding our problems in depth and for providing new means of lessening tensions and improving our common life. (NAS 1969:17)

How social science will lead to such benign outcomes is seldom made explicit. But the course of events would seem to be something like this:

1. Social science research produces "knowledge" about human and institutional behavior. "Knowledge" has connotations of fact, truth, and replicability.
2. Action based upon knowledge is more "rational" than action based on experience, judgment, or intuition. "Rational" connotes the apt fit of means to ends, an efficient use of resources, and an increase in the predictability of outcomes.
3. Rational action by government will lead to "good" outcomes. "Good" means that the consequences are beneficial to society.
4. The good effects of rational action by government will be shared uniformly and equitably by all groups in the society.

Some such thinking underlies the spate of pronouncements about the necessity for drawing upon the social sciences to solve the social problems that plague the nation and the world. How realistic are such expectations? It would perhaps be churlish to question the capacity of the social sciences to produce knowledge, at least "in the long run," but the expectations for timeless truth seem a distant dream. Much of what social science research has produced is limited in scope and incomplete in explanation; almost all of it is time- and situation-specific. As conditions change, research—which is inevitably based on past conditions and on only some of those—becomes outmoded. Like the French military planners of the 1930s who built the Maginot Line to win the previous war, social planners who devise policies to meet the earlier conditions revealed by research may find themselves outflanked by the blitzkrieg of events. This of course is not meant to suggest that partial knowledge is inferior to no knowledge—or to misperception. Not at all. Since policy too is made in the short run, current modes of social science research may suffice for many purposes. But the tendency to inflate the real contributions of the social sciences into eternal truths, good for all seasons, places a burden on them that they are not yet prepared to meet. And since each advance in research seems to uncover unsuspected complexities and new sources of variability, the quest for elegant and parsimonious laws of social behavior, on the model of the laws of the physical sciences, may never be successful.

Even more questionable is the expectation that knowledge-based action will inevitably benefit society. Many of the most critical problems afflicting the country remain problems only in part because of the absence of knowledge to solve them. As Rule has suggested:

> . . . a close look at the array of "social problems" in America today shows that few of them represent authentic "problems" in the sense of conditions equally undesirable from all political and social standpoints. Quite the opposite: conditions like pollution, racism, poverty, and the like are basically oppositions of interest—not social problems but social conflicts, overt or concealed. (Rule 1971:51)

Social science cannot fully depoliticize social problem-solving since choices among values are necessarily involved. Policies, however firmly based upon valid knowledge, will represent accommodations among competing interests and will tend to favor one set of interests over others. Unless there is total consensus about the ends to be achieved, the knowledge component is only part of the solution. In fact, the knowledge itself is often mired in value and interest assumptions. To expect that the application of knowledge will redound to the equal benefit of all, that in the words of the National Academy's report, it will "improv[e] our common life," is to overlook the intrinsically political nature of public policy.

Therefore, when observers look around them and see little visible impact of research on policy, or impacts that run counter to their reformist inclinations, they often seem to be judging the situation by simplistic standards. They expect research to be authoritative and potent enough to alter the direction of specific decisions in obvious ways, and they expect it to supercede the play of political forces and partisan interests in the bargaining over decisions. The implicit image is decision maker as fresh blotter: the decision maker is expected to soak up all relevant research. An even better metaphor might be decision maker as fresh stencil. Social science research imprints its message, and the decision maker is expected to transfer it to the stack of blank pages awaiting his action. If pressed to examine their assumptions, presumably no social scientist would make such extravagant claims. Yet much of the chorus of disillusion about the state of research use seems to rest on premises almost this farfetched.

Some of the expectations for the use of social science research are patently unrealistic. Yet with all the disclaimers and qualifications we have introduced, we have not removed the nagging suspicion that, even with more reasonable expectations, research is not being used as widely or as well as it might profitably be. The prevailing discontent bespeaks such low levels of appropriate research use that it is necessary to take it seriously. When knowledgeable and sophisticated observers as well as naive optimists report dismay over the neglect of research, we have to consider not only the internal standards of judgment that are being applied but also the external factors that account for the current state of affairs. And looking outward at the intersection of research and agency decision-making, we find that the road to application is by no means a royal highway.

Obstacles to Research Use

Many barriers limit the effective application of social science research to organizational decision-making. Observers, often writing on the basis of personal experience, have identified a series of constraints—cognitive, organizational, and political—that hinder the use of research. From the initial formulation of the research question to the point at which agency action is taken, the route is strewn with competing and conflicting influences. Even if we set aside allegations that decision makers are too ill-informed or too self-serving to bother about research, we still have a catalog of explanations for its neglect.

We can conceptualize the interaction between social science research and government decision-making in terms of three loosely coupled systems. First, there is the system that *produces* social science research, composed of research institutions and the social scientists who work within them. Second, there is the policy-setting and administrative system that potentially *uses* social science research, composed of government agencies and the officials who make consequential decisions within them. Finally, there is the *linkage* system, the array of institutions and arrangements, the staffs and advisers, whose task it is to transmit information from potential users of research to social scientists about the kinds of research that are needed and to transmit to potential users reports of relevant research that has been conducted.

Obstacles to research use can arise in any, or all, of these realms. The research-producing system may conduct research that is intrinsically deficient for decision-making purposes. Because the norms that govern research institutions are different from those that are operative in government agencies, the research that social scientists do may seem irrelevant or untrustworthy to decision makers. Specific claims about the sources of discontinuity include the following:

1. Social scientists, particularly those in universities, are often uninterested in issues of relevance to policy makers and program managers. Because of the system of academic incentives and rewards to which they respond, they tend to pursue lines of investigation that grow out of the core issues in their disciplines. These may be remote from concerns in councils of action.

2. Researchers' formulations of problems for study often do not match decision makers' definitions of problems. Even when they deal with issues on the policy agenda, such as health care or poverty, they may focus on different facets of the issue from those that engage decision makers and consider different sets of conditions as fixed and subject to change. If and when they make recommendations on the basis of their research, they may recommend options that are not feasible for government agencies (Israel 1966; Croker 1969; Ferman 1969; Cowhig 1971).

3. Researchers simplify problems in order to make them amenable to study. They may ignore conditions that are beyond the realm of their theories, their disciplines, or their interests. Decision makers must deal with problems in their multifaceted complexity (Simon 1976).

4. Social science has few theories or "laws" of wide generality that can provide a framework for policy research. Most applied inquiries derive at best from low-level propositions, often from ad hoc hunches. Each study begins from the beginning, largely in isolation from other research, and looks at each issue in its specific context. A good deal of research proceeds on a trial-and-error basis, and the results do not cumulate (Gans 1971; Barton 1973).

5. There are important limitations in social science methodology (Riecken 1967; Bernstein and Freeman 1975). Data sources are limited and sometimes inaccurate (Orlans 1973).

6. Researchers often conceptualize problems to fit the methodologies in which they are expert rather than to fit the nature of the question or the needs of decision makers.

7. Research takes time, and results may not be ready when an issue must be resolved (Price 1954; Sharpe 1977. Sharpe quotes Robin H. Jones's remark that sociologists' cry to government is "Give us the job and we'll spend the next seven years sharpening the tools.")

8. The concepts that undergird social science research are often unfamiliar to decision makers and sometimes incompatible with their assumptions about social behavior. Differences in conceptual premises, as well as poor writing, jargon, and lack of effort at communication, make social science research difficult for decision makers to understand (Reitz 1968; Lindsey and Lessler 1976). Increasingly sophisticated statistical analyses make comprehension even harder (Cohen and Weiss 1977).

9. Much social science research examines the effects of variables, such as race or socioeconomic status, that decision makers can do very little about. It does not concentrate on studying manipulable variables over which agencies can exercise some control (Riecken 1969; Davis 1973).

10. Much research concludes with inconsistent findings. There is on-the-one-hand, but there is also on-the-other. Such conclusions offer little direction for action (Cohen 1975; Uliassi 1977).

11. Some research conclusions are repetitions of the obvious. They indicate again what direct experience or previous research had led decision makers to expect. They seem to make little new contribution (Merton 1959. Belaboring the obvious is only one of the perils of social inquiry that Merton discusses; it is equally uncomfortable to find out that what people "know" is untrue.).

12. Some social science research studies conclude that things are not going well. People are in need; programs are not working. But there is often little in such reports to give guidance for effective corrective action (Horowitz 1969; Williams 1971).

13. Research is based upon experience in the past. Conditions in the future may differ in sudden and dramatic ways. Research results may be of little relevance under the changed conditions (Etzioni 1967).

14. In all applied research, to go from data to recommendations involves a "leap." The leap may be guided by the researchers' ideological predilections, practical lore, assessment of political feasibilities, judgments of clients' preferences and biases, or ignorance. Or researchers may not develop recommendations at all and let the decision maker determine the implications from the research. In any case interpretations of what the data "mean" for action can vary within wide limits. Interpretations are heavily in-

fluenced by the values of researchers and decision makers (Lazars-feld, Sewell, and Wilensky 1967; Meltsner 1976a; Mayntz 1977).

15. Social scientists tend to be liberal, left of center, reformist in orientation. Their political proclivities affect the kind of research they do and the implications of their work for policy. Their orientation may be at odds with the perspectives of government officials (Orlans 1973).

16. Social scientists are oriented toward originality and enjoy the counterintuitive and paradoxical. At least in academic settings, recognition tends to go to those with novel formulations and new models for interpreting experience. Challenge of the old and quest for the new tends to put them at odds with decision makers who have to cope with the world in the categories in which it is customarily perceived.

17. The results of a series of studies in the same substantive area do not necessarily converge and cumulate. Often they provide divergent and even contradictory conclusions. As more studies are undertaken to resolve the discrepancies, a range of new issues emerges and a more complex picture of reality appears. The decision maker is faced not with answers to what seemed like a straightforward question but rather with more questions and more problems than he had recognized at the outset (Cohen and Garet 1975; Cohen and Weiss 1977).

The decision-making system imposes its own constraints on research use. Even when a research study passes muster, officials are often unwilling or unable to use its insights as a basis for action. As individuals, they may avoid exposure to research, find it unintelligible, misunderstand it, consider it unreliable, or reject that which is antipathetic to their own interests. But even those who read social science research diligently and intelligently and are impressed with its conclusions may find little opportunity to use it. They do not function as isolated individuals but as members of complex organizations, and the organization sets limits on what they can and cannot do.

Moreover, when the officials serve in governmental agencies, they must function not only within the procedural, structural, and ideological framework of the organization but also within the parameters set by the larger political system. Major lines of policy and budgetary allocations are determined externally, by legislatures and political executives, and actions of the agency come under the scrutiny of the media, interest groups, and the public. The decisions for which officials may want to rely on social science evidence still have to conform to the political imperatives.

Observers have described characteristics of the decision-making arena that can interfere with the application of social science research. Even when decision makers are motivated to base their actions on the evidence that social science research provides, they may be checked by the nature of their environment.

1. Decision-making in public agencies is often a fragmented enterprise. Decisions are not necessarily the province of a single individual or even of a clearly defined set of individuals. Many actors in many locations both inside and outside the agency have a say, raising different questions and exercising different standards of judgment. Decisions are influenced by legislators, superordinate officials, subordinates, collateral divisions, other agencies, constituents, clients. No single set of research results is likely to be relevant to the concerns of all groups that participate in decision-making nor be persuasive to all (Truman 1951; Lindblom 1968: 70–100).

2. Decision makers change jobs with considerable frequency. Even when authority for decisions is clearly lodged with specific positions, occupants of the positions may stay for short periods. High turnover often precludes continuity of attention. Research of interest to one decision maker may be of little interest to her successor (Warner et al. 1963:172–74; Stanley, Mann, and Doig 1967).

3. Decision makers tend to be in a hurry. They want to solve problems and get on to the next item on the agenda. They may be too impatient to await conclusions from research (Cherns 1970; Redman 1973:230–31).

4. Decision makers have to deal with much of the world as given. They accept many aspects of social structure, agency organization, and social services as fixed, rather than as "variables" open to investigation. Therefore, they are often unreceptive to

social research that sees such features of the social world as problematic (Cobb and Elder 1976).

5. Policy issues shift rapidly. The concerns that give rise to a research study may have been resolved, forgotten, or drastically altered by the time the study is completed (Millikan 1959; Weiss and Rein 1969; Rossi and Lyall 1977).

6. Many decision makers have been immersed in the substance of program and policy issues for decades. They have rich firsthand experience and many sources of direct information. The contribution that social research studies can make seems marginal at best (Lazarsfeld and Reitz 1975; Caro 1977).

7. The findings and recommendations from social science research studies may not match the jurisdiction and authority of any agency. There is no body empowered to take the kinds of action that the research results imply (Rose 1974).

8. The findings and recommendations from social science research studies may call for action that is beyond the resources (funds, staff, skills) of the cognizant agency (Glaser et al. 1966).

9. The findings and recommendations from social science research studies may suggest changes in policy that are outside the ideological and philosophical boundaries of the administration, the agency, or the attentive public. When implications from social science research are beyond the range of acceptable options, the message is unlikely to be heeded (Shils 1949).

10. Policy makers are interested not only in the application of the best evidence to the resolution of problems but also in reconciling differences and reaching compromises that maintain the stability of the system. In the interests of responsiveness and consensus-building, they may be willing to sacrifice the "best solution" offered by research. Political rationality may eclipse scientific rationality (Dahl 1965; Lindblom 1968; Hofferbert 1974: 25–88).

Finally, there are limitations on the use of social science research in decision-making that arise from deficiencies in the transmission of information. The formal and informal bodies that are expected to communicate research to potential users may fail to get the word through. They may not know about relevant research, or they may not know for whom the research they know about is useful. Staff groups in research and planning offices, clearing-houses, consultants, newsletter editors may lack sufficient infor-mation to perform the linkage role effectively. Although the litera-ture on this component is sparser than that on the failings in research and decision-making, we can identify a number of pos-sible constrictions on the flow of research information.

1. Staff offices that commission research (often agency re-search, evaluation, and planning offices) are not always aware of the decisions that officials actually face and the types of informa-tion that would inform the decisions. Located outside the main decision line of the agency, they may be more responsive to the academic perspectives of the researchers with whom they deal than to the informational requirements of decision makers (Cole-man 1972).

2. Decision makers who call for social science research may be unable to specify their research needs appropriately. They some-times assume more than is known or perceive available options as excessively narrow, and therefore overspecify the research question. Sometimes they overgeneralize the problem, stating ob-jectives in vague and global terms without clarifying the con-straints that will limit their choices or the range of feasible alter-natives (Merton and Lerner 1951).

3. Research review committees that pass on applications for grant-funded research are primarily oriented to the technical merit of research proposals. Their review process may neglect considera-tion of the relevance of the research for decision-making.

4. Once research reports are received in an agency, few govern-ment offices perceive their mandate as systematic and effective dissemination to appropriate users. The dissemination function may be performed haphazardly, or it may not be undertaken at all.

5. Academic journals that publish social science research are likely to be inefficient channels for reaching government officials. Their primary audience is academic social scientists, and both in the selection of manuscripts and in style of presentation, they often bypass the interests of government audiences.

6. Conferences aimed at bringing decision makers and social scientists together for discussion of policy-relevant research have an erratic record. Only occasionally do the two groups share sufficient commonality of concept, language, and interest to make these efforts at "knowledge transfer" an effective enterprise.

7. Computerized information services, despite their sophisticated technology (or because of it), are infrequently used by decision makers to search for relevant research.

8. As a consequence of these factors, the reports of research that reach decision makers may be a small and biased subset of the research available in their substantive area. The studies that they learn about may be obsolete, poorly done, sensational, or partial, whereas sounder and more comprehensive work fails to come to their attention.

Thus, hurdles to effective research use can be identified at almost every point along the route from research to decision. Getting appropriate research information to one individual and having that individual incorporate the information in her selection of decision options begins to seem no mean feat in itself, but producing information that will influence the actions of a bureaucratic organization is several orders of magnitude more complex.

Toward a Sociology of
Knowledge Application

The insights provided by the speculative literature provide a richly textured view of the problems at the intersection between the social sciences and organizational decision-making. Most of them are illustrated by the personal experiences of social scientists or by case histories of the fate of particular studies (Sabatier 1978). They indicate a range of cognitive and structural factors that obstruct the use of social science research.

But which of them are important? Which are occasional hindrances and which are significant forces regularly impinging on the application of research? Which of them are paltry inconveniences and which are serious drawbacks to research use? No investigations have systematically examined their comparative effects.

The mission of our inquiry is to begin such comparative analysis. We start from the understandings, summarized in this chapter, that previous students of the subject have provided. Our concern is not so much with normative prescriptions and strategies for increasing the use of research as with understanding the situation as it exists. Our inquiry is a step toward development of what can be called the "sociology of knowledge application."

In 1949 Robert Merton called for systematic study of applied social science and the factors that facilitated or impeded its use for purposes of practical action. His luminous analysis discussed the cultural, organizational, situational, and cognitive contexts of applied social science research and identified such dimensions as the prevailing images of applied social science, including views of its objectivity, adequacy, political relevance, and cost. Such images, he hypothesized, would inevitably affect utilization. He suggested that empirical study, including study of the divergent values of policy maker and researcher, should help resolve questions about "the relevance, scope, and utility" of social science research. His theme was the "need for an 'applied social research on applied social research'" (Merton 1949, reprinted 1973:84, 77).

Paul Lazarsfeld devoted years to the development of what he called a "theory of uses" (Lazarsfeld, Sewell, and Wilensky 1967: xxvii). As the introduction to a collection of papers on "the uses of sociology," he developed a model of the relationship between sociologist and decision maker. The model posited a decision maker who had a problem; the decision maker called upon a sociologist to do research to help solve the problem; the sociologist formulated and conducted a research study; then he communicated the findings and recommendations to the decision maker. If all had gone well up to this point, the decision maker applied the findings to resolve the problem. Despite the limited nature of the model, it highlighted two particularly problematic points in the relationship: the "translation" of the client's problem into a research question and the "gap-leap" from empirical research findings to prescriptions for solution of the problem. Lazarsfeld saw the model as the core around which a theory of utilization could be built.

In his last book, Lazarsfeld took up the model again. Despite the additional case materials that he and his collaborators had collected, they discussed their efforts at a theory of utilization as "the bare beginning of such an effort. . . . The best one can hope for is a first classification of the ingredients that have to be added if one wants to move from knowledge to action . . ." (Lazarsfeld and Reitz 1975:37).

Within the last half-dozen years, a number of quantitative investigations on research use have been conducted. The best known is the survey by Nathan Caplan and his associates (1975) of over 200 decision makers in a range of federal agencies. Caplan found that most of the respondents reported at least one use of social science research. The reported uses generally involved "soft" social science generalizations rather than "hard," data-based findings. Other studies, such as those by Rich (1975), Patton et al. (1977), Knorr (1977), and Berg et al. (1978), are adding to our understanding of when and how social science research has an influence on decision-making.[4]

Recently Holzner has continued the conceptual discussion by suggesting the development of a new subspecialty, a "sociology of knowledge application," a sociology of knowledge "turned upside down" (Holzner 1978:8; Holzner and Marx 1979). Whereas the classical sociology of knowledge was concerned with the social basis of intellectual productions, a sociology of knowledge application would be concerned with the social consequences of knowledge. It would investigate the conditions under which knowledge is produced, diffused, and applied. He called particular attention to the need for understanding the multiple frames of reference with which people perceive knowledge and the discrepancies between the frames of reference of knowledge producers and knowledge users. Each group, he suggested, uses different reality tests as criteria for the certification of information as knowledge, and investigation could shed light on their views of the trustworthiness of different sources of knowledge.

A sociology of knowledge application, Holzner suggested, should include analysis of those organizational arrangements for knowledge production and use that encourage optimal learning. The societal styles and cultural patterns that affect research and its use also deserve attention. Where Merton called for an applied social science of applied social science, Holzner is in effect pointing the way toward a basic social science of applied social science.

Our inquiry is firmly within the field as Holzner defines it. It is intended to move the sociology of knowledge application forward.

NOTES

1. A prevalent assumption in the discussion of research and decision-making, as in any discussion of the relation of knowledge to action, is that research cannot provide a basis for the selection of goals. Rather it elucidates appropriate means for the achievement of goals, at best clarifying the implications of the pursuit of some goals at the expense of others, highlighting unanticipated consequences of the pursuit, pointing out conflicts among equally desired goals, and helping people grasp the corollaries of their choices.

In the day-to-day embroilments of agency decision-making, the connection between knowledge and action proves to be more complex and intertwined than the analytic model suggests. People often do not know with any exactness what their ends *are* until they begin to fashion concrete policies and have to confront knowledge of the trade-offs that any one policy inevitably entails (Schultze 1968:64 ff.). Debates over the ends of policy are fought out at least partly on empirical grounds. Policy arguments are often founded on what are empirically testable propositions (e.g., federal aid to educationally disadvantaged students will improve their achievement and adult earnings; mandatory prison sentences will deter crime). Means and ends, facts and values, research and decisions interact in complex ways. Just as we now recognize that values inevitably infuse the work of social scientists, so too do generalizations about social behavior—the stuff of which the social sciences are made—inevitably permeate the choices of ends (as well as means) in agency decision-making.

All of us base our actions on implicit theories about human behavior—psychological, sociological, political, and economic theories. Whether the theories come from folklore or analysis, from recent research or the lessons of past experience, or from a combination of all of these, they influence the goals we set and the actions we take. So too, is it inside the agencies of government.

2. The use of social science research for policy purposes goes back at least two hundred years. John Howard gathered facts and figures from prisons and prisoners in his drive to reform English prison management in the 1700s. Frederic Le Play (1806–1882) studied family budgets of the European working class not only because of scientific interest but also as a basis for practical proposals for social amelioration. Charles Booth's study of poverty among London working classes in the late 1880s had a decisive effect on English poor relief (Young, Schmid, and Rice 1939). The career of Charles E. Merriam was a particularly interesting example of a lifelong attempt to link social science and policy (see Orlans 1976).

3. Daniel P. Moynihan (1969) was among those who pointed out the tenuous research base on which much of the social scientific advice rested.

4. See also earlier empirical studies by Archibald (1968), Burt, Fisk, and Hatry (1972), and van de Vall (1975).

Chapter Two
FRAMEWORK
OF THE STUDY

OUR INTEREST is the reputed neglect of social science research by decision makers. Our aim is to understand the factors that affect decision makers' response to research. Review of the literature suggested a splendid assortment of hypotheses to be investigated. The first task was to decide specifically what to study, where, and how. This chapter presents the intellectual history of the choices we made.

What to Study:
Substantive Focus

The image of the three spheres of research production, research dissemination, and research use, described in chapter 1, provides a map of the territory we could explore. Given the number of places things can go awry both within each sphere and at the points of articulation between them, we had to select a point in the sequence for inquiry. To systematically study the gamut of activities from the formulation of research to its application in decision-making—and all the failings, distractions, and countervailing influences that can afflict those activities—is beyond the resources of a single project. If we tried to encompass all the relevant variables, we might at best do a small set of case studies, but case studies would not provide the kind of generalizable evidence that the present state of the subject calls for. Accordingly, we had to stake out a limited site for investigation.

We decided to focus primarily on the point at which decision

27

makers receive reports of completed studies. The studies have already been planned, funded, performed, and disseminated, and it is up to decision makers to decide whether and how they are going to use them. At this point, the *characteristics of the studies* are the critical variables, and we can analyze how the nature of the studies affects their usefulness for decision makers. The characteristics of decision makers may make a difference, too, and we can see if individuals' backgrounds and experience influence their reception of research studies.

The point for inquiry is the border between the research and decision-making spheres. Studies are produced by the research system, and once completed, they can influence the decision-making system. With the focus on studies, we can test a number of hypotheses about the operation of both spheres. For example, we can find out the extent to which decision makers reject social science research studies as intrinsically useless. If this is a prevailing response, if most studies fail to fit the expectations of potential users, it will suggest that the ways in which research studies are currently planned and performed militate against their influence on decision-making—or perhaps that decision makers are so uniformly indifferent to social science research that no efforts to perform relevant studies will win their acceptance. On the other hand, if certain studies are received with more enthusiasm than others, we will be able to identify the characteristics of studies that gain attention.

With the focus on research studies, we have the advantage of dealing with manipulable variables. Characteristics of research are subject to researchers' control. If we can identify features of research studies that gain them a hearing from decision makers, we will be able to give guidance to policy-oriented researchers on suitable modes of study design, analysis, and presentation. Another consideration that entered into the choice of focus was the interest of government research managers in issues of research funding. There is concern in many federal agencies with issues of peer review, grants versus contracts, the types of research organizations most appropriate for the conduct of policy studies, and so on. When we locate studies that are well received by decision makers, we can identify their funding mechanisms and organizational producers, and thus contribute to the discussion on strategies of research support.

With the focus on studies, we can talk to researchers and decision makers about the same body of evidence. We can collect their responses to identical stimuli and learn to what extent their perceptions converge or diverge, particularly about the usefulness of the work for decision-making. If decision makers and researchers view research with very different perspectives, we can identify the disjunctions and perhaps locate some of the sources of misunderstanding. By including in the sample members of research review committees, people who play a key role in deciding which proposed studies will be funded, we can learn their views, too, and understand some of the factors that govern the selection of research proposals.

Finally, by putting real, concrete studies on the table, we can move to discussion of other factors that influence reactions to research. The characteristics of social science research studies are not merely technical but substantive and political as well. Explicitly or implicitly, research results have implications that butt up against the realities of current policy. Decision makers respond to studies in terms of their match to the political constraints, organizational requirements, and individual expectations operative in the decision-making system. By focusing on particular studies, we can surface characteristics that fit—or fail to fit—the demands of decision makers. This can give us considerable information about the political and organizational imperatives that influence response to social science research.

For all these reasons, the study seemed a key starting point for systematic inquiry. Use of the study as the unit of analysis provides a framework within which we can address a range of issues. It gives us an entry into the complex domain of "social science research and decision-making" that is grounded in concrete, tangible detail and that evokes responses from actors from different spheres around common themes. It helps us learn which features of social science research are important in providing credibility and a sense of direction. The focus also allows us to widen out the inquiry and gain new insight into what "useful research" and "using research" mean in practice.

Where to Study:
Site of Inquiry

We wanted to study responses to research in an executive agency rather than in legislative or judicial settings. Accounts of the experience of legislatures and courts with social science (Wolanin 1976; Dreyfus 1977; Rosen 1972, 1977; Collins 1978) had alerted us to the special problems that plague the application of research to decisions in these systems. The overriding imperatives in legislatures (accommodating diverse interests) and in courts (settling controversial individual cases without rending the fabric of the law) relegate the rational contributions of research and analysis to peripheral consideration. In bureaucratic agencies, with their emphasis on expertise, long-tenured and stable staffs, and resources for the acquisition and support of research, social science research has greater opportunity to affect the execution of existing programs and the planning of new directions. Our original intent was to limit the study of decision makers to staff at the federal level. However, as chapter 3 explains, our experience during the early phases of the project broadened our scope to include decision makers at state and local levels as well.

The field we chose for investigation was mental health. Mental health is broadly defined to include alcohol and drug abuse, crime and delinquency, social problems, aging, as well as the prevention and treatment of mental illness and the operation of institutions that deal with mental illness. In essence, the definition accords with the institutional purview of the Alcoholism, Drug Abuse, and Mental Health Administration (ADAMHA) within the U.S. Department of Health, Education, and Welfare (HEW). There were several reasons for this selection. For one, ADAMHA— and particularly its senior institute, the National Institute of Mental Health (NIMH)—has a long tradition of support for social science research, encompassing both basic and applied research on a broad range of topics. NIMH has taken a leadership role in attracting capable social science investigators to the study of social issues. There is a history of concern for research and a body of relevant work (NIMH 1975).

Furthermore, the institutes in ADAMHA, which include the National Institute on Drug Abuse (NIDA) and the National Institute on Alcohol Abuse and Alcoholism (NIAAA) as well as

NIMH, have programmatic responsibilities. They support operating programs at state and local levels. While they fund basic as well as applied research for the benefit of the field as a whole, their own staffs—and the staffs of the state and local programs they support—are potential users of much of the research. Unlike the National Science Foundation (NSF), for example, whose research even in applied areas is destined solely for others, the institutes have a home-based research audience. And the intent of much of their research is to aid in carrying forward the missions of the agencies.

Finally, practical reasons indicated the choice of mental health as the field of inquiry. For many years it has been one of the few fields in which federal staff have taken an active part not only in funding social science research but also in disseminating its results to potential users in a variety of organizational locations. Rarer still, they have been willing to support the study of the diffusion and use of research. The interest of these staff members in the questions with which we are engaged provided the support and cooperation without which our inquiry would not have been possible.

Once having selected mental health agencies as the site for investigation, we found that they offered advantages for the development of a sociology of knowledge application. They are places in which the interplay between individual and organizational factors that influence receptivity to research becomes visible. These agencies are staffed by professionals who are aware of social science research, its canons, and its norms. Mainly psychiatrists, psychologists, and social workers, they are members of professions with a claim to scientific standing, and they pay allegiance to the quest for scientific knowledge. At the same time, their professions give them an alternative body of knowledge, based primarily on codified experience, with which to cope with issues of policy and practice. The not infrequent discrepancies between the understandings provided by social science research and the directions indicated by professional lore evoke an interesting set of issues, which are highlighted by the considerable measure of autonomy that professionals exercise over their work.

Mental health agencies are also bureaucratic organizations. Their members are professionals but they are bureaucrats as well.

They function within the context of hierarchies, rules, standard operating procedures, and domain interests that characterize complex organizations (Goode 1957; Litwak 1961). They are expected to accept the organization's needs for survival and growth and to give priority to the welfare of the organization—not only because their own careers are linked to its well-being but equally because the programs that they administer and in which they as professionals tend to believe are dependent upon the organization's stability. The organizational context sets limits on their freedom of choice. While their work allows much autonomy and discretion for professional judgment, they must function within the limits, and by the rules, of the organization. Their application of social science research to decision-making is bounded by the organization's hierarchical, procedural, and budgetary imperatives.[1]

The application of research is bounded, too, by the larger political framework. Supported in considerable part by public funds, mental health agencies are subjected to direction from superordinate executives and legislatures (W. R. Scott 1965; Hall 1972), and they have to be attentive to public concerns and political controversies that can influence their support. Recurrent conflicts over policy, budgets, and even survival have sensitized them to the need to be responsive to external demands and maintain good relationships with influential groups.

Thus, conducting our inquiry with officials in mental health agencies opens up a range of critical issues. While the application of knowledge is basically an individual act, the individual who works in a public or quasi-public agency acts within professional, organizational, and political constraints. Mental health agencies are not unique in this regard. Agencies in many other fields operate in the same kind of environment. The mental health field, encompassing as it does a wide range of substantive social issues, seems a strategic site for examining the latitudes and constraints.

How to Study:
Methodological Issues

The appropriate methodology for studying the questions with which we are concerned was not at all obvious. No off-the-shelf strategies seemed suitable. A survey was clearly one approach: we could *ask* people about the research that had been useful to them. Then either by asking them to describe what it was about such studies that made them useful, or by locating the studies they named and analyzing their characteristics, we might try to describe the studies that had had an impact. The limitations of such an approach were only too apparent. First, people often cannot tell you which studies they have used or found useful. They do not remember; they do not catalog references in their minds; they merge social science research with other sources of information; and as we shall discuss further, they are usually unclear about what using research means. They are likely to be particularly nonplussed by questions about *characteristics* of useful research—and even if they are responsive, they may often be inaccurate—as expert judges are often inaccurate about the basis for their judgments (Slovic, Fischhoff, and Lichtenstein 1977; Nisbett and Wilson 1977). Furthermore, we would not have a comparison with unused or unuseful studies, since it would be fruitless to ask people for nominations on that order. Not only would the questions sound silly, but even if one could prevail upon respondents to answer, such questions would call forth predictable stock responses.

A second possibility was case studies. Case studies can be genuinely fruitful, particularly in a field as empirically unplowed as this. But the number of cases we could examine in any depth would be small, and although we would learn about the influence of a wide range of variables on research use, we would not be able to generalize about the influence of any one set of variables, such as research characteristics, with much confidence. Moreover, given the vast assortment of factors at play, case studies have the disconcerting tendency to contradict each other, and we might be left with insufficient information to specify the variables that make a difference.

Laboratory experiments were another possible method of inquiry. Under controlled conditions, one can vary the types of research to which subjects are exposed with elegant flexibility. But laboratory conditions impose limitations on external validity. Answers to questions in a laboratory setting can be markedly different from those evoked under real-life conditions. And it was not at all clear that we could prevail upon the kinds of people in whom we were interested—decision makers, researchers, and research review committee members—to play our games. Students, even graduate school or professional school students, were not reasonable proxies. They lack the palpable knowledge of the field and its issues that comes from direct immersion, and they do not have the sense of agency options and constraints that workaday experience provides—and which was a critical component of our formulation.

After reviewing these and other modes of inquiry (Weiss 1977b), we developed a study design that combined the advantages of several different approaches. Interviews were the basic method of data collection, but instead of only asking people general questions, we presented them with actual reports of government-funded social science research. Then we had them rate each report first on its usefulness to their work and then on a set of research descriptors.

The interview was a simulation of an actual situation; it presented real research to real decision makers during their working day in their offices. The responses they report to the research, we assume, approximate their reactions to actual studies in the course of their ordinary work. The interview was not a simulation of the "hot cognitive processes" of decision-making (Janis and Mann 1977) but of the review and assessment of social science research studies—a rather commonplace occurrence in these offices. The analysis focuses on the relationship between their ratings of the usefulness of the studies and their ratings of the descriptive characteristics. This gives us information, based not on opinions but grounded in concrete examples of actual studies, about the characteristics of social science research studies that were judged to be useful to the work of decision makers in their daily job environments. We can identify which characteristics of studies are associated with high usefulness and which are associated with low usefulness to occupants of decision-making positions.

Operationalizing the Key Concepts

The next step was to define and operationalize the concept of "usefulness." Usefulness appears to be a soft concept, and it can be argued that what we should be interested in is not usefulness but actual use of research. The behavioral pay-off, the bottom line, is use. Why not formulate the study so as to make past use of research the dependent variable?

The basic reason is that "use" is just as soft and judgmental a concept as usefulness. One of the most important learnings from the first round of empirical investigation of research utilization (e.g., Caplan et al. 1975; Rich 1975; Caplan and Barton 1976; Patton et al. 1977) is the ambiguity of what constitutes a use. Its meaning is so unclear, its referents so foggy, that people who are asked to describe their use of research discuss vastly different behavior. Some limit the definition of use to the adoption of the explicit recommendations of a single study. At the other extreme, some people discuss their use of research in terms of sensitivity to social science perspectives (cf. Caplan et al. 1975:18–19). Depending on how they understand the idea of using research, and how the researcher classifies their responses, the interpretation of how much—and what kind of—use occurs can vary widely.[2] In fact, the perverse consequence of relying on "use" as a measure is that it implies specificity and certainty where little of either exists.

Besides the definitional difficulties with "use," there were other conceptual problems. If we are attempting to identify characteristics of research studies that make them more likely to be influential than other studies, we are in effect seeking to locate the appropriate constellation of characteristics for research that will prove to be useful. We are looking for characteristics that are *good* against the criterion of use. But if actual "use" (in the "nugget" sense) is taken as the dependent variable, we are building in troublesome assumptions. We are assuming that used studies have the right characteristics and unused studies have something wrong with them.

This is an undue burden to lay at the door of research. Given the nature of decision-making systems and their contingencies and perturbations, we know that some excellent and relevant social science research is inevitably ignored. In many cases, characteristics of the environment preclude use, whatever the characteristics of the studies. Even when we identify the characteristics of studies that are used, they may display little more than the quirks of fate. If instead we concentrate on research that decision makers deem useful—whatever may happen when such research gets enmeshed in the pushes and pulls, the politics and economics, of the decision-making process—we will be able to disentangle the characteristics of studies that are deemed to have something to contribute.

The concept of "use" also involves problems of incidence, memory, and bias. Incidence of research use (in the traditional sense) is assumed to be low. Caplan et al. achieved a high level of reported knowledge use only by counting in vague references to social science concepts and theoretical notions, unlinked to specific studies. If our aim was to identify the characteristics of used studies, we would probably have very few specific studies to analyze.

As for memory, decision makers often do not remember which research studies provided ideas or information that influenced their actions. They do not maintain files of bibliographic references in their minds. We did ask one question in our interview that asked for citation of a study that the respondent had found useful for his work, and we were confronted with respondents' severe problems in retrieving references on cue. Usually, research information is integrated into a person's perspective on events, and he finds it very hard to sort out the separate bits that went into constructing the perspective.

As for bias, some decision makers pride themselves on their experience and trained judgment. They like to claim that they are self-reliant in making decisions and are reluctant to credit research with substantial influence. In these cases, reports are biased by intentional underreporting of the use of research. Other respondents, who want to appear as knowledgeable supporters of social science, are likely to overstate their research use. Since social science research is (in Schon's [1971] term) "in good currency" in some professions and agencies, those who accept the normative injunction to base actions on research may report more use than fact would support. (Shifting to "usefulness" as a dependent variable, as we will see, does not obliterate this problem.)

Instead of "use," we chose to make the dependent variable the person's judgment that research was useful. Our aim was not to arrive at any absolute count of uses of research but rather to relate judgments of usefulness to characteristics of particular studies. In this context, we needed measures that reflected people's acceptance of a study as something worthy of their notice. However much external conditions might limit their ability to apply its learnings to concrete decisions, the measures should capture their sense that the study made a contribution to their work and their willingness to take it seriously. The distinction we were seeking to draw was between studies that people dismissed as they read them and studies that they found cogent, meaningful, and helpful in moving their work along. The central question was the basis on which people made this kind of determination: what are the characteristics of studies that lead to rejection or to acceptance and possible influence on action?

The basic measures we developed derived from two questions in the interview. After giving respondents summaries of actual research reports, we asked:

> Assuming your office had to consider the issues discussed in the study, how likely is it that you would take the study results into account?

Answers to this question give the respondent's judgment of the probabilities that he will pay attention to the research when the topic comes up for resolution. It is a measure of his likelihood of using the study. The wording also defines "use." In this wording, if a person "takes the study results into account," he is using the study—whether or not the decision made conforms with the study results. As the discussion in chapter 1 indicated, this seems to us a sound and realistic reflection of what research use means. It encompasses an array of conceptual and political, as well as instrumental, uses of research—without at the same time demanding that outside forces be too weak to have independent, competing influence on decisions.

The second question that attempts to capture the concept of usefulness asked:

> Focusing for a moment just on the study's findings, and not considering external constraints, to what extent does the study contain *ideas or information* that can contribute to the work of your agency?

Usefulness in this sense refers to the intrinsic contribution that a study can make. There is a normative overtone that the study should be used on logical-rational grounds. Whatever fallible people in a resource-constrained environment do, the research itself has met the test. It contributes to the decision maker's work.

As described in more detail later, we asked additional questions about research usefulness, to find out about the contribution that studies could make to other appropriate decision makers and the likelihood that they would use the results, and the kinds of functions that research can serve.

Two other concepts had to be operationalized: research and decision. The definition of research sounds simple enough, but as Caplan et al. (1975) and others have found, respondents can interpret it in remarkably different ways. We effectively solved the problem by choosing to employ 50 specific research reports and handing each respondent abstracts of two of these reports to read during the interview. These research abstracts thus embodied "research." We included both basic and applied research studies in the group, because we believed it possible that research intended to understand basic relationships without concern for practical applications might prove to be as useful to decision makers as research undertaken specifically for applied purposes. For a description of the process of selecting the reports, see the section on "The Research Studies" in chapter 3.

"Decision" was another problem. We came to terms with "decision maker" by selecting respondents who held positions above a given level in federal, state, and local hierarchies. Holding positions at these levels within federal and state mental health departments and local care-giving institutions implied responsibility for decisions about policy, program, resource allocation, and/or type of care. See the section on "The Sample" in chapter 3 for discussion of sampling procedures.

But when our pretest interviews asked people what kinds of decisions they made on their jobs, we were met with surprise, consternation, and rebuff. Many people, even those in high-ranked positions, disclaimed making decisions. "The only decision I make," said one federal respondent, "is where to spend my limited travel funds." There was a fairly general reluctance to admit making decisions of any substance.

There seem to be several reasons for this disavowal. One is that responsibility for decisions is so widely shared among individuals, sections, bureaus, divisions, institutes, administrations, and departments, that no one individual *can* make a decision. Even at the highest executive levels, the Secretary of HEW, the state commissioner of health, or the director of a hospital often needs legislative assent in order to take policy actions. This lateral dispersion of authority tends to leave individuals, even those in high executive positions, with a sense that they do nothing of moment without extensive consultation, coordination, and consensus.

Another reason derives from the intergovernmental system. Officials at the federal level often told us during the pretesting that federal officials do not make decisions; Congress passes laws that prescribe and limit their actions, they pass money down to states and localities where decisions are really made and service is given. Some state officials said that when they received funds from the federal government, it came hemmed about with restrictions from Congressional legislation and federal agency guidelines. All they did was pass the funds along to operating agencies in accordance with guidelined procedures. Local officials in hospitals and centers often said that when they received program funds, they were so restricted by federal guidelines and/or state regulations that they couldn't make decisions. They did what they were allowed to do. The fragmentation of authority both horizontally and vertically apparently limits the sense of authority for decisions that are made.

Of course, individuals holding the positions that we sampled do in fact set policy and program direction. But many of them lack the sense of discretionary latitude and authority that the word "decision" implies. As a consequence, we retained the "decision" wording in only one question in the interview. Instead we asked the respondents about the usefulness of research in their work and in the work of their office. The assumption is that work in these echelons includes the making of decisions about policy and program. When we select people to interview who hold responsible positions, we assume that making decisions (or preparing or influencing or participating in decisions) is a large part of what they do.

Having thus delimited the what, where, and how of the inquiry and come to terms with its central concepts, we were ready to begin the study.

NOTES

1. There has been extensive investigation of professional-organizational strains within one group—scientists in industry. See, for example, Marcson (1960), Kornhauser (1962), Pelz and Andrews (1966), Miller (1972). Other classics of divided loyalties (role conflict) are Wilensky (1956) and Merton (1968).

2. Caplan's (1975) conclusions represent some reorientation of his initial reading of the data. The Spring 1974 *ISR Newsletter* gave an early report on the study under the headline "Science Is Seldom Put to Good Use by U.S. Officials." The story was not as negative as the headline, but it did quote Caplan as saying that "officials often lack the skills and proper orientation to put scientific knowledge to good use" (2:2). It also cited Caplan's division of government officials into types of users and his conclusion that five out of ten federal officials fall into the "low usage" types. Apparently, it was through reconceptualizing and recoding what constituted a "use of knowledge" that more favorable conclusions were forthcoming. The reconceptualization subsumed the use of social science concepts, perspectives, and generalizations as well as specific data or research conclusions, and as discussion will indicate, makes eminent sense in light of the ways in which social science actually penetrates the policy world.

Chapter Three
CONDUCT
OF THE STUDY

T HE STUDY WAS BEGUN in 1974, with support from the National Institute of Mental Health. An interview schedule was developed and extensively pretested, a sample was drawn, and interviews were conducted in the summer of 1975. This chapter describes the sample, the interview, and the research studies that formed the central focus of the interview. A final section discusses the content of these studies against the backdrop of contemporary issues in mental health policy and programming.

The Sample

We interviewed 255 people: 155 decision makers in mental health agencies, 50 members of mental health research review committees, and 50 social scientists who had conducted mental health research. We included people from these different locations in order to illuminate the dynamics of the interaction between research and decision-making.

The original plan was to draw a sample of decision makers only at the federal level from the Department of HEW. Of these, 50 would come from the three institutes that dealt directly with mental health issues, the National Institute of Mental Health (NIMH), the National Institute on Drug Abuse (NIDA), and the National Institute on Alcohol Abuse and Alcoholism (NIAAA), and their parent body, the Alcohol, Drug Abuse, and Mental Health Administration (ADAMHA). The respondents selected would be branch chiefs and above, who had programmatic and policy responsibilities within the department for planning and operating mental health activities. Another 50 respondents were slated to be drawn from higher echelons within HEW. These were to be staff in the offices of the Assistant Secretary for Health, the Assistant Secretary for Planning and Evaluation, and the Secretary, who were assigned responsibility for mental health policy and programs.

Pretesting of the interview altered the sampling plan. During the pretests we learned two vital and compensating things. On the one hand, very few people above the ADAMHA level were either concerned with or well informed about mental health issues. Only when issues could not be resolved within ADAMHA did they rise to attention at the Assistant Secretary level. At the time of our interviewing, no unresolved mental health issue was visibly exercising the department (with the possible exception of the Administration's proposal for the gradual phase-out of federal funding for community mental health centers, but this was in stasis). So except for the four or five persons with regular legislative, budget, or program oversight responsibilities, few people in the upper tiers of the department seemed good candidates for an interview that focused on the use of mental health research in decision-making.

On the other hand, in the effort to avoid "using up" real respondents in the pretest of the interview, we were interviewing mental health officials in state and city mental health agencies. It early became apparent that they were very suitable respondents. They were dealing with mental health policy and programs, and they were well informed about issues in the field. Even more striking was the fit between the responsibilities at state and local levels and the topics and orientations of the research studies that NIMH and its sister institutes funded. The research results tended to be more relevant to their work and the kinds of decisions that confronted them than they were to the needs of federal officials concerned with directions for national policy. For example, many of the research studies that NIMH, NIDA, and NIAAA funded had to do with issues of treatment (e.g. short-term vs. long-term hospitalization), coordination (e.g. referrals from mental hospitals to community mental health centers), and demonstration programs (e.g. trials of behavior modification). These were more directly germane to the job responsibilities of directors of care-giving agencies and state departments of mental health than they were to the Secretary or Assistant Secretaries of HEW.

Accordingly, we shifted the sample frame. We decided to retain the sample of 50 officials from ADAMHA, NIMH, NIAAA, and NIDA, and add 50 officials at the top tier of state departments of mental health and 50 directors or chiefs of service in mental health centers, clinics, and mental hospitals.

The sample of federal decision makers was drawn from a listing of branch chiefs, division directors, and higher-level officials in the Alcohol, Drug Abuse, and Mental Health Administration and its component institutes NIMH, NIDA, and NIAAA. We checked off 86 persons in the ADAMHA listing whose titles suggested substantive decision-making responsibilities in the broad area of mental health. To the best of our ability we excluded purely administrative positions, such as "Acting Director, Office of Administrative Management," "Division of Grants and Contracts Management Director," "Deputy Equal Employment Opportunity Officer." We also excluded all intramural research staff. Three informants who were long-term employees of NIMH indicated which of the 86 positions actually involved high-level policy or program planning. From the informants' responses (which deleted some positions and added others), we compiled a list of 60 names: 50 were randomly designated as respondents, and the remaining 10 were numerically ordered to be used as replacements if needed.

To ensure a range of respondents at state and local levels, we selected 10 states and drew the state and local respondents (and the researchers and review committee members) from the main city[1] in each of these states. Two criteria were used in selecting states: geographical location and "progressiveness" of the mental health establishment. We selected states in all regions of the country, and we included a few states that were well known either for their forward-looking mental health policies and activities or for their backwardness. The final list of ten states in which we interviewed state officials was Washington, Arizona, Minnesota, Massachusetts, Maryland, Illinois, Indiana, Virginia, Mississippi, and Colorado. For the interviews with local mental health decision makers, researchers, and review committee members we used the same main cities plus the suburbs of Washington, D.C. (where we were already interviewing federal decision makers), and New York City and environs (where our own office was located).

At the state level, we did not include the commissioner or director of mental health, who in some states was a political appointee. We sampled from the next tier, which usually had seven to twelve officials. The names of agencies and positions were taken from the 1974 *Public Welfare Directory*. The positions that were on our preliminary list for state officials included the deputy/ associate director and directors of such functional areas as alcoholism, drug abuse, developmental disabilities/mental retardation, community services, supportive services, psychiatric facilities, and program planning and evaluation. We eliminated officials whose offices were distant from the state capital or main city (such as the director of a remote state mental hospital) and those whose functions were purely administrative. Then names were randomly chosen from the remaining list for five target interviews, and two or three additional names were held in reserve in case of interview loss.

The sampling process for local mental health officials was more complicated. We had two sources of information about mental health facilities in the sample cities: the *NIMH Mental Health Directory, 1973*, which listed treatment resources by city under the categories of (a) psychiatric hospitals, (b) general hospitals with separate psychiatric services, (c) other multiservice mental health facilities, (d) outpatient mental health clinics, and (e) components of other facilities, and also reported kinds of services offered and the auspices for each facility; and the *NIMH Directory of Federally Funded CMHCs*, issued September 1973, which identified community mental health centers (CMHCs) that were receiving federal funds.

In each of the sample cities, we drew a purposive sample of facilities. We aimed for diversity in type and sponsorship but gave priority to services that dealt primarily with mental illness and that were supported by federal funds. We thus included psychiatric hospitals, outpatient mental health clinics, children's psychiatric facilities, alcoholism treatment facilities, and psychiatric services within general hospitals. Their auspices were state, county, city, and nonprofit; all church-supported facilities and judicial system facilities were excluded.

Once the facilities were selected in the ten states and the metropolitan Washington area, the next step was to sample respondents. We called each facility and requested the names of the director, associate director, and the chiefs of major services. From the list, we generally selected one respondent per facility. In approximately half the cases, the selected respondent was the director of the facility, and in the other half, the associate or assistant director or chief of a service (inpatient, outpatient, children's, alcoholism, etc.).

Researchers were selected from the ADAMHA list of "Mental Health Research Grants 1974" and from a list of contract research on mental health maintained by the office of the Assistant Secretary for Planning and Evaluation (ASPE) in HEW. We checked off the names of those who were located in or near the ten state capitals/main cities and Washington, D.C. Scanning the titles of the grants and contracts, we eliminated those people whose projects were clearly not social scientific (e.g., physiological, pharmacological). From the remaining list, we randomly selected 50 names and a backup pool for replacements.

Names of members of research review committees were drawn from the publication *HRA, HSA, CDC, ADAMHA Public Advisory Committees: Roster of Members.* We used the October 1974 issue, and later supplemented the list from the June 1973 issue. We included members of twelve review committees of NIMH, NIDA, and NIAAA that reviewed research applications for basic and applied research, excluding those whose primary orientation was physiological or pharmacological. Again, location in or near a sample city was the key selection device for respondents. Because there were few researchers and review committee members in many of the sampled states, we added persons in the New York City area. In the final count, 25 interviews were done in New York, New Jersey, and Connecticut—7 researchers and 18 members of research review committees. Twenty-three interviews with researchers and review committee members were completed in the Washington, D.C. area.

Interviewing

We employed two interviewing firms to conduct the interviews, one for the Washington–Baltimore area and the other for the rest of the states. Our staff conducted training for the supervisors of the two organizations, and we gave the training course for the interviewers based in Washington. Supervision of interviewer performance was intensive. Our staff reviewed in great detail the first three interviews that each interviewer conducted. Subsequent interviews were checked on a spot basis. Since all interviews were tape-recorded as well as filled out from notes taken during the interview, we were able to locate such problems as changed wording of questions, inadequately probed responses, and leading probes. We called the interview supervisors and individual interviewers frequently with suggestions. Maintaining the quality of the fieldwork was a full-time task.

By and large, the interview completion rate was good. With decision makers, 82 percent of *all* attempted interviews were completed, and 90 percent of all attempted interviews with *eligible* respondents were completed (see table 3.1). But when an interview was not obtained with the designated respondent (see table 3.2 for reasons for noncompletion), a complicated reassignment was necessary. What made the business complicated was that for each respondent, two research reports were assigned to form the

Table 3.1. Attempted and Completed Interviews

Respondent Category	Interviews Attempted	Eligible Attempts[a]	Interviews Completed	Completion Rate (%) for Eligibles
Federal decision maker	63	55	51	93%
State decision maker	61	53	52	98
Local decision maker	64	64	52	81
Total Decision Makers	188	172	155	90%
Researcher	90	84	50	60
Review committee member	84	79	50	63
Total Sample	362	335	255	76%

[a]Interviews attempted with respondents who were eligible for inclusion. See table 3.2 for identification of reasons for noneligibility.

Table 3.2. Reasons for Noncompletion of Interviews

	Decision Makers			Researchers	Review Committee Members	Total
	Federal	State	Local			
Refused; did not reply to calls	4	—	9	9	16	38
Not available						
On vacation, on leave	—	—	1	8	7	16
Ill, deceased	—	—	1	2	1	4
Could not locate	—	—	1	5	3	9
Moved outside interview areas	—	1	—	10	2	13
Not eligible						
Left job, retired	7	7	—	—	—	14
Job responsibility not appropriate	—	1	—	—	—	1
Not on job long enough	1	—	—	—	—	1
Committee not suitable or not regular member	—	—	—	—	5	5
Project not appropriate or not principal investigator	—	—	—	6	—	6

core of the interview. These research reports were matched to the content of the respondent's job. For example, if the position was chief of children's services, study reports were chosen about treatment of children. If the designated respondent was unavailable, one possible procedure was to select a replacement from the same facility, for example, the director. However, this would necessitate reassignment of studies. Studies would have to be found that fitted a *director's* responsibilities and concerns, rather than those of a children's service chief. Since we were simultaneously intent on having each study abstract read exactly *ten* times, twice each by federal decision makers, state decision makers, local decision makers, researchers, and review committee members, the need to juggle reassignments of respondents and studies across ten states and the District of Columbia was a complex jigsaw puzzle.

The procedures for replacement were as follows: For federal and state officials, if the designated respondent moved to another position within the same agency, we interviewed him/her. For federal and state officials who had left the agency, we went to the next backup name in the replacement pool. Among local decision makers, those who had left the agency were replaced by those in a parallel position at another facility, insofar as possible. When we had exhausted all facilities on the list, we selected an alternate respondent from within the same facility.

Letters were mailed to each respondent outlining the background, purpose, and sponsorship of the study, requesting cooperation, and saying that an interviewer would call for an appointment. Interviewers made their own appointments. The interviewers were provided with tape recorders, and upon arrival asked if they might plug the recorder in. No respondent refused permission for taping. Interviewers also took notes during the interview, as close to verbatim as possible, as a hedge against malfunctioning recorders and as a way of avoiding the time-consuming process of total transcription of the tape. After the interview, the interviewer listened to the tape and filled out responses where notetaking had been inadequate. The interviewers sent in both completed interviews and tapes.

The tape recording generally worked very well. Respondents were comfortable, and the advantages were several. The tapes allowed the interviewers to amplify the responses they had jotted down and make them more nearly complete, and they allowed us to check on interviewer performance and to catch sloppiness very early. Thus we could provide immediate advice to the supervisor and interviewer, and if the interviewer's performance did not improve, we asked that he/she be replaced. Taping was a method of quality control and a basis for further training. A further advantage was that we could listen to the entire interview and, where the interviewer had not recorded everything said, we could hear the rest, with all its inflections, nuances, hesitations, irrelevancies, and anecdotes. During the coding of the open-ended responses, we decided to have many of the interviews completely transcribed. Having the tapes on hand allowed us the luxury of using a complete transcript for the coding of complex narrative responses and enabled us to capture many of the subtleties in respondent's replies.

The disadvantages of tape recording were few. There was the expense of purchasing and dispatching 14 recorders and about 270 tapes. It turned out that about two dozen of the recorded interviews were garbled or inaudible. But on balance, it was a highly useful procedure.

The Interview

The interview focused on the reading of actual research reports, reduced to two-page abstracts, of studies that had been supported by federal mental health funding bodies. Respondents were asked to rate each research abstract on several measures of usefulness, including the likelihood that they would use the study and the intrinsic contribution that its ideas and information could make to their work. They were next asked what would have made the study more useful and what might interfere with use of the findings. Then they rated the research abstracts on 29 descriptive characteristics, including such descriptors as technical quality, objectivity, compatibility with users' values, implementability of findings, and political acceptability.

The interview also collected information on the respondents' jobs, their pattern of research use on the job, their sources of research information, and their attitudes toward social research. Background information about each respondent was collected: length of time in the agency, prior experience, education, professional field, publications, political orientation, age, and sex.

What the interview aimed to do was to simulate the presentation of real research to real decision makers and discover their responses. It was expected that through analysis of responses, we could understand which research factors were associated with decision makers' willingness to pay attention to social research.

Decision makers' behavior in this simulated situation, we presumed, would approximate their actual behavior when confronted by social research information.

Our inquiry thus concentrates on the middle phases of the research utilization process. It starts once a decision maker has a report in hand. It does not consider means of getting research information *to* decision makers: appropriate channels, retrieval systems, the value of conveying information through trusted aides, or any social processes that direct attention to a particular piece of research.

At the other end of the time phase, our inquiry does not deal with what happens once a decision maker decides that a study makes a contribution to his work and that he will keep it in mind. We do not follow the sequence of events that provide support, reduce uncertainty, strengthen resolve, or give social reinforcement for doing something about the research results. We do not move to the point where research has a discernible impact on decisions.

The earlier and later stages are both critical phases of the research utilization process. We do not deal with them in this study; we leave it to other research to study their operation.

The Research Studies

The intention of the interview was to provide a simulated case of exposure to research. We wanted to give respondents reports of actual research studies sponsored by NIMH, NIDA, and NIAAA in order to learn their reactions. Therefore, we had to locate recent reports. Recency was important in order to maximize the relevance of the research to issues currently being considered by federal, state, and local mental health decision makers.

We expected to obtain reports of appropriate studies from NIMH, NIDA, and NIAAA grants and contracts offices. However, this expectation turned out to be chimerical. Only four reports of grant-supported research were available on initial petition to these sources. Three more dribbled in over the next few months. Intensive search through channels—the National Clearinghouse for Mental Health Information, Documents Control—failed to produce the expected research reports. The office of the Assistant Secretary for Planning and Evaluation had three volumes of abstracts of contract research studies that had been funded by "one percent evaluation funds" through mid-1973. However, the abstracts were not detailed enough to serve the purposes of our interview, and no abstracts were available for ADAMHA contracts paid from other funds. Contacts with other contracting offices finally yielded eight reports.

Thus the first empirical finding of our inquiry was that reports of ADAMHA-sponsored research are not systematically available. Even if decision makers should be motivated to seek out reports of research, they would have great difficulty in getting hold of them. In the granting divisions not all projects submit complete final reports, and when they do, one copy is put in the main Grants File (and cannot be removed from the office), and others are distributed on a haphazard basis—to staff members and officials who someone thinks may be interested. At the time we were there, no one seemed to be responsible for their distribution, and in a short time nobody remembered where they had gone.

Reports of contract research studies are tracked more closely. All reports are submitted, or the contractor does not receive final payment. A specific office is responsible for their procurement (e.g., Office of Program Development and Analysis in NIMH), and since it usually acquired the research to meet a specific informational need, that office tends to know where copies of the report are. However, when we applied to the cognizant offices, in many cases there were no spare copies available and staff referred us to the contractor.

Faced with the dearth of research reports, we contacted our project officers at NIMH for help. In an effort to obtain current information, they made calls to scores of principal investigators of ADAMHA grants asking them to submit "Final Report Summary Outlines" on the status of recently completed studies. When the summary outlines were received, they duplicated them and sent us copies. Most of the summary outlines were too skimpy in substance to be usable for our purposes. They then advised us to call the investigators directly and request reports.

We did. We telephoned every principal investigator of a study listed in the 1973 catalog of ADAMHA research grants that was then beyond its first year of funding and that was funded under a social science-oriented program. In all, we made close to 400 calls in an attempt to locate and contact 210 investigators. We finally reached a total of 147 investigators (or their associates) by phone. We sent out seventy letters either because they asked for an explanatory letter identifying ourselves and the reasons for our request or because we did not receive their report within six weeks of their promise to send it. Thirty investigators could not be reached by phone and were contacted by letter only. We were unable to either identify or locate the remaining 33 investigators. Some of these were researchers in contractor organizations; many firms list no authors' names on the report and, when we inquired, often could not remember either the contract or the author. Some were researchers poorly identified in the ADAMHA listing, e.g., Rose D. Jenkins, Los Angeles, California.

Through direct contacts, we received 127 reports of grant and contract research, 125 from investigators to whom we had spoken by phone and 2 from investigators to whom we had only written. Of the 22 investigators to whom we spoke who did *not* send reports, few refused outright. Several said that the research was still in progress, or that preliminary results might be misleading, or that a report was not yet available. In the case of contract studies, a few researchers said that they could not release the report without the consent of the contracting office. Several people said they had no available copies. One said all his papers had been destroyed in a fire, and one said his report was not available in English. Two insisted that their reports were on the way (one actually arrived about eight months later).

After five months of intensive effort, we had a total of 148 reports. The next step was to select those to be used in the interviewing.

Selection of Studies

One possible criterion for selecting the 50 research studies was representativeness of the population of ADAMHA-funded research. This would have called for a strategy of random sampling. However, two considerations made this a poor choice: one, the purpose of our study and two, the practical limitations of the universe with which we were dealing. The purpose of centering our study around the reading of actual research reports was to evoke realistic responses for the analysis of characteristics of research reports that made them more or less usable. Our interest was not in the absolute level of reported usefulness of ADAMHA-sponsored social research. Political attacks on government research programs were much in the news at the time, and we did not want our data to become entangled in the controversy. We were aware that our measures of reported usefulness, while serving well for relative comparisons between studies with differing sets of characteristics, could be misinterpreted if they were used as indicators of the absolute level of usefulness of mental health research. Therefore, we were not particularly concerned with the representativeness of the studies we used. We would be concentrating on the *relationships* between study characteristics and usefulness.

Moreover, there were practical difficulties in the way of random sampling. The reports that we had laboriously collected did not, as we had good reason to know, represent the universe of studies. The studies that we had *not* acquired were likely to differ in significant respects from those we had. Therefore, randomly sampling from the studies in hand would not yield a random sample of the total universe of ADAMHA-funded research. Furthermore, that universe is not stable over time. Any sample would be tied to (and limited by) the particular years from which the sample was selected. For example, studies on mental retardation had been funded by NIMH during the 1960s, but in 1974, when we were selecting reports, such research was being done under sponsorship of the National Institute of Child Health and Human Development in NIH. Other characteristics besides topic vary over time, according to the exigencies of the funding bodies. The balance of basic and applied research, the scale of studies in time and dollars, the populations studied—all may change from year to year. What was representative of ADAMHA research in 1974 would not necessarily be representative of ADAMHA research in subsequent years.

So despite the neatness of random sampling as a selection

strategy, there were problems in achieving real representativeness and there were no intrinsic reasons for seeking representativeness. Accordingly, we turned to other criteria.

Another possible method for selecting studies was through nomination by knowledgeable informants. Again there were problems. First, any procedure that called for nominations would be dependent on the visibility of the research and the unknown processes that affect visibility. Second, it would be even more time-bound than random sampling. Informants would probably be much more likely to remember recently reported studies than those even a year or two old. If there were any temporal eccentricities in ADAMHA-funded grants and contracts, the nomination procedure would be likely to magnify them. And while representativeness of all social research studies was not necessary, there seemed no reason to choose a selection procedure that might accentuate one specific time period of funding and its concomitant idiosyncracies. Third, a nomination procedure would create a new sampling problem—the sampling of informants. When we began to consider how to choose informants who would nominate studies, we recognized that every possible strategy would have biases. Choosing informants within ADAMHA, in universities, in mental health agencies—all would bias the type of research studies nominated, and in unknown ways. There was not enough information available about possible informants to choose people who were informed about a wide array of social research studies on mental health.

Accordingly, we chose a third option for selecting research studies—the construction of a typology of research studies and the selection of studies to represent each cell in the typology. There were three variables of research studies that we believed might particularly affect their usefulness to decision makers, and we wanted all combinations of these variables to be represented in the sample of studies. Furthermore, these were variables that we thought were apt to be confounded with each other; the typology selection procedure would avoid analytic problems with multi-collinearity by assuring that the variables would appear in different combinations. The three dimensions from which the typology was developed were: (a) the manipulability of the major independent variables, (b) the administrative implementability of the study's conclusions and/or implications, and (c) the political acceptability of the study's findings, i.e., compatibility with current philosophy and policy in the relevant governmental institutions.

The operationalization of the typology involved defining the categories in such a way as to achieve acceptable levels of intercoder reliability. This proved to have fruitful side effects. In clarifying categories in the typology, we also clarified questions to be asked of respondents.

The selection process began with the screening of all study reports that we had collected to ensure that they (a) had been funded by ADAMHA, (b) focused on a topic in the broad field of mental health, (c) were social scientific (thus eliminating, for example, a study of animal behavior, a legal-historical analysis, and a simple fact-finding count of activities), and (d) were conducted with minimal technical adequacy. This latter criterion was necessary to avoid bothering busy respondents with obviously inept research and losing their cooperation in the interview. The cutoff point was not very high. The remaining studies covered a wide range of scientific quality.

The studies that survived this screening were coded on the three typology variables by two coders; ratings were compared and differences reconciled. Then studies were chosen insofar as possible to fill each of the eight cells in the typology. Entering into the selection was a concern for ensuring a *spread* on several other characteristics of research that we thought might affect usefulness, such as funding by contract or grant, the type of research group performing the work, basic or applied focus. Although we did not give such descriptors as high a priority as the variables that went into the typology, in cases where several studies would fit the typology we took the opportunity to include variation on these dimensions.

One of the possibilities that we faced was that contract and grant research would differ in patterned ways. According to common stereotypes, contract research would be politically acceptable, with manipulable variables and implementable results, and grant research would tend to veer off into nonmanipulable variables, nonimplementable results, and political unacceptability. We tried, therefore, to find examples of both types of award in all cells of the typology, in order to be able to find out if there were residual distinctions between grants and contracts that would still make for differences in the data. As it turned out, there was no more trouble in locating contract studies that fit the cells than grant studies. In our final sample of 50 studies, we had 13 contract studies, and they were distributed across seven of the eight categories.

The 50 studies finally selected had the characteristics shown in table 3.3. As the table indicates, there are studies in all the cells. Optimally the cell frequencies would be equal, but even though they are not, the distribution helped to avoid the more severe problems attendant upon multicollinearity.

Other descriptors of the 50 studies included in the sample, as coded by staff coders, are shown in table 3.4. As the data show, the selection procedure yielded a diversity of studies covering a wide range of ADAMHA-funded social science research.

Abstracting the Studies

For each of the 50 studies, we wrote a two-page abstract. The abstract had a set format (see figure 3.1, which is the standardized form that abstracters followed), and covered (a) objectives of the study, (b) methods of measurement, data collection, and analysis, (c) findings, and (d) conclusions and (if any) recommendations. Enough information had to be conveyed to allow respondents to make judgments about the scientific merit of the study, the cogency of the findings, and their usefulness, without taking too much of their time or patience. Pretests suggested that two pages was the maximum tolerable length.

A standard two-page length turned out to be a Procrustean bed. Four-hundred-page reports and twenty-page articles were reduced to the same length. In abstracting long and complex studies, it became necessary to select a few aspects for the abstract rather than cover the studies in their entirety. Therefore, our study became an analysis not so much of the original reports as of the abstracts that we developed from them. When we talk of charac-

Table 3.3. Research Studies Selected, by Typology Category

	Results Politically Acceptable		Results Not Politically Acceptable		
	Results Implementable	Results Not Implementable	Results Implementable	Results Not Implementable	Total
Manipulable independent variables	16	3	6	5	30
Independent variables not manipulable	7	7	1	5	20
Total	23	10	7	10	50

Table 3.4. Characteristics of Studies Selected for Interviews, as Coded by Staff

Type of award:	
Grant	37
Contract	13
Year of research report:	
1975, 1974	21
1973	11
1972 or earlier	18
Type of research organization conducting study:	
Service agency	15
University	13
For-profit research organization	10
Nonuniversity nonprofit research organization	6
State or local government agency	4
Other	2
Type of population studied:	
Individuals	
Clients of CMHCs	9
Children, adolescents	8
Alcoholics	6
Criminals, delinquents	3
Drug users	3
Elderly	2
Other special population	2
"Normal" population	6
Institutions	
CMHCs	8
Other institutions, programs	3
Publication status of research report:	
Published	17
Unpublished	33
Type of data:	
Quantitative	41
Qualitative	2
Both	7
Direction of findings:	
Positive	16
Negative	22
Neither; mixed	12
Recommendations in report:	
Concrete explicit recommendations	23
Implicit or none	27

Figure 3.1 Standardized Form For Abstracts

Title, Author, Author's Institution, Year.

Objectives (Be brief!): To accomplish something (what?)
To evaluate something (what?)
To describe something (what?)

Method: (This is very important and should be comprehensive. Nothing should be included in *Findings* which is not explained in *Method!*)
Sample/Site: How many subjects? How were they selected? From what population do they come? What special characteristics do they have (age, sex, race, income, disabilities, etc.)?
Where does the research take place? Where are the data collected? If there is more than one site, how many were there and of what kinds? Examples: a CMHC or hospital, by mail, or a specific university, ten New York state prisons, etc.
Variables Investigated: What variables were considered in the research? Include those for which there were no significant findings. Separate independent and dependent variables. Dependent variables are the variables which you are trying to explain or affect, the outcome behaviors, attitudes, or conditions you are interested in. Independent variables are the variables which you use to explain variations in the dependent variables or outcomes. They are the factors which you hypothesize will make a difference in the outcomes. Example: If you want to evaluate the effect of two counseling techniques on drinking behavior in male and female subjects, then the independent variables are the two counseling techniques and sex, and the dependent variable is drinking behavior. *After each variable (or set of variables), record how it is operationalized.* E.g., drinking behavior, measured by self-report on questionnaire. Record if special instruments or tests are used or special validation techniques are used.
Data Collection and Analysis: How were the data collected? What techniques were used to get measures for each subject? Examples: Respondents were interviewed individually in their homes. Data were obtained from hospital records. Administrators reported on the practice in their institutions, etc. This should be detailed. What was the nature of statistical analysis and what tests of significance were used?

Findings: Carefully list major findings which are based directly on the data. Include actual numbers from the data where possible. Try to group findings to correspond to objectives. Note where findings are statistically significant. Include important null findings (i.e. findings which show no effect). Be clear!

Conclusions and Recommendations: Briefly list general conclusions, especially those which don't come directly from data, and recommendations for future action or research, if any. This section should be relatively short as the emphasis should be on *Method* and *Findings*.

teristics of reseach studies in following chapters, it should be noted that these are research studies as converted by us to abstracts. Since our focus is on the relationships between study characteristics and usefulness, it was not necessary that we preserve the actual characteristics of the original studies, although we conscientiously tried to do so. One alteration that we inevitably made was in the prose style of the abstract. In almost every case, by dint of extensive writing, rewriting, and revising, we achieved greater clarity of presentation than the original. Occasionally clarity was achieved at the expense of full exposition of complexity.

The presentation of research to decision makers in the form of two-page abstracts was an aid, rather than a drawback, to verisimilitude. As we learned, decision makers generally get their news about research reports in abbreviated form. While few of them have the time or inclination to read long technical documents, they do read short summaries. Our abstracts proved to be a good approximation of their usual introduction to research.

See Appendix A for two examples of study abstracts.

Assigning Abstracts
to Respondents

The most important principle guiding the assignment of study abstracts to respondents was that the topic of the studies they were asked to judge should match the issues with which they and their offices dealt. If we asked people to judge the characteristics of studies remote from their concerns, particularly the usability of such studies, we would get judgments with little weight or meaning. Our measures of usability and likelihood of use depended upon respondents' familiarity with the situation.

This principle was important, but in practice it had to be tempered because of the scope of our concern. NIMH and the other institutes fund studies on many topics that do not appear to be directly within *anyone's* official jurisdiction, e.g. the correlates of happiness, conditions under which alcohol is used to relieve tension. One of our long-standing assumptions was that studies not directly geared to current program or policy issues could still prove useful to decision makers. Therefore, in order not to foreclose the possibility that they would provide useful ideas and information, we included basic as well as applied research studies in the sample. We did not drop any study because of difficulty in matching it to an obvious "potential user."

Of course, this decision made the assignment task more difficult than it would have been had we chosen only studies commissioned by government bureaus or studies that fitted the responsibilities of identifiable decision makers. We had to try to maintain a reasonable match of studies with the work of respondents in order to keep the link to reality and still include these more basic investigations. The advantage was that we would be able to analyze decision makers' judgments of the usefulness of basic as well as applied social research studies for their work.[2]

A second criterion that governed the assignment of abstracts to respondents was the imperative of our research design. Each study had to be read and rated approximately the same number of times in order to have data of comparable reliability, and each study had to be read and rated by occupants of all five positions in the sample so that cross-position comparisons would be based on exposure to the same stimuli. So two people in each of five positions had to rate the same research abstract.[3] It took careful attention to jurisdictions of agencies, titles of positions, and information from knowledgeable informants, to match the content of jobs to the content of research studies. For researchers and review committee members, the analogous matching process was based on the subject of their own research, the jurisdiction of the research review committee on which they served, and their current position. Although there was no way to accomplish perfect fit, later responses indicated a reasonable match of research reports to respondents' jobs.

Content of the Studies

The studies dealt with a wide range of topics. Some were concerned with the origins and correlates of mental illness and/or deviant behavior, and they examined the effects of poverty, ethnicity, status inequality, marital status, family values, personal relationships, stress. Some described changes in individuals' problem behavior (drug abuse, delinquency, mental disabilities among the elderly) over time and changing conditions. A number were concerned with the ways in which treatment agencies functioned —their organizational effectiveness, interagency relationships, clienteles, use of innovations, citizen participation. Several evaluated the outcomes of particular treatment modalities or programs —day care for the mentally ill, group and individual aftercare for released patients, perceptual training for children with learning disorders, behavior modification strategies, psychological services for patients in prepaid health plans. A few studied community attitudes and responses—to suicide attempts, to released mental patients, to advertising campaigns alerting the public to the dangers of drinking.

In order to understand the relevance of the studies to the issues in the mental health field at the time of the fieldwork, it may be well to review the outlines of government policy in 1975. The basic policy of the federal government was support of community mental health centers (CMHCs). Over 500 federally supported CMHCs were functioning in communities around the country, providing a range of mandated services to residents of their "catchment areas." The basic services that CMHCs were originally required to provide—inpatient, outpatient, partial hospitalization, emergency, and consultation and education services—had been extended to include care for the elderly, for children, for alcoholics, and for chronically ill patients who are released from mental hospitals.

The support of community treatment on this scale, with plans for continuing expansion of the number of CMHCs, was a marked departure from earlier government policy. For over a century, the primary mode of care for the mentally ill had been state-supported mental hospitals, large institutions often in rural areas, where psychiatric patients tended to stay for lengthy periods of time (Deutsch 1949; Greenblatt, York, and Braum 1955). By the 1940s there was growing disillusionment with the efficacy of such institutions in providing therapy and rehabilitation. They were coming to be regarded as warehouses and "snake pits" where people were shunted aside, often for life, to live in conditions of apathy and isolation at best, and at worst of humiliation, exploitation, and filth.

The movement to get patients out of the depersonalized state hospitals gathered adherents through the 1940s and '50s, and came to be known as "deinstitutionalization." With the success of psychoactive drugs in reducing disturbing symptomatology in the mid-1950s, it became possible to release patients to their homes, to group care facilities and halfway houses, and to other small facilities in the community. Cognate to deinstitutionalization was "community care." Community treatment facilities were expected not only to provide care for patients released from hospitals and prevent their rehospitalization; they were also expected to provide early treatment for people in the beginning stages of mental illness, to provide emergency and short-term intervention, and to prevent the onset of serious illness (Joint Commission of Mental Illness and Health 1961).

The Community Mental Health Act of 1965 marked the beginning of federal support for mental health treatment. Under this act and its renewals, funding was provided for construction of CMHCs and for staffing. Federal money for staffing each center was to continue at declining levels for a total of eight years, at which time the center was expected to be self-supporting. Each center was expected to serve a contiguous population of 150,000 to 200,000 (Foley 1975).

The CMHC was the basic framework of government mental health policy at the time of our interviews. Although Presidents Nixon and Ford had both made efforts to cut federal support for CMHCs, the Congress had kept appropriations intact. Professionals in the field were in substantial agreement that CMHCs were a vital element in mental health care. Federal, state, and local mental health officials rallied around their protection and expansion. Nevertheless, reports critical of the CMHC program were appearing (USGAO 1974; Chu and Trotter 1974; for an analysis of the content and methods of these reports, see Siegel and Doty 1979), and threats to the renewal of the CMHC legislation continued.

Other policy controversies that engaged the field—and there

were inevitable controveries in a field that had never come to consensus on what mental illness was, how it originated, or what modalities of care were most effective—tended to focus on institutional arrangements and methods of service. Opinion was divided on such matters as what the appropriate role of state mental hospitals should be, how community care could be organized and operated to meet the needs of the chronically mentally ill, what modes of service were most suitable for the elderly, the drug addict, and the alcoholic, what were effective strategies for early identification of those vulnerable to mental illness, how poor people and minority group members might most effectively be treated and retained in treatment, whether there were techniques adequate for the prevention of mental illness, whether CMHCs and other community treatment agencies should seek to provide a range of "reality services" (such as aid in employment, housing, education, child care, household financial management) to help people in distress cope more effectively with their environment, how mental health services could be provided through other agencies—schools, courts, probation services, social welfare agencies—to serve people in need, how mental health services could best be coordinated in a community.

These were the major kinds of issues in the studies that we used for the interviews. Some of the studies' conclusions harmonized easily with current policy paradigms, others were more controversial, a few raised fundamental criticisms. Our respondents reacted to the social research studies that we presented them within the general context of mental health policy as it had evolved at this time.

NOTES

1. In seven states, the "main city" was the state capital, but in Illinois, the main city was Chicago because the department of mental health was located there; in Washington, Olympia and Seattle were both included; for Maryland, Baltimore was used because again the department of health and mental hygiene maintained its office there.

2. It might be well to mention here that our assumption about basic research received some support. As the data turned out, studies that we classified as "basic research" were not rated significantly less useful than the other studies in the sample.

3. In the pretests, an order effect appeared in respondents' ratings of research studies. They tended to be harsher on the study rated first in the interview. Therefore, in the main study we systematically varied the order in which each abstract was presented in the interview. This meant that each study was assigned to be read once in first position and once in second position by each category of respondent. Analysis of the final data showed no significant order effect.

Chapter Four

RESEARCH CHARACTERISTICS: FRAMES OF REFERENCE FOR ASSESSING RESEARCH

M OST PEOPLE WOULD AGREE that the properties of social science research studies have some effect on the degree to which decision makers pay attention to them. Some studies are so poorly done or so disconnected from the context within which officials work that they must seem less useful than better conducted or more relevant studies.

But what are the actual properties of research that are viewed as critical by decision makers? Or to phrase the question the other way, what are the criteria that decision makers use in judging whether or not studies are useful to their work? All of us have criteria, explicit or implicit, that govern the weight we give to particular pieces of research. In essence, they represent our "frames of reference," the dimensions through which we filter incoming studies before deciding whether to take them seriously or to disregard them. Among social scientists, the key frames of reference are expected to be the methodological soundness of the study and the theoretical orientation underlying the study, but even social scientists use other criteria—the relevance of the topic to their area of specialization, perhaps the fit of the findings with their expectations, the reputation and affiliation of the researcher, and so on. Among decision makers, the central frames of reference—as well as the collateral frames—are less consensually defined. The aim of this inquiry is to discover which frames of reference decision makers actually apply in assessing the usefulness of social science research studies for the work in which they are engaged. Because of the difficulty that most people have in expressing the standards of judgment that they use, we investigated this question by giving decision makers abstracts of actual studies to read, having them rate the studies both on usefulness and on research descriptors, and then analyzing the relationship between the two sets of ratings.

Theoretical Framework

The basic assumption with which we began was that each decision maker in a public agency is expected to perform multiple functions with competing and potentially contradictory demands. Specifically, mental health decision makers as potential users of social science research face three competing sets of demands.

First, they are expected to be managers, administrators of programs, supervisors of staff—people who get things done. They are executives who organize resources for the performance of tasks that will forward the mission of their agency. The norms associated with the executive orientation relate to action and accomplishment.

Second, they are members of professional fields that have claims to a scientific basis. As such, they are expected to pay attention to research (including social science research) that advances the state of knowledge in the field of mental health and the expertness of its practice. Their scientific orientation gives them a responsibility to examine the validity of research studies before accepting them as guides to action. The norms associated with the scientific orientation relate to concern with the validity of research that enters into policy and program development.

Third, they are also upper-level members of bureaucratic organizations. Because they hold positions in public or quasi-public organizations, they have a political orientation which alerts them to the needs for protecting and advancing the position of their agency in the surrounding political environment. They are expected to be concerned about the survival and growth of their bureaus, their programs, and their budgets. At the same time, they have responsibilities for promoting the policy positions that they believe are beneficial to the clients of the agency. It can uncharitably be said that decision makers' policy positions are determined by self-interested concerns for power, influence, and career advancement. With more generosity and possibly more truth, it can equally well be hypothesized that officials in service agencies, particularly professionals, believe in the programs they manage. While their organizational location no doubt affects the way they view issues, their recruitment into the profession, the agency, and the job was influenced by belief in the value of what the agency does, and once they are in the field, their professional socialization should increase their sense of the value of their mission. Their interest in preserving and extending particular programs is thus likely to be affected not only by commitment to the welfare of their unit and their career but also by an overlapping commitment to the welfare of the public they serve. They believe in what they do and they want to promote the agencies and programs in which they do it. The two "political" interests seem to be inherently intermingled. The norms associated with the political orientation relate to the protection and enhancement of their programs and agencies and the advancement of their own beliefs and policy positions.

The theoretical premise from which we started was that occupants of executive positions in mental health agencies are responsive to all three sets of norms. Each set makes valid demands on them, and to the extent that they call for different responses in a concrete situation, decision makers must make difficult choices. Fortunately, at any particular time, not all of the three orientations are likely to be salient. If the program is not under threat, the political orientation may have low priority. If the program is operating efficiently, the need to increase attention to managerial issues may not be great. But our assumption was that the nature of executive status in a professional service bureaucracy requires attention to diverse and competing expectations.

Hypotheses

The managerial, scientific, and political orientations that we posited for decision makers led us to hypotheses about their standards for useful social science research. We expected that they would screen research according to three general criteria: a criterion of implementability corresponding to their managerial orientation, a scientific criterion corresponding to their scientific orientation, and a political criterion corresponding to their political orientation. They would exercise all three standards simultaneously or in rotation, because each corresponds to a facet of their organizational role.

Specifically, we hypothesized that decision makers would consider social science research studies more useful to the extent that studies (a) provided implementable conclusions, (b) were methodologically competent, and (c) conformed with users' beliefs and agency policy. These three criteria would represent dimensions to which decision makers are alert and therefore would constitute dimensions that they use to *describe* research and to *assess* its usefulness.

The concern with implementability derives from the need to get the job done in order to achieve the agency's mandated goals. As managers, decision makers can be expected to look at a social science research study with an eye toward the feasibility of implementing the study's conclusions.

Certainly many commentaries on social science research as an aid to decision-making have stressed the need for practical conclusions. Critics often complain that social research studies deal with social issues in global terms and make grandiose recommendations. For example, a study dealing with the financial crisis of an American city concludes with a recommendation for fundamental redistribution of income in the United States. There is little that any city official, or anyone else, can do about making changes of that order.[1] Or else research offers data but no interpretation of those data for action, so that busy executives are left to ferret out whatever guidance they can from the turgid prose and complex tables. Many social research studies deal with the effects of unbudgeable or "sticky" variables, such as race and socioeconomic status, which government decision makers cannot alter, and they ignore the manipulable variables, such as program availability or eligibility for services, which decision makers can change. When social research studies do not match the decision needs and scope of authority of decision makers, then they are likely to have limited influence. Therefore, it seems reasonable to expect that decision makers would describe and judge research in terms of the practicality, feasibility, and implementability of study conclusions.

From a scientific perspective, decision makers should be concerned about relying on social science research only when it provides valid knowledge. In this mode, therefore, we expected them to be alert to the technical quality of the studies from which the conclusions derive. Incorporated into this frame of reference should be sensitivity to scientific canons of design, measurement, analysis, objectivitiy, and generalizability. We anticipated that research of poor scientific quality would be regarded as lower in usefulness than more competent research.

Not all observers of the use of research in government agencies agree that the technical competence of research affects its use. Many of them, particularly social scientists, are skeptical that decision makers pay any attention at all to methodological soundness; it is the conclusions of the research that matter, and whether or not they are compatible with what officials want to do. There is some tentative evidence to support this formulation (van de Vall 1975; Useem and DiMaggio 1978). Although we were not sure how salient a frame of reference technical merit would be, we believed that professionals in mental health would be sensitive to methodological quality. At the very least, they might screen out shoddy or obviously biased studies.

From a political perspective, we believed that decision makers would describe social research in terms of its political acceptability. This dimension would reflect the importance of the value orientations of potential users of the research and the compatibility of a study's conclusions with these values. Also relevant here would be the congruence between a study's conclusions and the institutions, structures, and program arrangements currently in place. It semed probable that a research study would be seen as particularly useful when it supported the position that potential users held and legitimated their programs. Decision makers might well regard research that challenged things-as-they-are as less useful than research that could be used as ammunition in their own and their agency's cause.

These, then, were our original hypotheses. In operational terms, we expected that factor analysis of decision makers' ratings of specific studies would yield three factors—one having to do with implementability, one with scientific merit, and one with political acceptability. This would be the underlying structure in respondents' views of social science research.

We expected these factors to be related to respondents' perceptions of the usefulness of studies for their work. Given the multiple roles that decision makers performed on their jobs, each factor would tend to distinguish studies that were viewed as more useful from those viewed as less useful. We expected that the background and experience of decision makers and the types of positions they occupied would affect which criterion had greatest weight on their judgments of the usefulness of studies.

In addition to the three anticipated factors, we believed it necessary that studies be relevant to the substantive content of decision makers' work, that they fit the decisions that decision makers actually faced. We tried in several ways to ensure this fit in advance. First, in assigning research studies to respondents, we made every effort to match topic to job title and responsibilities. Second, in the wording of the question about likelihood of use, we tried to build relevance into the context. We asked, "*Assuming your office had to consider the issues discussed in the study*, how likely is it that you would take the study results into account?" Finally, we asked respondents to tell us who "the most appropriate user" of each study would be. Besides answering the usefulness questions for themselves, they responded to questions about the study's usefulness for occupants of the "most appropriate" position as well.

With all our efforts to assure a high and stable level of topical relevance, we knew that there would be variation in the degree to which the substance of the research abstracts matched respondents' jobs. We expected that variation in relevance would affect respondents' ratings of the usability of studies. Therefore, we asked a specific question about the extent to which the topic of the study was "relevant to the issues your office deals with." We thought that relevance would be a dimension separate from the other hypothesized factors.

Such were our expectations. It is time to see how the research characteristics actually clustered.

Factor Analysis of Descriptor
Ratings

Each respondent rated two studies on the 29 descriptive characteristics listed in figure 4.1. We factor-analzyed the ratings. The total number of (analytic) cases for factor analysis was 510, which represents ratings of two studies by each of 255 respondents.

Factor analysis as used here is more than a data reduction technique. It isolates those analytically separable dimensions of real studies that respondents use in their ratings. The factors sum-

Figure 4.1 Descriptors on Which Respondents Rated Studies

To what extent is the general topic of the study relevant to the issues your office deals with?

To what extent do you think that the findings are valid?

To what extent do the findings agree with your sense of the situation?

Please indicate the extent to which each statement applies to the study:

a. Deals with a high priority issue
b. Adds to descriptive, causal, or theoretical knowledge in the field
c. Adds to practical knowledge about the operation of policies or programs
d. Compatible with the ideas and values of the potential user
e. Analyzes the effects of factors that decision makers can do something about
f. Has direct implications for a course of action
g. Implies the need for major change in philosophy, organization, or services
h. Targeted, i.e. focuses on a narrow set of dependent, or outcome, variables
i. Contains explicit recommendations
j. Supports a position already held by the user
k. Recommendations are supported by the data
l. Implications of the findings are politically acceptable
m. Consistent with a body of previous knowledge
n. Findings can be applied within existing agencies and programs
o. Challenges existing assumptions and institutional arrangements
p. Raises new issues or offers new perspectives
q. Inexpensive to implement
r. On time for a pending decision
s. Findings are unexpected or novel
t. Provides quantitative data
u. Generalizable to equivalent populations
v. Comprehensive, i.e., includes most of the potentially explanatory variables in analysis
w. Statistically sophisticated
x. Technical quality of the research is high
y. Findings are internally consistent and unambiguous
z. Objective, unbiased

NOTE: All descriptors were rated on a 5-point scale from "to a great extent" to "not at all."

marize the patterns of covariation in respondents' descriptions and, as such, represent underlying constructs that people use in describing research.

From the factor analysis, we located four stable factors.[2] The four factors were very similar when we analyzed the ratings of the total sample, the decision maker subsample, and the researcher and review panel subsample.[3] They represent dimensions of research that people distinguish as they assess research. Obviously the factors derive from the list of research characteristics that we provided. Our list was developed from extensive study of the literature on research utilization and organizational receptivity to knowledge, refined by repeated pretests, and it attempted to represent the dimensions of research that have been found to affect use. In factor-analyzing the data, we found that omission of some of the items (e.g., because of a large number of missing values) left the factors unchanged. In effect, they appear to be tapping constructs about research that tend to remain stable.

Figure 4.2 lists the items in each factor and their loadings. The four factors do not agree completely with the three factors hypothesized. Two of them, however, are very close. One is the factor that includes the items:

Contains explicit recommendations
Analyzes the effects of factors that decision makers can do something
    about
Targeted, i.e., focuses on a narrow set of dependent, or outcome, variables
Has direct implications for a course of action
Findings can be applied within existing agencies and programs
Adds to practical knowledge about the operation of policies and programs

This factor is much like the hypothesized factor relating to the implementability of study conclusions. A study that is rated high on this factor deals with manipulable variables, has clear implications for action, which are explicitly spelled out, and which are implementable within existing programs and structures. This is just the kind of research that managers can put directly to use. Perhaps the only surprise is that the item "inexpensive to implement" did not load this factor. "Inexpensive" did not load on any factor, in effect forming a separate factor of its own. An explanation is suggested by the fact that respondents had difficulty in

Figure 4.2 Factors of Research Characteristics

Loading	Factor I	
.922	Technical quality is high	
.890	Statistically sophisticated	
.794	Objective, unbiased	
.745	Provides quantitative data	
.702	Findings internally consistent, unambiguous	
.634	Recommendations supported by data	RESEARCH QUALITY
.625	Comprehensive set of explanatory variables	
.612	Generalizable to equivalent populations	
.569	Findings are valid	
.560	Adds to descriptive, causal, theoretical knowledge	

Loading	Factor II	
.745	Supports user position	
.718	Consistent with previous knowledge	
.663	Compatible with user ideas and values	CONFORMITY WITH USER EXPECTATIONS
.613	Agrees with respondent's sense of situation	
-.550	Findings unexpected or novel (negative)	

Loading	Factor III	
.706	Contains explicit recommendations	
.703	Manipulable independent variables	
.664	Targeted—few dependent variables	ACTION ORIENTATION
.661	Direct implications for action	
.605	Applicable within existing programs	
.526	Adds to practical knowledge	

Loading	Factor IV	
.764	Challenges existing assumptions and arrangements	
.738	Implies need for major change in philosophy, organization, or services	CHALLENGE TO STATUS QUO
.574	Raises new issues or perspectives	
-.437	Findings are politically acceptable (negative)	

NOTE: Factors are derived from 510 ratings of 50 research studies.

rating inexpensiveness; this item had a large proportion of missing answers (36 percent of the total sample, 35 percent even among decision makers). If some people were unable to rate it, others may have rated it unreliably. There is considerable complexity involved in figuring out (a) what implementation would involve, (b) how much it would cost, and (c) what scale of expense to apply in order to determine whether it fell within the range of "inexpensive." It seems likely, in retrospect, that the inexpensiveness item was vulnerable to excessive measurement error.

In all events, we do have a factor related to the feasibility and practicality of applying the results of the study to program or policy decisions. We call it Action Orientation.

A second factor that appears much as expected has to do with the scientific aspect of the work of mental health officials. It contains the cluster of items relating to the technical competence of a research study. Loading on this factor, which we call Research Quality, are (in order of loading):

Technical quality of the research is high
Statistically sophisticated
Objective, unbiased
Provides quantitative data
Findings are internally consistent and unambiguous
Recommendations are supported by data
Comprehensive, i.e., includes most of the potentially explanatory variables in analysis
Generalizable to equivalent populations
Findings are valid
Adds to descriptive, causal, or theoretical knowledge in the field.

Most of these items deal strictly with the methodological competence of the study. They are concerned with the logic and rigor of research. Two of them relate to the norms of science: "objective, unbiased" and "recommendations supported by the data." It thus appears that characteristics of objectivity are integrally related to characteristics of scientific competence.

Another two of the items that load on the factor have to do with how the results happen to turn out: the internal consistency and unambiguousness of the findings and the addition to descriptive, causal, or theoretical knowledge. In practice these two characteristics of a study are beyond the control of the researcher; they are the luck of the draw. Even an elegantly designed and executed study conducted with great objectivity can yield inconsistent, on-the-one-hand-but-on-the-other-hand results. And even an elegant and objective study can add little that is new to the corpus of knowledge, either because it replicates what is already known or because it fails to confirm the hypotheses that stimulated its development. Nevertheless, our respondents' answers show that consistency of findings and addition to knowledge add to the authoritativeness of research. They merge with considerations of technical competence. The Research Quality factor thus represents not only the methodological soundness usually associated with technical quality but also the cogency of the research.[4]

So far, so good. The pattern of ratings has tended to confirm the dimensions of administrative feasibility and research quality. However, the hypothesized political factor, it turns out, separated into two factors. One of them contains the items:

Supports a position already held by the user
Consistent with a body of previous knowledge
Compatible with the ideas and values of the potential user
Agrees with [the respondent's] sense of the situation
Findings are unexpected or novel (negative)

The underlying theme of this factor appears to be compatibility of a research study's conclusions with what the potential user believes. The emphasis is on the user, rather than on the agency or program or the larger political system. There is certainly some sense, among the items clustering in this factor, that a study is congenial to the user's values and policy position and as such is in his interest. But there is a more pervasive sense that it conforms with what he knows is so, that it supports his construction of reality. Studies rated high on this factor would confirm the user's image of the way things work. They are plausible. They are intuitively congenial. Therefore, we have labeled the factor Conformity with User Expectations.

The Conformity factor addresses research studies mainly in terms of their consonance with prior knowledge. In this form, it becomes grounds for believing a study's results, because they are consistent with one's own knowledge and experience. The Research

Quality factor provided technical grounds for trust in a study: it was good research. The Conformity factor appears to offer a separate and independent source of trust or distrust in a study's results. If a study is high on Conformity, it is credible because it fits into one's existing framework of concepts, causal theories, and empirical information. An experienced executive relies on his experience as an alternative source of information to that provided by social science research. When the two sources conflict, he may criticize the research for its methodological inadequacy, not out of peevishness or even self-interest but because the methodology that was used yielded results contrary to his informed judgment. The results seem to be "wrong," and therefore the methodology of the study is suspect.

The Conformity factor is not related to radicalism-conservatism in the broader arena of national politics. It does not have to do with partisan orientations or broad social ideologies. In the context of this inquiry, it relates to agreement with users' knowledge and beliefs about mental health institutions, programs, and philosophy. We examined the possibility that the Conformity factor contained an element of political conservatism by computing its correlation with respondents' reported political orientation. (They had reported their political orientation on a 5-point scale from radical to conservative.) The correlation for decision makers was .04, for researchers and review committee members .02, and for the total sample .03.

Items about institutional policy cluster in a separate factor which has a more overtly political cast. The items in this factor are:

Challenges existing assumptions and institutional arrangements
Implies the need for major change in philosophy, organization, or
  services
Raises new issues or offers new perspectives
Implications of the findings are politically acceptable (negative)

This factor represents major disagreement with current institutional policy or practice. The items concern the organizational structures through which (in this context) mental health services are provided. If we define politics as the process of allocating resources such as power, money, and prestige, then it is these organizational structures whose course is largely determined by politics. The factor, therefore, has a distinctly political flavor, and as the negative loading on the last item indicates, studies rated high on this factor tend to be politically unacceptable. We call the factor Challenge to the Status Quo.

Our hypothesized political factor has become two factors. One of them almost depoliticizes the individual's own values, beliefs, and self-interest, and integrates them with prior knowledge. This factor, Conformity with User Expectations, is so firmly organized around the user's sense of the situation that it contains only a mild suggestion of research as a tool in the struggle for advantage. It is explicitly about the individual's beliefs, knowledge, and point of view. The other factor, Challenge to the Status Quo, becomes the repository of political considerations. It deals with assault on the current practice of (mental health) organizations.

Although it appears likely at first glance, Conformity and Challenge are not opposite ends of a continuum. The two factors are not negatively correlated. They are essentially not correlated at all (Pearson $r = .05$). The factors vary independently. This independence indicates that decision makers are almost as likely to agree as to disagree with research findings that challenge institutional practice. Mental health institutions are not monolithic in belief. There is apt to be an underground, perhaps even a sizable overground, that questions policy, program, or structural arrangements. At the least, respondents differentiate between organizational behavior and their own values and beliefs.

An example may clarify the distinction between Conformity and Challenge. In 1975 when we were conducting our interviews, the accepted premise in mental health policy was that most psychiatric patients would fare better in the community than in state mental hospitals. Policies promoted diversion from hospitalization to community treatment, wherever possible, and early release for patients who had been hospitalized. However, in many places community treatment facilities were inadequate, and the care that released chronic patients received was not well suited to their needs. Many mental health officials were aware of the shortcomings. Thus, when one of our studies reported that released mental patients were making poor adjustments to reentry into the community and that contact with community mental health centers neither contributed to successful reentry nor reduced rehospitalization, the conclusion "conformed" with the beliefs of not a few mental health officials. But at this period, it "challenged" the assumptions and arrangements of the mental health systems in most states and implied a need for major change.

The Challenge factor points toward change. In this respect, it has something in common with the Action Orientation factor, which also represents a push to reform. Unlike Action Orientation, however, which has a practical bent, studies rated high on Challenge suggest fundamental criticism and major change. There is a relationship between the two. In the final oblique factor solution, Challenge and Action Orientation are correlated ($r = .30$). (See table 4.1.)

The four factors account for twenty-five of the twenty-nine items on which studies were rated. Four items did not enter any of the factors. One was inexpensiveness which, as mentioned earlier, was only minimally correlated with any of the other variables. The other three items formed a cluster: relevance of the topic to the issues that one's office deals with, timeliness of the research for a pending decision, and the high priority of the issue.

As it turned out, there were a large number of "no answers" on the timeliness item (51 percent of all ratings, 41 percent among decision makers). It seemed that in many cases respondents did not know the time schedule of decision on a topic or felt that discrete decisions could be made—for example, about adoption of

Table 4.1. Intercorrelations Among Factors Describing Studies
(*Pearson Correlation Coefficients for Decision Makers' Ratings on Factors*)

	Conformity	Action Orientation	Challenge	Relevance
Research Quality	.19	.37	.15	.13
Conformity to User Expectations		.26	.05	.21
Action Orientation			.30	.25
Challenge to the Status Quo				.28

a treatment strategy—at many times at hundreds of decentralized sites. Whether or not a study was "on time" for such decisions was a feature less of the study than of the agencies, and their awareness and readiness. What we learned is that where decisions pertain to something other than a national issue on which sides have been taken, support mobilized, and pressure for action exerted, the definition of "timeliness" of research becomes remarkably amorphous. Because of the large number of missing values, there were statistical difficulties in including the item within a factor, and because of the flaccidity of definition, we were not sure it would add to clarity.

As for relevance of the topic for one's work, there were two procedural reasons for not trying to combine it with other items. First, unlike the other two items in the cluster, it was asked only of decision makers and not of researchers or review committee members. Therefore, any combinative factor would have to be disaggregated for analysis of researchers' and review committee members' responses, and analyses would not be comparable. Second, among decision makers, relevance logically pertained to usefulness of a research study only for themselves and not for those whom they designated "most appropriate users." Again, the issue of comparability argued for keeping the relevance item separate. Accordingly, we treated relevance, inexpensiveness, high priority, and timeliness as separate variables and will discuss them in the appropriate section.

To sum up, the factor analysis of respondents' ratings of 50 specific studies has yielded three types of factors. First, there is relevance to issues being considered by one's office (and its related items of priority of the topic and timeliness). Second, there are two factors that provide a basis for trust in a research study. These are Research Quality, which gauges the soundness of a study according to the canons of science, and Conformity with User Expectations, which subjects study results to the test of experience. Third, there are two factors that provide direction. Action Orientation, with its characteristics of explicitness and practicality, offers guidance for incremental change within existing programs. Challenge to the Status Quo, which questions intellectual, organizational, and political perspectives, points toward fundamental change.

Revised Hypotheses

Having empirically discovered the dimensions on which respondents describe research, we have to reconsider our original hypotheses about the effects of these dimensions on the usefulness of research studies. We retain the expectation that the multiple roles that decision makers perform within agencies evoke multiple standards for judging social research. Four of the standards that we expected them to use have in fact appeared: scientific merit, implementability, political acceptability, and relevance to their work. In addition, we have located another factor, Conformity with User Expectations, that enters respondents' judgments of research. It represents a dimension associated with the compatibility of research with the individual's beliefs, values, knowledge, and practical experience. The existence of the Conformity factor suggests that decision makers can be expected to screen research through the filter of their own knowledge and beliefs.

The political factor that we expected has changed shape. We originally conceptualized it as advancing the users' own interests and policy positions and the well-being of their agencies. However, analysis has shown that decision makers make a distinction between their own values and policy positions and those of their institutions. Accordingly, the political factor that emerged represents a challenge only to current philosophies and operations of institutions.

It is necessary to revise our hypotheses. Our revised hypotheses are that relevance is positively related to decision makers' perceptions of the usefulness of research studies, that both Research Quality and Conformity are positively related to usefulness, and that Action Orientation is positively related to usefulness. Challenge to the Status Quo, with its push toward fundamental change in policy, is no longer necessarily a threat to the user's own beliefs and values. But because it runs counter to prevailing political feasibilities, we hypothesize that it will be negatively related to judgments of usefulness. We now turn to the data.

NOTES

1. "It would probably be helpful if future research was directed at solving day-to-day problems and arriving at workable solutions. Most articles in the *APSR* and other jour-

nals do not deal even remotely with the real world and those that do come up with solutions that are totally unworkable. The suggestion that the income distribution in the United States should be restructured does not really help a city that is looking at an immediate budget deficit of $50 million and may have to lay off a third of its work force" (Michael Updike in Nagel and Neef 1975:95).

2. The specific solution presented here is the result of an oblique rotation, using a direct oblimin criterion, of the factors with eigenvalues greater than 1.00. The factors emerged from a principal components factoring of a matrix of Pearson correlation coefficients. Missing values were deleted pairwise. Because of the use of pairwise deletion in the correlation matrix, some method was necessary for estimation of the effects of missing values in calculating factor scores. A number of methods for weighting missing observations were tried. The factor scores from each method were correlated with the original items. The matrix was compared to the primary factor structure matrix obtained in the factor analysis, and the method of computation was selected which best reproduced the original matrix. It involved total estimation with missing observations assigned the mean value of the item. The factor score of a respondent was deleted if more than half of the items with loadings greater than .40 (in the factor pattern matrix) on that factor had missing observations.

3. We elected to adopt the solution for the total sample in our analysis, because one of our interests was comparison of the perceptions of different groups, and only when the factor structure was constant could we compare the scores of decision makers, research review committee members, and social science researchers. The factor solution for the decision maker subsample was very similar.

4. Not included on the interview schedule for decision makers, but included for research review committee members and social science researchers, were items on six additional characteristics of research. All of the additional descriptors had to do with research quality and called for technical judgments beyond those that decision makers might be qualified to make. The items on which only researchers and panel members rated studies were: "fit of the research design to the problem," "appropriateness of sampling methods," "appropriateness of sample size," "appropriateness of data sources and instruments," "appropriateness of comparison(s) made," "appropriateness of statistical procedures."

When we factor-analyzed *all* the rating items (including the additional six from the panel and researcher respondents), four of these six items loaded, as expected, on the Research Quality factor. They were elaborations of the same concept. The two items that did not load on Research Quality were the items on sampling methods and sample size; they formed a separate factor of their own. The suggestion is that sampling characteristics are distinguishable from other features of research quality, such as design, measurement, analysis, objectivity, consistency, etc. Nevertheless, they are related to quality. The correlation between the Sampling factor (composed of the two items) and the Research Quality factor is .43. The correlation between the Sampling factor and the most similar item on the decision maker schedule, "generalizable to equivalent populations," is .53, and its correlation with the other quality items from the researcher and panel schedule ranges from .54 for "fit of design to problem" to .63 for "appropriateness of comparisons made."

The additional items, which spell out technical merit in finer detail, thus tend to confirm the substantive meaning of the Research Quality factor. The factor does contain within it considerations of design, data collection, and analysis.

Chapter Five

EFFECTS OF RESEARCH CHARACTERISTICS ON DECISION MAKERS' JUDGMENTS OF USEFULNESS

To test the effects of the research characteristics on decision makers' judgments of the usefulness of research studies, we employed multiple regression. The intent was to find out the direction of effect and the relative importance of each factor for the usefulness of research. There were four different dependent variables, i.e., four measures of usefulness. The usefulness measures and the interview questions from which they derive are:

Usefulness Measure	*Interview Question*
Likelihood of own use	"Assuming your office had to consider the issues discussed in the study, how likely is it that you would take the study results into account?"
Substantive usefulness in own agency	"Focusing for a moment just on the study's findings, and not considering external constraints, to what extent does the study contain ideas or information that can contribute to the work of your agency?"
Likelihood of use by most appropriate user	"How likely do you think it is that these decision makers [those named by respondent as occupants of the

	one position for which the findings are most appropriate] would actually take the study results into account?"
Substantive usefulness for most appropriate user	"Focusing just on the findings, and and not considering external constraints, to what extent can the information or ideas in the study contribute to their work?"

All four measures were rated on a scale from 1 to 5, from "to a great extent" to "not at all."

Correlations among the four measures are high but not extremely high. They range from a low of .35 to a high of .55. Respondents make distinctions about usefulness in the four specific situations.

Of the correlations among the four measures of usefulness, the two that are highest occur when the user is the same—either oneself or the designated most appropriate user. For oneself, the likelihood of use and substantive usefulness are correlated .55; the same two measures for the position designated by the respondent as most appropriate user are correlated .53. Respondents' ratings indicate that there is a firm connection between the contribution that a study can potentially make to a decision maker and the decision maker's likelihood of using the study—but it is by no means a perfect connection.

Table 5.1. Intercorrelations Among Measures of Usefulness
(Pearson Correlation Coefficients for Decision Makers' Ratings)

Measures of Usefulness	Substantive Usefulness in Own Agency	Likelihood of Use by Most Appropriate User	Substantive Usefulness to Most Appropriate User
Likelihood of own use	.55	.40	.47
Substantive usefulness in own agency		.35	.46
Likelihood of use by most appropriate user			.53

Another sizable correlation is between one's own likelihood of using a study and its substantive usefulness to others, i.e., one's belief that it can contribute ideas or information to them (with the clear suggestion that others *should* use it). The correlation is .47. A similar correlation appears between the two substantive usefulness measures ($r = .46$). The lowest correlation in the set of measures is between the substantive usefulness of a study for oneself and the likelihood that others will use it ($r = .35$). (For a description of the positions named as most appropriate users, see chapter 6.)

Because of the distinctions that respondents make in answering the usefulness questions, we will keep the measures separate rather than combine them into a composite score. Our analysis highlights the contrasts as well as the similarities among relationships between research characteristics factors and the different measures of usefulness.

Effects of the
Research Characteristics Factors

Table 5.2 shows the effects of the characteristics factors on each of the usefulness measures as derived from the responses of the 155 decision makers in the sample.[1] For the ratings of the respondent about himself and his own office, relevance of the topic also appears. For most appropriate users, relevance is not given, because these users are "appropriate" precisely because the subject matter of the study is relevant to their work.[2] The table also shows the total variance in usefulness explained (R^2) by the factors.

We find first of all that characteristics of research are important predictors of usefulness. Depending on the measure used, they account for from 23 percent to 42 percent of the total variance in usefulness. Research characteristics clearly make a difference in decision makers' response to social research studies.[3]

A second observation is equally apparent at first glance. All the factors are positively related to usefulness. While the size and order of the standardized regression coefficients (betas) vary on the different usefulness measures, the higher the score on each factor, the higher are the usefulness scores. Further, the betas fall

Table 5.2. Effects of Research Characteristics on Usefulness
*(Standardized Regression Coefficients for Measures of Usefulness
Regressed on Research Characteristics, as Rated by Decision Makers)*[a]

Research Characteristics	Likelihood of Use	Substantive Usefulness
In the Work of Respondent:		
Research Quality	.39**	.24**
Conformity with User Expectations	.18**	.11*
Action Orientation	.12*	.18**
Challenge to the Status Quo	.19**	.22**
Relevance to issues office deals with	.15**	.19**
R^2	.42**	.35**
In the Work of Most Appropriate User:		
Research Quality	.13*	.19**
Conformity with User Expectations	.20**	.20**
Action Orientation	.23**	.25**
Challenge to the Status Quo	.18**	.32**
R^2	.23**	.38**

NOTE: N (for inference):

	Likelihood of use	Substantive usefulness
For respondent	275	266
For most appropriate user	275	273

[a]See note 1.
*Significant at .05 level.
**Significant at .01 level.

within a fairly narrow range. Since the positive association was predicted for all the factors except Challenge to the Status Quo, we have initial confirmation of these hypotheses. We will return later to discussion of the relationship of Challenge to the usability of research.

Let us first mark out the parameters of the discussion by looking at the percentage of variance explained by research characteristics for the different measures of usefulness. Research characteristics explain more of the variance for one's own likelihood of using research (42 percent) than for any of the other measures. The suggestion is that one's own conduct is fairly predictable, and one's use of research is influenced relatively strongly by the attributes of that research. One's behavior is therefore viewed as rationally ordered: response depends on features of the stimulus. In contrast, other people's use of research is less well explained by the characteristics of the research. The research characteristics factors account for only 23 percent of the variance in likelihood of research use by others, even though these others have been designated as the people most appropriate to use the particular studies. Decision makers evidently believe that it is hard to predict how other people will actually behave. *Their* use of research will depend not only on the attributes of research but also on other factors, perhaps including their personal characteristics and aspects of their situation and the environment.

When it comes to the substantive usefulness of a research study, i.e., the contribution that its ideas and information can make, research characteristics explain about the same amount of the variance for one's own work and for the work of others (35 and 38 percent respectively). These figures suggest that the contribution that a study *can* make, if people pay attention, is dependent in a consistent way on its characteristics. The degree of intrinsic utility of a study that is explained by its characteristics stays very much the same, no matter who the potential user is.

Research Quality

The factor that best predicts both decision makers' likelihood of taking a study into account and the substantive contribution that its ideas and information can make to their work is Research Quality. Although we had hypothesized that Research Quality would be positively related to a study's usefulness, its salience is surprising. Many social scientists contend that Research Quality is almost irrelevant to decision makers, that what counts is whether a study supports a position that they want to take. The importance of Research Quality in these data does not conform to such expectations. What accounts for its unexpected showing?

One possibility is that the respondents, knowing the norms of social science, are engaging in blatant idealization of their own conduct. But remember that the data do not come from *asking* people which factors affect the usefulness of a study to their work. They come from analysis of two sets of ratings of each study— ratings of its usefulness and ratings of its descriptive characteristics —and represent the statistical relationships between the two sets of ratings. In order to come up with the pattern of responses reported here, a respondent who rated his likelihood of using a study as high would have had to rate the study high on many of the ten items that went into the Research Quality factor, and a respondent who rated her likelihood of taking the study into account as low would have had to rate many of the Research Quality items low—whatever the other characteristics of the study or the situation. It is possible that there was a tendency to respond along these lines—that finding a study useful influenced the respondent to be somewhat more generous in rating the Research Quality items. Nevertheless, other responses during the interview suggest that this tendency was neither so extensive nor so conscious as to invalidate the importance of Research Quality.

For example, one question did ask respondents' *opinions* about the characteristics of research studies that would affect their use. Early in the interview, they rated the importance of research characteristics (items identical in wording to the items on which they later rated the research reports) on their decision to use a study. (These data are reported in chapter 10.) This question can be expected to show clearly any bias toward "socially desirable" answers. Some of the items that were part of the Research Quality factor did receive high importance ratings but others did not, and comparison between individuals' opinions about importance and the statistical association of the same items with their ratings of the usefulness of specific research reports indicate little correspondence. When we examined the items associated with a study's usefulness rating for each respondent, we found that they did not match the items which he rated high on "general importance" at all closely. There is little support here for the assumption that respondents purposely slanted their ratings of specific studies to accord with their notions of socially desirable characteristics.

Also, during the interview some respondents were outspokenly skeptical about the usefulness of social science research. They were not averse to articulating such responses. Other comments, recorded during the rating procedure, indicated the care with which respondents tried to give fair and responsible judgments.

Finally, we can look at respondents' ratings for the "most

appropriate user" of each study, in the lower half of table 5.2. Clearly their ratings indicate a judgment that *other* users will accord Research Quality much lower importance than they do in taking a study into account. For likelihood of use by oneself, Research Quality has a standardized regression coefficient of .39; for likelihood of use by other appropriate users, the standardized regression coefficient is .13. In fact, the difference in the effects of this one factor largely accounts for the difference in the predictive power of all characteristics (R^2) for likelihood of use by self and by others. For the substantive usefulness of a study's ideas and information, the difference in the effects of Research Quality is nowhere as big ($\beta = .24$ for self, $\beta = .19$ for others).

What may well be happening is that the ratings of Research Quality and likelihood of own use represent what respondents would like to do. They are conveying their subjective disposition to give a hearing to research of good quality. They know themselves from the inside, with all their noble intentions, and their ratings reflect the mode that they would like to follow. For other people, on the other hand, their ratings may represent what they observe—the fact that when they look at other people's behavior, they do not see much of a relationship between Research Quality and use. They judge other people by what they do rather than what they think. Without deliberate misrepresentation, they may be giving themselves the benefit of taking account of what they intend to do.[4]

Their hypothetical behavior in the interview simulation appears to be highly influenced by Research Quality. Whether their actual behavior when confronted by research on the job is likely to be so influenced is an important question. Our interpretation, based on all the evidence, is that although there is probably some inflation in the relationship between Research Quality and respondents' own likelihood of use, Research Quality is by no means unimportant. Even in their fairly jaundiced views of the behavior of other users, Research Quality has a positive and significant relation to likelihood of use.

After all, the major reason that decision makers turn to research rather than to alternative sources of information is because of the truth claims of science. When they rely on social science research rather than, say, anecdotal accounts, program records, or the fruits of the agency grapevine, the rationale is that research provides more accurate information. Consequently they want some assurance that the studies they rely on are methodologically sound enough to warrant their trust. In considering policies and programs with important budgetary and human consequences, they want to have confidence that the research that enters into their judgments obeys the canons of science.

Other data from the interviews provide further understanding of the value of Research Quality. We asked a set of questions about the specific functions each research study could serve if it were used, such as raising an issue to attention, formulating new policies or programs, or improving existing programs. (These data are reported in chapter 8.) Respondents rated the extent to which each study would be appropriate for seven possible functions. Analysis revealed that Research Quality was an especially important feature of studies that were appropriate for two purposes: mobilizing support for a position or point of view, and changing ways of thinking about an issue. This suggests that Research Quality is a particularly valued characteristic of studies that enter the arena of debate and negotiation. When decision makers rely on evidence from research in adversarial situations, they want the research to provide effective ammunition for convincing others and mobilizing support. If it can be discredited by opponents on scientific grounds, they are left out on a limb. Thus, Research Quality not only assures decision makers that they are basing a case on good evidence; it also serves the vital political function of protecting the case from methodologically based criticisms by adversaries.

Thus, the salience of Research Quality may not only connote a scientific orientation, as our original hypothesis posited; it may also represent a recognition of the instrumental utility of valid, well-conducted research in organizational controversy. Poorly performed research crumbles under attack. Scientifically competent research is better apt to withstand attack and may actually help to bolster supporters and convince waverers.

The association between Research Quality and usefulness is based upon decision makers' ratings of the research quality of studies. It thus becomes important to find out whether they know Research Quality when they see it. Since we have ratings from 50 social science researchers and 50 members of research review committees on the same 50 studies that decision makers rated, we can compare their ratings of Research Quality, study by study, with the ratings given by specialists in research. The intraclass correlation between decision makers' ratings and the ratings of researchers and review committee members combined on Research Quality is .30 ($p = .015$). Although positive and significant, the correlation is not very high. However, the intraclass correlation between the ratings of Research Quality by researchers and by review committee members, two groups who are expected to be experts in judging the technical merit of research, is lower ($r_i = .17$, n.s.).

Other investigators have reported similar evidence that social scientists do not exhibit high agreement on ratings of research quality (Bowen, Perloff, and Jacoby 1972; Scott 1974; McTavish et al. 1975: app. 5; Ward, Hall, and Schram 1975; Lindsey 1978). The consistency of ratings by natural and biological scientists of the research quality of research proposals has also been found to be relatively low (Cole and Cole 1978). The level of agreement between Research Quality ratings by decision makers and by social scientists in our inquiry falls within the same range as the agreement levels reported among social scientists.

Conformity with User Expectations

Conformity with potential users' knowledge, values, and experience is also associated with the usefulness of research. Studies that score high on Conformity with User Expectations are more likely to be used and more likely to be considered substantively useful. They support the views that decision makers have already formed; they fit within their accustomed frameworks of understanding. By reinforcing and elaborating what decision makers already know from their education, experience, reading, and direct involvement, such studies are intuitively plausible and thus are likely to be taken into account.

Conformity with User Expectations shows similar effects on respondents' own likelihood of using studies ($\beta = .18$), on others' likelihood of use ($\beta = .20$), and on the substantive contribution for others ($\beta = .20$). It is slightly less important for substantive usefulness in their own work ($\beta = .11$). In fact, Conformity has less effect on substantive usefulness for their own work than any of the other factors. Apparently conformity to what they already know and believe gives a study a ho-hum quality; it is old hat to them and contributes relatively little additional information. Therefore, while conforming studies are likely to be taken into account because they are congenial and supportive, they are less likely to add to a decision maker's own stock of knowledge.

Action Orientation

Action Orientation, too, increases studies' perceived usefulness. Studies with direct and practical implications for action and explicitly formulated recommendations are substantively useful and likely to be taken into account. But Action Orientation is perceived as more consequential for other users than for the respondents themselves. In fact, analysis shows that it is the factor that ranks first for other people's likelihood of taking a study into account ($\beta = .23$), but last for their own likelihood of taking a study into account ($\beta = .12$). As we shall see when we examine the perceptions of social science researchers (chapter 11) and members of research review committees (chapter 12), these respondents show the same pattern when talking about appropriate users of research. Social scientists' ratings tend to stress the importance of Action Orientation (and minimize the importance of Research Quality) in making research useful to decision makers, even more than do decision makers' ratings with reference to other users.

The importance of Action Orientation is part of the traditional wisdom. Studies that score high on Action Orientation, with its focus on manipulable variables, explicit recommendations, and feasible actions, give clear direction to users. Decision makers' ratings indicate a recognition of the value of such characteristics, but they show a tendency to ascribe higher salience to them when discussing other users; they have a more variegated view of their own behavior.

Relevance to the Work
of One's Office

Relevance of a study to the issues that one's office deals with is also positively associated with usefulness. We tried to ensure relevance before the fact by assigning research studies to respondents for whom the topic sounded suitable on the basis of their job titles. (That we at least partly succeeded is shown by the ratings of the relevance of studies: 75 percent of the ratings were three or better on a scale of one to five, and 57 percent were in the top two categories.) We also worded the question on likelihood of use to incorporate the assumption of relevance. The question asked: "Assuming your office had to consider the issues discussed in the study, how likely is it . . . ?" Despite these efforts to minimize variation (and thus the predictive power of relevance), relevance retains an association with the usefulness of a study for one's work. Obviously research on topics that engage decision makers' interest and concern is more likely to make a contribution and get attention. For other users, relevance is controlled. They were nominated by respondents as most appropriate users precisely because of the relevance of the study for their work.

Challenge to the
Status Quo

In terms of our hypotheses, the data so far have supported the importance of Research Quality, Conformity with User Expectations, Action Orientation, and relevance, for the usefulness of social science research. But the expected negative association of Challenge to the Status Quo with usefulness does not materialize.

We had expected that research that suggested fundamental changes in agency philosophy or practice would not be regarded as useful. Responses indicate otherwise. Challenge is a positive feature of research. As seen in table 5.2, high scores on Challenge are associated with high substantive usefulness both for oneself ($\beta = .22$) and for other users ($\beta = .32$), and even show a positive relationship to the likelihood of a study's being used (by self, $\beta = .19$; by others, $\beta = .18$).

The significance of Challenge is reinforced by other data. The question asking which purposes a research study can serve (reported in chapter 8) listed seven purposes and asked respondents to rate how well each study, if it were used, could serve each purpose. Analysis of this set of ratings shows that Challenge to the Status Quo is the factor that ranks first for six of the seven purposes. Studies that are high on Challenge are perceived as especially suitable for changing ways of thinking about an issue, formulating new policies or programs, raising an issue to attention, and improving existing programs. These responses offer some understanding of why Challenge is a valued attribute.

As table 5.2 indicates, Challenge to the Status Quo is perceived as contributing less to the likelihood of use of studies than to their substantive usefulness—particularly for other users. Challenge ranks first in predicting substantive usefulness for others. The suggestion here is that other decision makers stand in particular need of research that questions existing political and administrative arrangements. Officials may view themselves as familiar with "the big picture"; it is other decision makers who need exposure to broader views.[5] Their ratings imply that challenging research can be particularly useful to those who may lack the knowledge and insight that they themselves have.

We had expected that the political orientation of officials in decision-making positions would dictate a concern for preserving the status quo, not making waves, staying within the bounds of accepted philosophies and structural arrangements, and continuing programs and policies much as they were. Although the factor analysis had indicated a separation between their own beliefs on the one hand and the operation of mental health agencies on the other, it still seemed as though the maintenance of existing arrangements would be the accepted position and that concern for stability would govern their reception of research.

That hypothesis is not supported. Decision makers in mental health are receptive to research that runs counter to policy and practice. They do not reject studies that score high on Challenge, but instead find them particularly useful. What accounts for the contradiction of so much previous writing about the defensive stance of agency officials and their rejection of information that casts doubt upon their agencies and their programs?

A number of possible explanations occur to us:

1. Perhaps the respondents are lying. But as the earlier discussion about Research Quality explained, it is not easy to lie with this kind of rating procedure. It is not a direct answer that we are analyzing but the *relationship* between a set of answers describing a study and a set of measures reporting usefulness. Moreover, the relations with Challenge are consistent over eleven measures of usefulness (the four in table 5.2 and the seven in table 8.1). Furthermore, whereas with Research Quality there are relatively clear norms about what is good research, in this area there is little consensus about what is good, what is a socially desirable answer, or what the interviewer or study director wanted to hear.

Finally and most persuasive of all, the interview gave the respondents an opportunity (before any questions about specific studies were asked) to enumerate their own criteria for useful research. Open-ended questions were asked on this topic, and then respondents were handed a checklist of the same research characteristics as they would later use for rating studies and asked, "How important are each of these characteristics to you when you choose to use a research study?" Both on the open and closed questions, items that related to Challenge were down near the bottom of the list of preferred criteria. (Chapter 10 presents these responses in detail.) Challenging research characteristics were apparently viewed neither as wanted nor as socially desirable enough to lie about. Deception in the Challenge ratings does not appear an adequate explanation.

2. Perhaps decision makers in mental health agencies in this period were not "members of the team" and were out of sympathy with current mental health policy and programs. Perhaps they did not see rewards to their programs or themselves ensuing from commitment to current practice but saw advantage from major changes in policy and program.

There appears to be some element of truth in this claim, in the sense that decision makers' ratings of research studies showed essentially no relation between the Challenge factor and the Conformity factor ($r = .05$). Decision makers' ratings were about as likely to indicate that challenging research was in accord with their beliefs and knowledge as to indicate that it contravened them. A research study that challenges current mental health ideology and organization is about as likely to find supporters as opponents among decision-making officials. As a colleague suggested, in mental health fields there is some tendency to believe that "whatever is, is wrong." So much is unknown, and so many programs result in failure, that leaders in the field must have many doubts if they are to be considered forward-looking.

Their willingness to listen may have been enhanced by the fact that the studies that they rated dealt with mental health policy and programming in a range of locations and were not limited to their *own* agencies. They could apparently accept fundamental criticisms in this context when their commitments to the programs that they themselves managed (and their own careers and influence) were not necessarily on the line.

3. Another possible reason that Challenge appears as a positive characteristic is that mental health is a field in flux. It does not have a single orthodoxy or a dominant "policy paradigm," and perhaps this absence makes it particularly tolerant of a range of divergent views. Unlike fields with more fixed allegiances, mental health encompasses divergent "schools" which have different beliefs about the origin of mental illness, appropriate treatment modalities, and the proper organization of services (Susser, 1968; Mechanic 1969).

The social science research studies that respondents rated were concerned with just these kinds of issues—need, treatment, prevention, organization of services, coordination, consultation. It is possible that mental health decision makers are willing to entertain a particularly wide spectrum of notions. The mental health field may be more tolerant than most in giving consideration to a variety of perspectives on program design and operation.

4. Perhaps the social research studies that we presented to respondents were not provocative and challenging enough to the mental health system to trigger rejection. Perhaps they were so tame that decision makers could accept the likelihood of giving them consideration in their work. It is true that they were not excessively radical. None of them raised questions about the basic institutions in the society or challenged fundamental economic arrangements. The studies that were rated highest on Challenge to Status Quo were those that:

a. Challenged prevailing intellectual assumptions in the field, e.g., assumptions that poverty is a cause rather than a result of mental illness, or that stress has a causal relation to mental illness,
b. Showed that current accepted programs were functioning poorly, e.g., community care for former mental patients,
c. Offered evidence in support of emergent program schemes not yet put into practice, e.g., community control of community mental health centers,
d. Supported out-of-fashion programs that had been supplanted by newer developments, e.g., long-term hospitalization for schizophrenics.

These were not brand new ideas. In fact, looking at our factor solution, we see that the item "Findings are unexpected or novel" does not load high on the Challenge factor. The ideas had been in circulation; some were being actively promoted. The research studies presented evidence that supported nonestablished and controversial positions. The ideas, if accepted, would result in reorientation of mental health policy and programming. They would require some fairly major shifts. While they were not extremely radical, their acceptance would in fact call for fundamental change in mental health practice.

Our investigation tests the Challenge factor only within the range of challenge represented by studies that had been funded by the institutes within ADAMHA. If the range were widened to include research that embodied very radical criticism or very controversial proposals, the effect of Challenge on usefulness might prove to be curvilinear, falling off at very high values of challenge. However, one might question whether government agencies fund research studies of such fundamental challenge—and even whether social science researchers propose them. Our search for mental health social research studies funded by ADAMHA did not uncover studies more challenging than those that were presented in the interviews.

5. Perhaps Challenge enhances the usefulness of social research studies for mental health decision makers because of the operative definition of use. Most definitions of "using" research involve the direct application of research findings to a decision. Our definition of use refers to "taking study results into account," and our definition of substantive usefulness refers to the contribu-

tion of ideas or information that a study can make. These broader formulations require only that decision makers give serious hearing to research and that they believe the research has something relevant to say. (Cf. Berry 1976; Cohen and Garet 1975; Boeckmann 1976; Janowitz et al. 1976; Caplan 1977.) Our definitions of use and usefulness are consistent with what respondents told us early in the interview about their prior uses of research. Their narrative reports discussed research use not so much in terms of adopting specific study conclusions as in terms of taking research into consideration as they identified problems and searched for suitable responses. (See chapter 9.)

Therefore, when we confront the salience of Challenge as an asset to usefulness, it is within this context of use. Research that challenges accepted ideas, arrangements, programs, and institutions cannot readily be put to work in a direct and immediate way. It cannot be plugged in to solve problems, particularly when it runs up against the antagonism of interests embodied within the current political balance. But decision makers' ratings of research indicate that such research can contribute to their work and the work of other appropriate decision makers. It can *enlighten* them.[6] They do not necessarily apply it *in the short term*, but it affects the way they think about issues and gradually it can affect what they do.

Thus, research is useful not only when it helps to solve problems. It is also useful when it questions existing perspectives and definitions of the problematic. Decision makers indicate that research can make contributions *to their work* by challenging ideas currently in vogue and providing alternative cognitive maps. Even if the implications are not politically acceptable at present, such research helps to develop alternative constructions of the world and its problems, which in time yield new ways of addressing policy problems. It is an optimistic conclusion, suggesting that service bureaucracies are not always the conservative, cautious, self-protecting, self-seeking entities of much of the scholarly literature on bureaucracy. At least in attitude and intent, the people who staff mental health agencies at all levels are open to research that provides controversial ideas. Whether this receptivity is special to, or better developed in, mental health than in other fields is an open question. But it clearly emerges from the data of this study.

But what of the political frame of reference? Do the findings suggest the absence of a political approach to decision-making in mental health? Are these decision makers immune from the zeal to further their own policy positions and ensure the survival and growth of their agencies which observers have long described as a hallmark of public bureaucracies? Don't they evince tendencies to use research in such self-serving ways?

The positive relationship of Conformity with User Expectations to measures of the usefulness of research studies suggests that supporting the user's position, ideas, and values is not irrelevant to use. For all the intermingling of values with knowledge, respondents' ratings still indicate that the compatibility of a study with users' beliefs and philosophy enhances both the usefulness of a study to them and their likelihood of paying attention.

As for the use of research to further the fortunes of their agencies, such use is still within the zone of possibility for mental health decision makers. The key point is that they can advance their policy predilections and agency welfare by challenging and fundamentally changing programs as well as by adhering to the status quo. Once we recognize this point, then the possibility of political use of research is reinstated. The use of research to *change* programs becomes a way of protecting the agency, its appropriation, and its influence.

Mental health decision makers, as professionals, have commitments to humanitarian values, to service, and to particular modes of treatment, such as community-based care, preventive care, short-term crisis intervention, government support for mental health care for the poor and minorities. That they also have commitments to their agencies, programs, and their own careers is no doubt also true, but these concerns are intermingled with their professional values. If a mental health official believes firmly, as a professional, in the value of alcoholism prevention programs, then almost inevitably she believes that she, her program, her agency, and its budget are indispensible. But she is also willing, even eager, to improve and even radically restructure the program if she believes that change will enable it to do a better job.

Or at least, and this is as far as our data actually take us, to think about radical restructure.

Summary
We have identified five attributes of social science research studies that are associated with their substantive contribution and with the likelihood that they will be taken into account. They are Research Quality, Conformity with User Expectations, Action Orientation, Challenge to the Status Quo, and relevance to the issues that the office deals with. All five characteristics are positively related to the perceived usefulness of research.

The positive contribution of Challenge to usefulness was unexpected. But research that questions current programming and offers divergent perspectives can provide ideas that stimulate thought, and much of the use that decision makers make of research is to aid them in thinking about programming. They tend to conceptualize their work not so much as making a series of discrete decisions, for which research provides direct guidance. Rather they view their work as an ongoing stream of planning, suggesting, advising, managing, and doing, and in this context, challenging ideas and information are useful for the conceptual orientation they provide.

The other unexpected finding was the salience of Research Quality. Decision makers' ratings of studies indicate that they are more likely to take account of methodologically competent and cogent research—although their ratings also show that they are less sanguine about *other* decision makers' proclivities to do so. The association between Research Quality and usefulness suggests that when decision makers turn to research rather than to other sources for information, they expect the research to be methodologically sound. Other data in the interview show that high-quality research has value for convincing others and mobilizing support, purposes for which research that is vulnerable to methodological criticism is less well suited. Although there may be some inflation of the importance of Research Quality in respondents' ratings, it does appear to be significantly related to the usefulness of research studies among mental health decision makers. Whether decision makers in other fields, who have had less exposure to social science research and its methodologies, would show similar reliance on Research Quality remains to be seen.

As chapter 9 will explore in detail, mental health decision makers are exposed to a great deal of research, and when they read a report, they seldom do so with an immediate decisional application in mind. Rather, they usually read research as part of the job of keeping informed. (In that sense, the "simulation" of research use in the interviews was very much in keeping with their usual procedures.) If they believe that a study is not "useful," they are apt to dismiss it out of hand and forget it. If as they read it they consider it useful, they tend to store it in their minds, along with their other knowledge; it deposits a residue. Then when events on their job call for action on an issue, they draw upon the stock of knowledge they have amassed. It is within this context that the importance of Research Quality, Conformity to User Expectations, Action Orientation, Challenge to the Status Quo, and relevance should be considered.

When rating studies in terms of their usefulness for other users, decision makers apparently disregard some of what they know about their own use of research. They revert to a more decisionistic perspective, for example by giving greater weight to the Action Orientation of a study for its usefulness to others. Nevertheless, there are strong similarities in their ratings of studies for themselves and for others, and the association of the research characteristics factors with all the measures of usefulness reinforces their importance for understanding what makes social science research useful.

Interactions Among Research
Characteristics Factors

Having established that each of the research characteristics factors is associated with the usefulness of social science research studies, we then examined their effects in combination. We wanted to find out whether their effects are additive or whether certain configurations of factors elevate or depress usefulness.

One possibility is that there are two frames of reference that govern decision makers' reception of research. One is a testing for validity and the other a testing for direction. Decision makers can assess the validity of a study on two alternative bases: they can use the standards of methodological rigor associated with the scientific method (Research Quality) or they can judge the study by the extent to which it agrees with the prior knowledge they have derived from their education, observation, personal involvement, and experience (Conformity with User Expectations). The hypothesis is that the importance of Research Quality will be contingent on the degree to which the study Conforms with Expectations. The more closely it fits with what they already know, the easier it will be to accept the study as valid and therefore the less important Research Quality will be. On the other hand, the more it diverges from what they know, the more important Research Quality will be in overcoming their doubts about its truth.

Similarly, there are two bases on which a study can provide direction. It can give clear and explicit guidance for feasible reform (Action Orientation), or it can challenge current practice on fundamental grounds and suggest new perspectives and orientations (Challenge to the Status Quo). The hypothesis is that the more it provides Action Orientation, the less important it is that the study provide the reorientation embodied in Challenge, and the less action-oriented it is, the more necessary it is for a study's usefulness that it be challenging. Similar effects are expected when a study is high or low on Challenge to the Status Quo. Action Orientation and Challenge are *alternative* ways of providing direction.

In terms of interactions, the hypotheses lead to the expectation that the two factors that relate to validity, Research Quality and Conformity, are mutually compensatory, and the two factors that provide direction, Action Orientation and Challenge, are also mutually compensatory. In statistical terms, the hypothesis is that the interactions of the factors in each of the pairs will have significant negative effects on usefulness.

Another possibility is that decision makers employ the factors as filters for research in temporal sequence. In this model, decision makers first examine a study for its relevance to their work. If it does not pass the relevance test, they discard it. If it passes, they go on to look at Research Quality and/or Conformity. If it does not pass either of these tests, they discard it. If it passes, they examine Action Orientation and Challenge. The pattern of time-sequencing would show up as interactions between the factors in a different configuration from that posited above.[7]

To investigate such possibilities, we examined the interactions among the factors.[8] We did this by constructing product terms using the continuous factor scores. The unit of analysis is the study rating by decision makers ($N = 310$). We regressed the dependent variable, likelihood of use, on the five factors (what we have called the four factors and relevance) and the ten two-factor interaction terms.[9]

Two of the ten interaction terms show significant effects on likelihood of use. They are the interaction of Research Quality and Conformity, and the interaction of Action Orientation with Challenge. The regression coefficients for both interactions are significant at the .01 level. None of the other interactions is significant.

In both cases, Research Quality × Conformity and Action

Table 5.3. Effects of Research Characteristics and Truth and Utility Interactions on Likelihood of Use
(Regression Coefficients for Likelihood of Use Regressed on Research Characteristics Factors and Factor Interactions)

Independent Variables	Unstandardized Regression Coefficient	Standard Error	Standardized Regression Coefficient
Relevance	.13	.05	.14**
Research Quality	.55	.07	.39**
Conformity to User Expectations	.26	.07	.19**
Action Orientation	.13	.07	.10
Challenge to the Status Quo	.28	.07	.20**
Quality × Conformity	−.20	.07	−.12**
Action Orientation × Challenge	−.19	.07	−.12**
Constant	3.14		
	$R^2 = .45**$		

NOTE: N (for inference) = 272
**Significant at .01 level.

Orientation × Challenge, the combination of the characteristics factors predicts a *lower* likelihood of use than a simple addition of the two factors would have suggested. When Conformity is high, high scores on Research Quality lead to lower increments in usefulness than when Conformity is low. Research Quality still has a positive relation to usefulness when Conformity is high, but the positive relationship is substantially less than when Conformity is low.

By calculating the first partial derivative of the regression equation for Research Quality, we see that the effect of Quality on likelihood of use is $.55 - (.20 \times \text{Conformity})$. When the value of the Conformity factor is 0 (its mean), the slope of Quality is .55. For each unit increase in Conformity, the effect of Quality is attenuated by .20, so that studies with Conformity scores of $+1.0$ would show increases of .35 in likelihood of use for each unit increase in Quality. For each unit decrease in Conformity, the effect of Quality is increased by .20; studies with Conformity scores of -1.0 would show increases of .75 in likelihood of use for each unit increase in Quality. Research Quality has more than twice as large an effect when Conformity is low as it has when Conformity is high. When a study yields counterintuitive results, it is much more important for its likelihood of use that it be high in Research Quality than when its results are compatible with users' expectations.

Similarly, when we look at high ratings on Action Orientation, high ratings on Challenge contribute less to likelihood of use than a simple additive combination would predict. When Action Orientation is low, high scores on Challenge have more effect on usefulness.

The same pattern holds when Challenge is high or low. For Action Orientation, the slope is $.13 - (.19 \times \text{Challenge})$. For Challenge, the slope is $.28 - (.19 \times \text{Action Orientation})$. Thus, when a study is low on Action Orientation, high values on Challenge can in effect compensate for the lack of Action Orientation and increase usefulness, and when Challenge is low, Action Orientation can compensate and raise usefulness. The trade-off demonstrates that the two bases of direction are alternatives to each other.

These data show that a temporal sequence of filters for research does not appear. But decision makers do seem to apply two tests to determine their likelihood of using a research study. One test has to do with the trustworthiness of the study, and either Research Quality or Conformity or both can add to the study's usefulness. We call this "the truth test." The trade-off effect shows that the importance of Research Quality is contingent upon the level of Conformity. (Although the interaction term is symmetric, we do not consider the possibility that the importance of Conformity is contingent upon Research Quality, because decision makers' knowledge and beliefs antedate their review of the study and cannot depend on its Research Quality.) When Conformity is low, Research Quality adds more to likelihood of use than an additive model would posit. Conversely, when Conformity is high, Research Quality adds less—although within the range of our data, it always adds something to likelihood of use.

The second test we call "the utility test." Action Orientation is much more important when a study offers little Challenge, and Challenging results are more important for likelihood of use when a study is low on Action Orientation. A study does not benefit proportionally from high levels of Action Orientation and of Challenge simultaneously. When a study's results are feasible to implement, it does not add much to its likelihood of use to show fundamental deficiencies in current practice or the promise of alternative perspectives. When a study suggests reconceptualization or redirection of policy, respondents are receptive to its ideas but they are less receptive to advice on practical steps to implement its recommendations.

The truth test and the utility test are composed of interdependent components whose effects are contingent on each other. As table 5.3 shows, the factor interactions that represent the two tests together add 3 percent to the variance explained by research characteristics, an amount significant at $p < .01$. The research characteristics factors and the factor interactions explain 45 percent of the variance in likelihood of use.

The truth test and the utility test, along with the relevance of the content of the study to their sphere of responsibility, represent decision makers' frames of reference for social science research. They constitute the standards that decision makers apply in judging their likelihood of using research.

Truth test. Is the research trustworthy? Can I rely on it? Will it hold up under attack?

1. Research Quality. Does the research meet scientific criteria?
2. Conformity with User Expectations. Are the results compatible with my experience, values, and knowledge?

Utility test. Does the research provide direction? Does it yield guidance either for immediate action or for considering alternative approaches to problems?

1. Action Orientation. Does the research indicate how to make feasible changes in things that can feasibly be changed?
2. Challenge to the Status Quo. Does the research challenge current philosophy, program, or practice? Does it offer variant perspectives?

Respondents' Own Words:
Operation of Research Factors

Having presented the research characteristics factors statistically, we can give a more palpable sense of their operation by quoting the verbatim comments of decision makers as they rated specific studies. During the rating process, they were asked the reasons why they gave a study the usefulness rating they did. (This question was asked before they rated the characteristics of the study.) Many of their answers are almost encapsulated descriptions of the factors.

Answers that relate to the Research Quality of a study include the following:

It's a carefully focused study with care given to research design and execution. Within its modest limits it does its job competently. I'm mainly concerned when I look at a study that it be competently done. It's my job to worry about the implications. (174)[10]

I like the variables, the things they looked into. They were well-chosen. And the number of interviews appeared adequate. The sample was adequate. [The procedure of] randomly chosen blocks was fair and unbiased. (176)

It wouldn't be good enough for a masters thesis. . . . It can be used politically if it supports a position we hold, but by the same token it can be picked apart by someone who doesn't support that position. (161)

That study is making a breakthrough, but I wouldn't give it wholehearted support because the N is very low. (206)

Some of the comments capture the essence of the Conformity factor. It is apparent that most of these respondents use Conformity as grounds for rating a study as useful, but notice that at least one respondent (209) cites Conformity as the reason for a low rating of usefulness and another one (127) is at best ambivalent.

Results have been the same in other studies. The staff feeling and the departmental staff would agree very much with these findings. (255)

It makes sense. It agrees with my gut-level feeling. (348)

It doesn't agree with my experience, fairly long-term experience. . . . There are certain things which I would consider crucial that are not mentioned here. (316)

It agrees with our conclusions generally, and to that extent it isn't much use to us. (209)

The study does not demonstrate anything new. It's rather a confirmation of understanding that already exists. (127)

A number of respondents explained their rating of a study's usefulness by referring to its Action Orientation.

It has aspects that could be implemented, and it makes a good case for an alternative way. . . . It could be used to make a point of additional programming. (264)

I think it provides some concrete findings upon which decisions could be based. The business about the alcohol counselors. We might look at that as indication that further utilization of similar kinds of people in similar settings would be advantageous. (106)

. . . the type of program they are running there is fairly successful with certain types of clients. We would be able to, hopefully, incorporate that in our program. (223)

It gives you the kind of data you need in terms of functioning, rehospitalization, and costs, to make certain kinds of policy decisions. (120)

Challenge to the Status Quo also appears in these open responses. Here are a few answers that explain decision makers' ratings of their likelihood of using a study on the basis of its Challenge. We include one (255) that points to Challenge as the basis for a low usefulness rating.

It highlights some important shortcomings in present program development, and the conclusions and recommendations are very much to the point. (201)

[The study shows that] specific things that community mental health centers are offering are not appropriate. I think we ought to take a look at what we're doing. (335)

It identifies some weaknesses in terms of the program itself. And some costs that need to be examined. . . . (145)

This would not sell politically. This would not sell within the bureaucratic organization. (255)

It could point out some of our delinquency here, the groups we're not reaching, and some conclusions that we have arrived at that may be . . . partly erroneous. (338)

Thus, in their open-ended answers decision makers give a sense of how the factors play out in practice. As they reviewed a study, the criteria that they volunteered as the basis for their judgments often parallel the factors that we extracted from the ratings that they later gave.

With greater effort, we located narrative responses that suggest the nature of the truth and utility tests. Here is a quotation from a local decision maker that expresses the trade-off between Research Quality and Conformity. He is answering a question about what would make him favor the results of one study over another study on the same topic.

One would begin by looking at the scientific merits of the study. Was it methodologically sound? In the final assessment of a study, its value is how it accords with one's own scientific and clinical experience when evaluated reasonably in a clear-thinking manner. . . . I might agree with the conclusions of an author on the basis of my experience while having the feeling that his data does not support those conclusions. But the data I'm carrying around inside of me does. . . . Unfortunately, the literature is full of so much useless drivel that one has to be selective in applying some of the things that come out. That's another reason clinical experience is so critical. (304)

A federal respondent suggests the interaction between Action Orientation and Challenge. As we pick him up, he is answering a structured question on the importance of research characteristics for his decision to use a research study, and he has come to the item

"Implies the need for major change. . . ." He is trying to form a numerical rating of the importance of this characteristic, and he says to the interviewer:

If one has in mind a theoretical or etiological study that implies the need for major change, it may be very important to know in a theoretical conceptual fashion. If the concern is with practical application, feasibility in terms of its use, it [implies major change] would become somewhat undesirable. In other words, if one has to change the entire criminal justice system before one can even do that, it's going to take one hell of a long time to ever be able to apply it. (134)

That is a fair country approximation of the interaction between Action Orientation and Challenge to the Status Quo.

NOTES

1. All regression equations have been calculated from matrices of Pearson correlation coefficients which have been constructed using "pair-wise" deletion of missing observations; that is, only the pairs of variables with missing data are excluded in calculating each correlation. This method does not bias results when there is a large number of cases and a small number of missing observations (Mackelprang 1970). It has the advantage of preserving as much of the data as possible for analysis.

In calculating probabilities for statistical inference when using pair-wise deletion, the number of cases considered is the smallest number in any of the bivariate correlations. This is a conservative estimate; it avoids capitalizing on the use of pair-wise deletion to inflate statistical significance. In the tables, we show this "N (for inference)," but most of the simple correlations from which the regressions are calculated are based on considerably more cases.

In table 5.2, for instance, the "N for inference" ranges from 266 to 275 for the four regressions. These are the fewest valid observations that occur in any of the bivariate correlations used to compute the respective regression equations. However, most of the correlations used for these computations are based on 290 or more cases.

2. The three items not included in any of the factors (on time for decision, inexpensive to implement, and high priority issue) show no significant relationship to any of the usefulness measures independent of the four factors and relevance.

3. Scores on the research characteristics derive from the ratings given by the individual. This means that each person uses his own situation and experience in determining the extent to which a characteristic is descriptive of a study, e.g. the extent to which it conforms with prior knowledge, is politically acceptable, has clear implications for action. Although this procedure can lead to intersubject variation in ratings, it is the most appropriate way to determine how the respondents react to a study; only their judgments about the characteristics are meaningful inputs to their judgments about the study's usefulness. Since our intent is to model the standards that they apply in judging usefulness, we rely on their ratings of study attributes.

4. In terms of attribution theory, this would say that they are making a *situational* attribution for their own behavior; it is circumstances that lead them to do what they do.

They make *personal* attributions for the behavior of others; *they* do because that is the kind of people they are (Shaver 1975: 81–82, 126–37).

5. This interpretation is supported by Arnold Meltsner: ". . . when I got feedback on PPBS [Program Planning Budgeting System], the decision maker almost always thought it of value for shaking up people's thinking. He was the big thinker himself, but the rest of the organization needed new perspectives." Personal communication, July 27, 1976.

6. For pioneering discussions of enlightenment vs. social engineering functions of social research, see Crawford and Biderman (1969), Janowitz (1970).

7. Since the data do not support this hypothesis, we relegate its technical construction to a note for the intrepid reader. Consider first decision makers' ratings on the relevance of a study to their work. Among those who rate relevance high, Research Quality and Conformity should be more highly associated with usefulness than among those who rate relevance low. Among those who rate relevance low, Research Quality and Conformity should have little effect on usefulness because they would have already discarded the study on grounds that it was not pertinent to their work. For those who rate Research Quality or Conformity high, the association of Action Orientation and Challenge with usefulness should be higher than for those who rate Research Quality and Conformity low. Among those who rate Research Quality and Conformity low, Action Orientation and Challenge should make little difference. If such conditions obtained, then the interaction terms (relevance by Research Quality, relevance by Conformity, Research Quality by Action Orientation, Research Quality by Challenge, Conformity by Action Orientation, Conformity by Challenge) should be significant.

8. For discussion of the application and interpretation of interaction terms in multiple regression analysis, one can consult almost any text on multiple regression. One of the more complete appears in chapter 8 of Cohen and Cohen (1975:291–342). A more abstract discussion of theoretical models and their relation to applications is presented by Kenneth E. Southwood (1978).

9. We performed a similar analysis with substantive usefulness as the dependent variable. Since the pattern was similar, although not as sharp, reporting the results would be redundant, and we limit presentation here to likelihood of use.

10. Numbers in parentheses are the code numbers of the respondents. The 100s are federal, the 200s are state, and the 300s are local decision makers.

Chapter Six

MOST APPROPRIATE USERS
OF RESEARCH STUDIES

R ESPONDENTS WERE ASKED about the usefulness of study reports not only for themselves but also for the persons whom
they characterized as the most appropriate audience for the studies.
They specified potential users in terms of the positions they held
and the types of organizations in which they worked, e.g., clinician
in a community mental health center, director of a state mental
health department, the Secretary of HEW. Thus, a by-product of
the questions is a description of the suitable audience for
ADAMHA-funded social science research studies.

When we look at the 310 responses from decision makers
(155 decision makers each discussing two studies), we find that
more than half of the "most appropriate users" named are service providers at the local level. Decision makers locate most
appropriate users of the studies in:

Federal government	15 percent
State governments	15
Local mental health agencies	34
Local service agencies other than mental health	20
Other	17

(N = 310 responses)

A third of the mentions refer to administrators and staff in mental
health care-giving agencies, and 20 percent to staff in other local
agencies, primarily schools and criminal justice agencies. The federal users identified range from the President and the Congress
to staff in ADAMHA and other federal agencies and departments.

The "other" category is a varied assortment: local government, voluntary organizations, parents, consumers, the public, "everybody," nobody.

That federally funded research studies should appear primarily applicable to *local* service providers may seem surprising. But this situation is evidently not unique to the field of mental health. The recent National Academy of Sciences report indicates that less than one-third of the total federal investment in "social knowledge production" is devoted to the interests of federal users (NAS 1978:36–37). The same report states that of the $1.2 billion spent by the federal government in fiscal 1976 for knowledge production on social problems (which in their definition includes research, evaluation, "policy formulation demonstrations," and general purpose statistics), $443 million, or 37 percent, was spent on behalf of nonfederal "third parties."[1] Much of the rest was devoted to the "advancement of knowledge" (14 percent) and "statistical collection" (19 percent), categories for which potential users are vague and uncertain. Only 31 percent of the investment in knowledge production was directed to federal users: 14 percent was classified as aimed at improvement of federal policy and 17 percent at improvement of federal programs.

Our data about ADAMHA-funded research studies, although examining a much narrower slice of knowledge production activities and based on analysis of a limited number of individual projects, also highlight the nonfederal bent of much federally funded research. With federal officials designated as most suitable users in only 15 percent of the responses, it becomes obvious that most federally funded mental health research is not geared to their concerns. Thus, in the search for reasons why research has had so little discernible effect on federal policy, one plausible explanation is that little of the research that federal agencies fund addresses issues relevant to federal policy.

We took a special look at the thirteen studies in our sample that had been funded under contract. Contract studies, which are initiated and developed by federal offices, might be expected specifically to serve a federal audience. Yet even in this group, only 29 percent of the mentions of most appropriate users were federal officials of any kind. Certainly it is vital for the effective operations of "federal programs," such as the community mental health center program, that the nonfederal people who run the programs at state and local levels be well informed, and research addressed to their needs is not irrelevant to federal interests. Nevertheless, the relative infrequency with which federal users were named came as a surprise.[2]

There are three other kinds of information that we can derive from the data on most appropriate research users. We can see how clear-cut the distinctions are between studies useful to one user group and those useful to others. That is, do studies divide crisply into "useful-for-federal-officials," "useful-for-state-officials," and so on? Second, we can examine the effect on usefulness ratings of the location of the most appropriate user. Finally, we can see whether the effect on usefulness of the research characteristics (Research Quality, Conformity to User Expectations, Action Orientation, and Challenge to the Status Quo) changes depending on whether designated users are federal, state, or local decision makers. That is, do decision makers perceive that different research attributes will enhance usefulness to people in the different sites? Those are the issues to which we now turn.

Decision makers' agreement on appropriate users. How clearly do the studies line up in federal, state, and local columns? Do decision makers agree on the category of user for whom each study is best suited? The answer is no. On no study is there total agreement on the level of government for which it is most appropriate. For 15 studies out of the 50, more than half of the respondents agree on the level of user, and for another 13 studies, exactly half the respondents agree. These 28 studies, which show some measure of congruence on audience, are perceived as directed toward:

federal users	2 studies
state users	3 studies
local users in mental health agencies	16 studies
local users in other agencies, e.g. schools, courts	7 studies

There are another 4 studies for which half the decision makers or more agree that rightful users are in none of these locations, although even then, they differ in designation of the alternative. For 18 studies there is essentially no agreement.

The disarray in the responses prevented us from analyzing whether those of our respondents who held a position designated as most appropriate for a specific study rated it as more useful than did others. But the general pattern of the data suggest that this would not be so. Over all, the local decision makers in the sample tended to rate studies somewhat less useful than did others, despite the predominant reported suitability of the studies to people in local positions.

Disparities in designation of most appropriate users for each study can be considered evidence of "unreliability" of the measure. But we think that such an interpretation would miss the important substantive implication. What the responses highlight, we believe, is the fluidity of the decision-making process in an intergovernmental system. There are no sharp demarcations between the kinds of information that are useful at one locus and those that would inform action at another. If a study is useful for one group of users such as local providers of service, it is likely also to be seen as useful for the state and federal officials who plan the programs, write the regulations, and dispense the program funds. Support for this observation comes from the fact that decision makers at each level are somewhat more likely to cite their *own* level as appropriate users than are decision makers at other levels. They appear to be sensitive to a study's potential for contributing to the work that they know best. For example, a study that shows the kinds of difficulties encountered in maintaining adequate liaison between community mental health centers and state mental hospitals has utility for people in many different places. In a similar vein, as we will see in chapter 8, studies that are viewed as useful for one functional purpose are highly likely to be viewed as useful for other purposes as well.

Therefore, the lack of general agreement on specific user groups appears to be intrinsic to the interlocking division of responsibility in mental health. It arises from the "marble cake" of federalism where human services are a partnership among federal, state, and local agencies. It is part of the same phenomenon that leads to planning for "concerted intergovernmental, interagency efforts" and rhetoric about "Federal/State/local partnership in services" (NIMH 1977:11–13).

Effects of "most appropriate user" on ratings of research usefulness. Is there a difference in the ratings of the usefulness of studies when the appropriate user is federal, state, or local? By and large, there *is* a difference in the ratings of the study's likelihood of use, but not in its substantive usefulness (ideas and information).

When the proper user is identified as staff of a local care-giving agency, decision makers rate the likelihood that such people will take the study into account *lower* than when perceived users are occupants of other positions ($p < .05$). Most of the difference occurs when the designated users are in care-giving agencies outside the field of mental health. Decision makers judge local mental health personnel almost as likely as state and federal personnel to make use of research studies; they are more doubtful when they are referring to teachers, school superintendents, social workers, probation officers, nursing home directors, and the like.

In terms of the substantive contribution that the study can make, there are no significant differences by category of user. Decision makers judge the study to have an equivalent potential to contribute to the work of appropriate users wherever they are located.

As far as our data go, there seems to be some merit in their perceptions. Although we have no evidence about non-mental health personnel, there is evidence (discussed further in chapter 7) that local mental health people are somewhat less apt than federal and state officials to take research into account in their work.

Effects of research characteristics for different types of users. Let us see whether the location of the most appropriate user affects the relative importance of the research characteristics in promoting usefulness. We have seen that Research Quality, Conformity, Action Orientation, and Challenge are positively associated with usefulness both for the decision makers themselves and for those they designate as appropriate users. It turns out that the relative contribution that each of the factors makes to usefulness remains very much the same whoever the respondent identifies as most appropriate user. In terms of likelihood of use, there are no differences. In terms of substantive usefulness (the contribution of ideas and information that a study can make), again there are no differences by level of position of the most appropriate user. But when we look at local users *in mental health agencies* only, there are hints that studies can contribute more (and correlatively, that users can profit more) when the studies Conform less to prior expectations and Challenge current operations more. The associations are not significant, but the overtones are that it is local mental health personnel who can particularly benefit from an influx of new information and ideas.

Designation of most appropriate users by social science researchers and members of research review committees. Social science researchers and members of research review committees designate most appropriate users in almost exactly the same fashion as do decision makers. They, too, name staff in local caregiving agencies over half the time (55 percent of all mentions, compared to 54 percent of mentions by decision makers). They designate federal officials (16 percent of their mentions) and state officials (14 percent) much less often. The equivalent percentages among decision makers are 15 percent each for federal and state users. Residual categories—city or county officials, voluntary organizations, everybody, and others—account for the remaining 15 percent of the users they name.

The extent of agreement with decision makers on who appropriate users are, both in the aggregate and study by study, shows that researchers and review committee members have a relatively realistic grasp of where studies can be used. With reference to the level of user, they share both the perceptions and the lack of clear-cut discrimination among levels that characterize the responses of decision-makers who are close to the action.

NOTES

1. Their classification of audience, which the report describes as "difficult and judgmental," was based on the overall mission of the funding agency, not on analysis of projects funded (NAS 1978:36).

2. These data suggest that our sampling strategy, i.e., the inclusion of state and local decision makers, was wiser than we knew at the time.

Chapter Seven
EFFECTS OF DECISION MAKERS' LOCATION, EXPERIENCE, AND BACKGROUND CHARACTERISTICS

S O FAR WE HAVE BEEN talking about the characteristics of social science research studies and how they affect judgments of the studies' usefulness. We have found that research characteristics explain 45 percent of the variance in the likelihood that decision makers will consider study results in their work. Now we turn to characteristics of the decision makers to see whether their location, experience, and background explain more about their response to social science research.

It seems reasonable to expect that personal characteristics make a difference in the extent to which people in positions of authority rely on social science research. In fact, Patton et al. (1977) conclude from a series of interviews about the impact of twenty evaluation studies in the health field that "the personal factor," i.e., the leadership, interest, enthusiasm, determination, commitment, aggressiveness, and concern of one or two key people, was a central factor in accounting for whatever kinds of effect occurred. These kinds of personal attributes are obviously difficult, if not impossible, to measure, and to make investigation even more difficult, it appears that they are highly situation-specific. A person who shows strong commitment and enthusiasm for one study under one set of circumstances will often be uninterested in other studies under other circumstances. It may be the fit of a study to the special concerns and interests of a person at a particular time that accounts for her energetic advocacy of it, rather than any generalized qualities of skill or leadership.

Nevertheless, there is a literature about the effects of characteristics of individuals in a collateral field—the adoption of innovations. Much work has been done to discover which individuals are most likely to adopt new technologies and what features of their organizational environments promote innovation. Although the adoption of innovations differs in some basic ways from the willingness to take account of social science research—innovations are relatively concrete products or processes whose adoption is clear-cut, visible, and relatively formal—this work points to some personal and organizational attributes that tend to enhance innovativeness. It suggests the kinds of variables that we should examine in investigating the less palpable, more diffuse topic of incorporating social science research results into one's repertoire for addressing organizational problems.

Although the findings are not always stable across studies, some of the individual characteristics that have been found to influence the adoption of innovations are age (Rogers 1962; Lippitt et al. 1967; Marcum 1968; but Rogers and Shoemaker 1971), education (Rogers 1962), professionalism (Evan and Black 1967; Rogers 1967; Aiken and Hage 1968; Marcum 1968; Havelock 1969b; Becker 1970), and extensive contacts, communication, and exposure to information (Katz 1961; Hemphill, Griffiths, and Fredericken 1962; Rogers 1962; Coleman, Katz, and Menzel 1966; Marquis and Allen 1966; Rogers and Shoemaker, 1971). Organizational attributes that have been found to foster innovation include size (Mansfield 1963 and 1968; Carroll 1967; Schon 1967), closeness to sources of innovation (Lippitt et al. 1967; Rogers 1967; Havelock 1969b) or the inclusion of an internal "intelligence" unit (Miles 1965; Watson 1967; Glaser and Ross 1971), and representation of a number of occupational specialties on staff (Aiken and Hage 1968; Hage and Aiken 1970; but Havelock, 1969a).

In our study, we have information on respondents' backgrounds and jobs that allow us to examine several of these concepts. We grouped respondent variables into three categories that might be expected to increase the likelihood that they will use social science research. The categories are:

1. Autonomy—the extent of freedom that individuals have to make choices in their work. Included here are the intergovernmental level at which they work and the type of position they hold.
2. Receptivity to social science research. In this category are attitudinal variables, education and profession, experience in doing research, length of time on the job, and personal characteristics that might affect receptivity.
3. Exposure to social science research. Included in this category are respondents' reported previous use of research on the job, reading of research reports, and prior knowledge of the research report they rated.

Our expectation is that these attributes will increase the likelihood that respondents consider the studies presented to them during the interviews as useful for their work.

Tables 7.1, 7.2, and 7.3 show the variables that were analyzed. The first column gives the zero-order correlations between the variable and the person's rating of his likelihood of using the studies. The second ("beta in") column shows the standardized regression coefficients for each variable *after* the five research characteristics factors (what we have called the four factors plus relevance) and the truth and utility interactions have been entered into the equation. "Beta in" indicates what the standardized regression coefficient (β) would be if this item were the next item entered. All of the items were entered as dummy variables (unless otherwise noted) so all members of a set could not be entered simultaneously; the "beta in" data come from different—but strictly comparable—equations.

Autonomy

The items in this category—level of position and type of position—are indicators of the latitude that decision makers have for making choices in their work. In general, federal officials can be expected to have more autonomy in planning and promoting change in mental health programming than those who work at state and local levels. As our interviews indicated, state and particularly local decision makers consider themselves fairly constrained in setting new program directions of the type implied by the social science research studies that we presented to them.

Table 7.1. Effect of Decision Makers' Autonomy on Likelihood of Use
(*Correlations and "Beta In" for Characteristics of Decision Makers*)

	Relation to Likelihood of Use	
Autonomy	*Zero-order Correlation*	*"Beta in" after Factors & Interactions*[a]
Intergovernmental level		
Federal	.19**	.09*
State	−.03	.04
Local	−.16**	−.13*
Type of position		
Policy maker	.03	−.01
Program manager	−.04	−.01
Administrator	.10*	.07
Clinical supervisor	−.13*	−.09
Information manager	.07	.03

[a]"Beta in" is the value that the standardized regression coefficient of the variable would take if it were added to the regression equation in table 5.3, which includes the research factors and truth and utility interactions.
*Significant at .05 level.
**Significant at .01 level.

(Work at the federal level may have other connotations as well, such as greater proximity to sources of research information, since the ADAMHA institutes maintain extensive research programs.)

The second attribute is type of position. From their descriptions of their jobs during the interview, we classified decision makers' jobs into five categories: policy maker, who had responsibility for or major input into decisions on policy directions; program manager, who managed a program at the federal, state or local level (directors of community mental health centers were classified here); administrator, who managed a "staff" function in the line-and-staff terminology, such as budgeting; clinical supervisor, who supervised patient care; information manager, who did planning, analysis, evaluation, expert consultation, data systems operation, or research management. Our sense from reading respondents' descriptions of their work is that policy makers, program managers, and information managers have more autonomy for program choice than do administrators and clinical supervisors. We hypothesized that decision makers with greater job autonomy would find the studies presented to them more useful.

If we look at the autonomy items in the first column in table

7.1, we see that at the zero-order, four of the correlations are significant. As anticipated, federal decision makers are most likely to find the research studies useful and local decision makers are least likely. However, only one of the expected relationships with type of position materializes: clinical supervisors are less likely to judge research useful. Since there is considerable overlap between clinical supervisor and local level (all 14 clinical supervisors held local positions), even this relationship must be explored further. Contrary to expectations, a job as administrator correlates positively with likelihood of use.

The second column of the table presents the standardized regression coefficients for each item after the research characteristics factors and factor interactions have been entered into the regression equation. Once research characteristics have been taken into account, type of position is no longer significant. All the relationships with position tend to diminish. The importance of "level" remains. Decision makers at the local level in mental hospitals and mental health facilities are significantly less likely to say they will pay heed to research studies; federal-level decision makers are significantly more likely. While we originally defined level as an indicator of autonomy, let us examine other relationships in the data before we accept this interpretation.

Receptivity to Research

A general receptivity to social science research can be expected to increase ratings of usefulness of specific studies. The first set of indicators of receptivity comes from a battery of opinion items. We presented respondents with a set of statements and asked them to indicate the extent of agreement or disagreement with each item on a 4-point scale. (These data are discussed in chapter 13.) One of the items was "Good research *should* be used whether or not its conclusions are politically acceptable to high policy makers." A positive response should indicate receptivity. Another item was: "The social sciences are too limited in methodology to be able to make significant contributions to government decision making." A negative response on this item would indicate confidence in social science and therefore perhaps a tendency toward receptivity. A third statement was: "Government agencies have a

Table 7.2. Effect of Decision Makers' Receptivity on Likelihood of Use
(*Correlations and "Beta In" for Characteristics of Decision Makers*)

	Relation to Likelihood of Use	
Receptivity	Zero-order Correlation	"Beta in" after Factors & Interactions[a]
Attitudes		
Agree strongly: Good research should be used whether politically acceptable or not	.04	.02
Disagree strongly: Social science methodology too limited to make contribution	−.03	−.04
Disagree: Agencies have limited options	.13*	.11*
Education and profession		
Number of years of higher education	−.11*	−.02
Psychiatry, medicine	−.09*	−.04
Psychology	.01	.04
Social work	−.05	−.05
Other profession	.13**	.06
Full-time experience in care-giving agency or professional practice	−.13**	−.10*
Experience doing research		
Previous full-time employment in research organization	−.09	−.03
Author of social science research		
Number of written reports, books, articles (continuous)	.07	.06
Number of reports (categ.)		
No reports	−.02	−.05
1–3 reports	−.16**	−.04
More than 3 reports	.11*	.07
Number of published research articles, books (continuous)	.12*	.09
Tenure		
Time in position	−.09	−.10*
0–3 years	.11*	.13**
4–10 years	−.07	−.08
Over 10 years	−.09	−.11*
Time in agency	.06	.04
0–3 years	.05	.07
4–10 years	−.11*	−.11*
Over 10 years	.08	.06
Time in government	.17**	.09
Personal Characteristics		
Age	.10*	.03
Sex (male)	.07	.06
Political orientation (radical, very liberal)	−.02	−.00

[a]"Beta in" is the value that the standardized regression coefficient of the variable would take if it were added to the regression equation in table 5.3, which includes the research factors and truth and utility interactions.
*Significant at .05 level.
**Significant at .01 level.

limited range of options for action, and research findings that fall outside that range are of little use." Again, disagreement should indicate receptivity to the use of research, since there is more latitude for action.

The opinion items show mixed effects: one is positively and significantly related to decision makers' ratings of usefulness, one is positively related but not significant, and one is negatively related but not significant. A belief that agencies have a wide enough range of options to make consideration of social research worthwhile is the one item that correlates significantly with judgments of usefulness. Even after the characteristics factors and interactions have been taken into account, this belief is still associated with ratings of the likelihood of use of specific studies.

The other variables expected to indicate receptivity were derived from data on respondents' education, profession, and experience. Years of higher education was a rough measure; longer immersion in higher education might be expected to increase one's understanding and appreciation of the social sciences. We recognized, of course, that certain professional schools were less likely to impart such lessons, and so we also include here the profession with which the respondent identified himself. Prospectively, we expected that psychologists would be most receptive to social science research and perhaps social workers the least.[1] Another item that might reduce receptivity was experience in professional practice. Professionals who have had experience in providing direct care are often more attuned to the idiosyncratic attributes of clients and the value of clinical judgments than with the probabilistic conclusions that social science research derives from studies of population samples. We therefore examined respondents' prior full-time employment in care-giving agencies or other direct service in the expectation that such experience would reduce ratings of research usefulness.

Length of education is a poor predictor of the likelihood of decision makers' using social research studies. In fact, the longer their education, the less receptive they are, largely because of the presence of psychiatrists and physicians at the upper end of the "years of education" scale. At the zero-order, "other" professionals are more receptive than any of the main professional groups. They defined their professions in varied ways from public administrator to biostatistician. Their most important characteristic in this context is the relative shortness of their education compared to the other decision makers in the sample; "other professional" correlates $-.42$ with years of education. Once the research characteristics factors are entered into the regression, none of the educational or professional variables survives. However, experience in direct service is significantly related to perceptions of usefulness in the expected negative direction. Those respondents who had been professional practitioners are less likely to find research useful. There is, of course, a strong overlap between this variable and local level.

Experience in actually doing social science research might be expected to increase receptivity. We asked decision makers two questions about their experience as researchers. First we asked if they had ever worked *full time* in a university social science research institute, or a for-profit social research or consulting organization. Those who reported such experience appear in table 7.2 as having had full-time employment in an organization whose primary orientation was social research. A second question inquired about their writing of research reports. We asked: "Have you ever been author, coauthor, or editor of a book, article, or unpublished research report that was based on social science research? [If yes:] About how many of the following kinds of publications have you authored or coauthored: books, articles in professional journals or books, unpublished research reports?" A positive response could derive from the respondent's current position or from any other position, or even from his graduate school years or a nonjob avocation. When we combined all listed categories, we produced a continuous variable that appears in the table as "number of social science research reports written." Analysis of this variable indicated that it behaved nonlinearly; having written one, two, or three publications was worse for ratings of research usefulness than writing none at all. (Perhaps having written only unpublished reports such as masters' essays or doctoral dissertations turns people against research.) Accordingly, we constructed another variable that eliminated unpublished reports and included only published books and articles. This variable also appears in the table.

Three of the items about doing research and writing research reports are significant at the zero-order. Having written one to three research reports is negatively correlated with the likelihood of using research studies; writing more than three reports based on social science research and the total number of published research articles and books are both positively correlated with likelihood of use. After the factors have been taken into account, however, none of the relationships remains significant.

The next set of items that we expected to affect likely use of social science research has to do with tenure. We thought that time on the job would reduce receptivity. Old-timers would get to know the ropes, they would rely on their experience, they would tend to trust their own judgment and give short shrift to research findings that aimed to offer guidance for their work. With this expectation, we looked at three items: time in position, time in agency, and time in government.

As expected, time in position is negatively associated with judgments that the research studies are useful; people new to their jobs are particularly likely to indicate that they would use the studies. The effect of time in position is linear; the longer decision makers have been in the same position, the less likely are they to find the research studies useful. The relationship is significant after the characteristics of the research are controlled. Thus, no matter what kind of research is involved, people who have spent a longer time in the same position are less likely to expect to use the research.

Time in agency works differently. Effects are curvilinear, with people in the middle category (four to ten years in the agency) less favorable in judgments of usefulness than those either newer or older. Length of time in government shows still another pattern. The longer in government, the more useful decision makers find the studies. However, unlike the other tenure variables, the significant effect of time in government in the zero-order correlation washes out after the research characteristics factors are controlled. The most clear-cut finding is that people who have been on the job and in the agency for a short time are more likely to consider research studies useful.

There were reasons to expect that age and political orientation would be related to judgments of the usefulness of research. People

Table 7.3. Effect of Research Exposure on Likelihood of Use
(*Pearson Correlations and "Beta In" for Characteristics of Decision Makers*)

	Relation to Likelihood of Use	
Research Exposure	*Zero-order Correlation*	*"Beta in" after Factors & Interactions* [a]
Prior use of research		
Extent of use of research		
Often	−.03	−.01
Some	.06	.04
Little or none	−.06	−.05
Extent of seeking out research	.16**	.14**
Often	.14**	.11*
Some	−.03	.10
Little or none	−.14**	−.14**
Completeness of citation to useful study	.07	.03
Sources of research information		
Research reports read per month in professional publications	−.14**	−.07
Best sources of research include journals	−.10*	−.08
Best sources of research include people	.07	.04
Personalness of best source	.06	.05
Preference for written reports	−.08	−.04
Heard of study before	.17**	.02

[a]"Beta in" is the value that the standardized regression coefficient of the variable would take
if it were added to the regression equation in table 5.3, which includes the research factors
and truth and utility interactions.
*Significant at .05 level.
**Significant at .01 level.

of younger age and more liberal disposition might give higher
ratings of usefulness. As it turned out, older age is related to judgments of higher usefulness of studies when we use the simple correlation coefficient, but its effect is erased when the factors were
considered. Political orientation (and sex, which we also examined)
has little effect.

Exposure to Research

The interview asked a number of questions that relate to
previous exposure to social science research. The questions are
grouped under three headings: a set that deals with their current

use of research on the job, a set on their sources of research information, and an item on whether they had previously heard of the study that we gave them to rate during the interview.

About their use of research, we asked decision makers: "Do you consciously use the results of social science research in reaching decisions on your job?" and "In what ways do you use social science research on your job?" and elsewhere in the interview, "Do you seek out research information when you're considering policy or program alternatives? About how often does this happen?" These questions were coded and analyzed; answers to the first two questions were coded into "extent of use of research," and answers to the latter two questions were coded into the "extent of seeking out research." There was also a question that asked decision makers to cite a specific study that they had found useful for their work; we asked for as much identifying information about the study as possible, including author, title, date, where published, or (if the reference was incomplete) the topic of the study and where the respondent saw or heard of it. We coded the completeness and clarity of the reference.

Let us look at the effects of these variables. In the set of items on prior use of research, the three measures of the extent to which decision makers seek out research when considering policy or program alternatives are significantly correlated with the likelihood of finding the research studies useful. All three relationships remain significant when they are entered in the regression equation following the factors and factor interactions. Experience in searching for research enhances decision makers' likelihood of finding studies useful, even after the characteristics of the studies are controlled. People who report seeking research in the past are more likely to find research reports useful in the present. They are "users."

The next group of items on exposure has to do with the sources decision makers use to learn about research. Nine questions in the interview inquired about types of sources used, frequency, and their relative ranking. From these, we constructed five measures: number of research reports read per month in professional publications, whether "best sources" of research information include journals, whether "best sources" of research information include people (colleagues, researchers, conferences, word of mouth), the personalness of the single best source of research information (rank ordering best sources placing informal discussion with people highest and mass circulation magazines lowest), and a preference for written over personal sources of research information.

The responses on these items show that familiarity with written research reports, and preference for written over personal sources, tend to be negatively associated with the perceived usefulness of the studies. However, none of the relationships reaches significance once the research characteristics have been controlled. The unexpected *direction* of the relationships—i.e., the negative relationship of heavy research reading and reliance on written sources with ratings of usefulness—may perhaps be explained by the fact that broad acquaintance with other research studies reduces the contribution made by the studies that the interviewer gave respondents to read during the interview, and that decision makers who prefer to receive research information through personal contact were more favorably disposed toward research in an interview situation in which they were interacting with a personal purveyor of research—the interviewer. However, since the relationships are not significant, they should not be overinterpreted.

The final item on exposure asked respondents whether they had heard of the study that the interviewer presented to them prior to the interview. In 14 percent of the 310 cases (155 decision makers each rating two studies), the decision maker had previously heard of the study. Hearing of the study is significantly correlated with high ratings of usefulness at the zero-order. It is possible that this variable captures a number of dimensions—the relevance of the study to the respondent's work, the aggressiveness of the respondents' outreach for research, the size, visibility, and perhaps the quality of the study. However, when hearing about the study is entered into the regression equation after the factors and factor interactions, its relationship to usefulness drops to near zero.

Of all three sets of exposure items, i.e., prior use of research, sources of research information, and familiarity with the study rated, only one item increases the usefulness ratings after the factors have been taken into account: the extent to which decision makers have actively sought out research in the past. There is an active dimension to this item that betokens more than mere exposure. People who seek out research show a reliance on and receptivity to research that raises their likelihood of using other research studies.

In the foregoing discussion, we have noted a number of cases in which characteristics of the respondents showed a zero-order correlation with their ratings of the usefulness of specific studies (i.e., when only two variables were considered) but the relationship diminished when the characteristics of the studies were controlled. What is going on in such cases? A likely interpretation is that such respondent characteristics are working through the research characteristics factors. As discussed in chapter 5, ratings of research characteristics may depend to some degree on characteristics of respondents. The data in the present chapter suggest that respondents with particular characteristics (e.g., administrators, authors of more than three social science research reports) may be more likely than others to rate one or more of the *research factors* high (or low), and the research factors are all significantly associated with the usefulness ratings. Accordingly, once the research factors are entered into the regression equation, the additional amount of variance explained by the *respondent* characteristic decreases. And if one accepts some conventional cutoff point, such as .05, for statistical significance, then the respondent characteristic dips below the significance level. In a later section of this chapter, we look at the possibility that certain respondent characteristics interact with a specific research factor to affect judgments of usefulness. If this is so, then we can pinpoint which types of individuals put more (or less) emphasis on particular factors in judging the usefulness of the studies they read.

Let us summarize the effects we have located. These are the variables that show significant effects on decision makers' likelihood of using research studies after controlling for the research characteristics factors and interactions. The sign in parentheses indicates the direction of effect on likelihood of use.

Level: federal (+), local (−)
Opinion: Disagree that agencies have limited options (+)

Experience in care-giving agency or other direct service (−)
Tenure: years in position (−), 4–10 years in agency (−)
Extent of seeking out research (+)

Given the number of variables we have examined, this is not a particularly long list, and there are intercorrelations among several of the items. The possibility that some of them are chance relationships has to be recognized.

We now enter the variables simultaneously into the regression equation to see how much additional variance they explain.

**Table 7.4.   Effects of Research and Decision-Maker Characteristics on
Likelihood of Use**
(*Standardized Regression Coefficients for Likelihood of Use Regressed on
Research Characteristics, Truth and Utility Interactions, and Selected
Decision-Maker Characteristics*)

Characteristics	Standardized Regression Coefficient	
Characteristics of the Research Studies		
Research Quality	.39**	
Conformity with User Expectations	.17**	
Action Orientation	.11*	
Challenge to the Status Quo	.19**	
Relevance to work	.14**	
R^2 for characteristics factors only		.42**
Interactions of Research Characteristics		
Research Quality × Conformity with User Expectations	−.12**	
Action Orientation × Challenge to the Status Quo	−.12*	
R^2 for characteristics factors and factor interactions only		.45**
Characteristics of Decision Makers' Position, Experience, Background		
Federal level	.02	
Local level	−.05	
Extent of seeking out research	.13**	
Disagree that agencies have limited options	.10*	
Experience in direct service	−.06	
Years in position	−.08[+]	
R^2 for all variables		.50**

Note: N (for inference) = 270.
[+]Significant at .10 level.
*Significant at .05 level.
**Significant at .01 level.

Regression Analysis

The six added variables account for over 4 percent more variance than did the characteristics of the studies alone. This addition to the variance explained is significant at the .01 level. The only additional variables that attain statistical significance at the .05 level when all the variables are entered are the sense that agency options are broad enough to make nonroutine research useful and the extent to which decision makers have sought out social science research in the past. Both of these variables are associated with decision makers' judgments of higher likelihood of using studies. Near significance is length of time in position. The longer decision makers have held their particular jobs, the lower is their likelihood of taking specific research studies into account in their work.

The characteristics of research studies are far more important predictors of likelihood of use than are attributes of decision makers. The only decision-maker attributes that show significant relationships with likelihood of use, above and beyond the research characteristics factors, have to do with: (a) active use of research in their work and (b) a belief that research can have effects on agencies. Our earlier classification of decision-maker attributes into autonomy, receptivity, and exposure can probably be collapsed into one general category having to do with successful prior use of research.

Interactions with the Factors

On conceptual grounds, it seems likely that certain characteristics of respondents' structural location, experience, and background will not so much increase the usefulness rating directly as increase the salience of certain research characteristics. Decision makers with certain attributes will place more emphasis on Research Quality, others more on Action Orientation, and so on, in judging a study's usefulness. For instance, decision makers with research backgrounds might rely more on Research Quality in assessing a study's usefulness than decision makers with no research experience. Respondent characteristics should, in this sense, work through specific factors to affect ratings of usefulness.

To specify the effects of decision makers' background characteristics on the factors, we compute interaction terms and enter them into the regression equation. The procedure is similar to a three-way cross-tabulation. We are, in effect, trying to find out whether differences in response on one variable affect the *relationship* between the other two.

The purpose of examining the effects of interactions between research characteristics and decision-maker characteristics on research usefulness is not only to increase explanatory, or predictive, power. More basically, it is an effort to identify categories of decision makers who apply particular standards in the assessment of social research studies. In a substantive sense, the analysis of interactions is a search for identifiable "types" of decision makers who give priority to one set of standards in deciding whether or not to take specific studies into account in their work. The analysis helps us to find out whether there is "a scientific type," "a managerial type," and so on—whether there is a category of decision maker who exercises a particular criterion in judging the usefulness of social research.

Let us look at the decision-maker attributes that might be expected to inflate (or deflate) the relationship between each of the factors and usefulness.

Research Quality

We expected certain respondent characteristics to increase the association of Research Quality with usefulness. Characteristics that have a scientific cast might be expected to heighten the salience of Research Quality. We believed it likely that research experience, a Ph.D., authorship of research articles, a position in analysis, planning, or data management, belief that research should be used, and belief that the social sciences have adequate methodology would all enhance the importance of Research Quality. We anticipated that incumbency in a program manager position would decrease the importance of Research Quality because of a manager's needs for other features (e.g., implementability) in research studies.

There was no reason for expecting a federal position to elevate the salience of Research Quality—or of Conformity or Action

Orientation. There was reason to expect that the greater autonomy of federal positions might enhance the positive effects of Challenge on research usefulness. Nevertheless, we entered federal position in all the interactions in an effort to discover the mechanisms through which the zero-order correlation between location in a federal agency and reported likelihood of using research operated.

Therefore, we considered the relationship between Research Quality and each of the following items:

Program manager position (negative effect expected)
Information manager position
Full-time experience in a research organization
Ph.D. degree
Author of published articles or books based on social science research
Number of publications based on social science research
Strong agreement that good research should be used whether or not
  its conclusions are politically acceptable
Strong disagreement that the social sciences are too limited in meth-
  odology to contribute to decision making
Federal level position

We constructed interaction terms for each of these characteristics with the Research Quality factor. After regressing ratings of likelihood of use on the research factors and research factor interactions, we entered the first-order terms (federal level, program manager position, etc.) and then looked at "beta in" for the interactions with Research Quality. "Beta in" shows what the standardized regression coefficient (β) would be if this were the next term entered in the regression equation. Examination of the F-values for the interaction terms shows that four of the interactions with Research Quality are significant: program manager position, information manager position, research experience, and federal position. All are significant at the .05 level. Full-time work experience in a research organization, a managerial position in planning, analysis, or data systems, and working at the federal level all increase the effect of Research Quality on usefulness. Occupancy of a program manager position diminishes the salience of Research Quality on usefulness; although the effect of Research

Quality for program managers is still high, it is not as high as for those in other types of jobs. These effects are all in the anticipated direction. The other attributes we tested did not interact with Research Quality to affect usefulness, even at the .10 significance level.

Conformity

The Conformity factor is essentially a measure of reliance on one's own knowledge, values, and experience. We believed that certain decision-maker attributes might increase its relationship to research usefulness. The length of time that a decision maker had been in the agency might increase his reliance on his own judgment. A brief time in a new job might reduce such reliance. A position as clinical supervisor, where knowledge derives largely from experience, might heighten the importance of Conformity. Also acting in the same direction might be agreement with the statement that decision makers tend to ignore social science information that does not conform to their beliefs. This opinion item in essence reflects a belief that other people use Conformity as a filter for social science information. Finally, we also examined the effect of federal position.

These interaction terms were entered into the regression equation:

Length of time in agency
Time on job 0–3 years (negative effect expected)
Clinical supervisor position
Strong agreement that decision makers tend to ignore social science information that is not consistent with their beliefs
Federal position (direction of effect unclear)

None of these items showed a significant interaction with Conformity. None of them raised (or lowered) its effect on the usefulness of research studies.

Action Orientation

This factor represents the practical applicability of a research study's conclusions. A reasonable expectation was that this factor would be more important to people in charge of running programs. Also those who were relatively new to the agency, and those who believed that agencies had scope for action, might be more reliant on the criterion of Action Orientation. Therefore, we tested the following items for interaction effects:

Program manager position
0–3 years in agency
4–10 years in agency
Disagreement with the statement that agencies have a limited range of options and research findings outside that range are not useful.
Federal position

The only item that showed an effect on the relationship between Action Orientation and usefulness was decision makers' disagreement that agencies' constraints make research useless—and that only at the .10 level. The other items did not interact significantly with Action Orientation.

Challenge to the Status Quo

We thought that several variables might increase dependence on this criterion for judging research useful. A position as policymaker would give a person greater latitude for making basic changes in policy; therefore, challenging research might have a special attraction. Also, a federal position might give greater scope of action for using challenging research. Similarly, a radical or very liberal political orientation might dispose a decision maker to heed challenging research.

Two of the opinion items might also be relevant: "Government policies are arrived at through political processes that pay little or no attention to research" and "Government agencies tend to ignore research findings that are not in line with agency assumptions and philosophies." Respondents who disagreed with both those statements would tend to believe that even politically unacceptable research studies could have an effect on policy. Therefore, they might accord Challenge a higher importance. Accordingly, we tested the interactions with Challenge of the following items:

Policy-maker position
Federal level
Radical or very liberal political orientation
Disagreement that policies are made by politics and not research
Disagreement that agencies ignore incompatible research

None of the relationships was statistically significant even at the .10 level. None of these characteristics of the position or attitude of decision makers significantly affected the salience of Challenge for the likelihood of using research studies.

Summary of Interactions

If we accept the .05 level of significance as a cutoff point, four interactions of decision-maker attributes with the factors are significant. They all affect the salience of Research Quality. Prior experience in a research organization, a position in information management, and working at the federal level heighten the importance of Research Quality; position as program manager reduces it. At the .10 level of significance, one other interaction is significant: Action Orientation with a belief in agency options. Those who disagree that agencies operate within a limited range of options and that research outside that range is useless tend to place more weight on the Action Orientation of a study in assessing its usefulness.

We entered these interaction terms into the regression equation reported in table 7.4 after the other variables.[2] See table 7.5. None of the interactions between research characteristics and decision-maker characteristics is significant at the .05 level. Two are significant at .10—the interaction between research experience and Research Quality and the interaction between belief in agency options and Action Orientation. The other three interaction terms are not significant.

The regression equation with the research characteristics factors and interactions, the decision-maker variables, and the five interaction terms, explains 53 percent of the variance in decision makers' likelihood of using specific studies. The five research

Table 7.5. Effects of Interactions Between Research and Decision-Maker Characteristics on Likelihood of Use
(*Standardized Regression Coefficients for Likelihood of Use Regressed on Research Characteristics, Decision-Maker Characteristics, and Selected Interactions*)

Characteristics	Standardized Regression Coefficient
Characteristics of the Research Studies	
Research Quality	.34**
Conformity to User Expectations	.19**
Action Orientation	.03
Challenge to Status Quo	.20**
Relevance to work	.14**
Interactions of Research Characteristics	
Research Quality × Conformity with User Expectations	−.10*
Action Orientation × Challenge to the Status Quo	−.12*
Characteristics of Decision Makers' Position, Experience, Background	
Federal level	.04
Local level	−.03
Extent of seeking out research	.14**
Disagree that agencies have limited options	.11*
Experience in direct service	−.09⁺
Years in position	−.08⁺
Experience in research organization	−.01
Program manager position	.00
Information manager position	−.07
Interactions of Research Characteristics and Decision-Maker Characteristics	
Research experience × Research Quality	.12⁺
Information manager × Research Quality	.01
Program manager position × Research Quality	−.11
Federal position × Research Quality	.08
Disagree that agencies have limited options × Action Orientation	.11⁺
R^2	.53**

NOTE: N (for inference) = 270.
⁺Significant at .10 level.
*Significant at .05 level.
**Significant at .01 level.

characteristics factors alone explained 42 percent of the variance; the research characteristics interactions brought the variance explained to 45 percent. The six additional terms relating to decision-maker characteristics which were added during the first step of the analysis in this chapter (see table 7.4) increased explanatory power by over 4 percent. The three first-order variables included in the interaction terms (research experience, program manager position, and information manager position) added almost nothing by themselves. The five interaction terms explain an additional 3 percent of the variance.

The intent of examining the interactions between research characteristics and decision-maker characteristics was to identify categories of decision makers who apply a particular standard in judging the usefulness of specific social science studies. Within the limits of the decision-maker characteristics that we are able to examine, there do not seem to be such clear-cut single-criterion groups. The evidence of this conclusion is that we examined twenty-five interactions, almost all of them interactions for which there were reasonable grounds for expecting relationships, and none had significant effects on research usefulness at the .05 level. The interaction of decision-maker characteristics and research characteristics does not appear strong.

We have not been able to identify particular characteristics of decision makers that are associated with the exercise of particular standards of judgment to affect the usefulness of research. This is not to say that there may not be people who pay more attention to one standard (research quality, conformity, etc.) than another in assessing the usefulness of social research. But within the range of variables analyzed in our research, individuals do not seem to differ systematically; they do not form identifiable categories. If decision makers differ idiosyncratically, there are situations where this is important to know, for example when a researcher is conducting a study for a particular group of people. But it apparently will have to be discovered anew each time. Our data reveal no decision-maker characteristics that interact significantly and systematically with research characteristics to affect judgments of the usefulness of social science research studies.

NOTES

1. One indication of the low status in which social workers hold research is its ranking in several surveys of social work professionals and students (Rosenblatt 1968; Kirk and Rosenblatt 1977).

2. Of course, we also entered the first-order terms which were components of the interaction terms that had not already been entered. There were three: prior experience in a research organization, program manager position, and information manager position.

Chapter Eight
SPECIFIC FUNCTIONS SERVED
BY RESEARCH STUDIES

Decision makers use information for a variety of purposes. We have already identified two basic purposes: the instrumental purpose associated with Action Orientation, where research provides practical, incremental, implementable recommendations that can be applied directly to policy or program; and the conceptual purpose associated with Challenge to the Status Quo, where research questions fundamental premises on which policies or programs are based and provides a basis for rethinking those premises. But so far, we have not considered specific types of decision situations to which research information might apply. Are there specific decisional activities for which some kinds of research are particularly appropriate? It is this topic which forms the focus of this chapter.

The literature on the use of social science research often suggests that there are different functions that research can serve (e.g., Merton 1949; J. Weiss 1976; Rein and White 1977; Rich 1977; Pelz 1978). Most discussions emphasize use of research for problem solving; applied research is primarily expected to weigh the relative advantages of alternative schemes for dealing with problems (Schultze 1968; Rivlin 1971; Coleman 1972; Lazarsfeld and Reitz 1975). But clearly there are other possible functions for research in the decision-making process, such as gaining attention for a problem, identifying causes of the problem, providing new modes of conceptualizing the problem, developing strategies for coping with the problem and its causal factors, "making sense" of the current operating policies (uncovering their latent logic), legitimating either current or alternative policies, assessing the nature of support and opposition to policies, justifying inattention to a problem or delay in dealing with it, and so on (C. Weiss, 1977a).

Writers on decision-making often present the concept of stages or phases in the cycle of decision-making (Lasswell 1956; Agger, Goldrich, and Swanson 1964; Rose 1969; Brewer 1974; Janis and Mann 1977). The stages are variously conceptualized but tend to include: identifying the problem, canvassing for alternative solutions, weighing the relative advantages and disadvantages of each alternative, selecting a solution, implementing the solution, and evaluating the results. The notion of decisional stages provides another, if overlapping, construct by which to differentiate the contributions that research information makes.

What we want to examine is whether research that is useful for one decisional activity is also useful for others, or whether different kinds of studies tend to "specialize" in usefulness at different points of the decision cycle. We have two kinds of data to use in this analysis. We have information on the properties of the studies, and we can see whether the same or different study characteristics are associated with usefulness for different decisional activities. We also categorized the 50 studies by research type (description, causal analysis, study of process or implementation, outcome evaluation), and we can see whether different types of research are perceived as suitable for different phases of decision-making.

The Measure

After decision makers rated the usefulness of each study for themselves and for other appropriate users, they were asked about the appropriateness of the study for seven decisional activities. The question was:

Study results can be used for many purposes. Assuming these study results were used, which of these purposes would they serve? Please rate from 1 to 5, where 1 means this is a very appropriate use and 5 means not appropriate at all.

—Raising an issue to the attention of government decision makers
—Formulating new government policies or programs
—Evaluating the merit of alternative proposals for action
—Improving existing programs

—Mobilizing support for a position or point of view
—Changing ways of thinking about an issue
—Planning new decision-relevant research

The structure of the question was designed to gauge the degree to which different decision-making activities make use of different informational inputs. That is why ratings were done on a scale of appropriateness and why the respondent was told to assume that the study results were used. These seven ratings are not intended to serve as alternative measures of usefulness. They are indicators of *how* the study could be used (if it were used).

Similarities and Differences
Among Uses

A first step in the analysis was generating the correlations among the seven ratings of appropriateness. As table 8.1 shows, the ratings are highly intercorrelated. The correlation coefficients range from .41 to .76, the median is about .47, and all the correlations are positive. Decision makers who see a study as useful for one purpose are likely to regard it as useful for other purposes. There is a generalized quality about judgments of usefulness— and uselessness. Even such disparate items as mobilizing support for a position and planning new research have a correlation of

Table 8.1. Intercorrelations of Ratings of Appropriateness for Different Uses
(*Pearson Correlation Coefficients for Decision Makers' Ratings*)

Purpose	Formulate	Evaluate	Improve	Mobilize	Change	Research
Raising an issue	.76	.42	.44	.41	.42	.47
Formulating new policies or programs		.51	.54	.51	.46	.47
Evaluating alternatives			.62	.46	.50	.47
Improving exist- ing programs				.49	.50	.43
Mobilizing support					.59	.41
Changing ways of thinking						.49

.41 and thus share 17 percent of the variance in decision makers' assessments of appropriateness for use.

A similar pattern was reported in a recent study on the use of technology assessments (Berg et al. 1978:59–62). The authors of that study found very high intercorrelations among ratings of the use of technology assessment studies for such diverse purposes as obtaining background information, advising or informing others, defining policy options, and selecting policy options.

For all the similarity, our study found that decision makers do make some distinctions. If we look at the correlations in table 8.1, we see that certain pairs are much more closely linked with each other than with other items. The pair, raising an issue to attention and formulating new policies or programs, has a coefficient of .76. We can consider these two items as representing the activity of "agenda setting." Ratings on another pair, evaluating alternatives and improving existing programs, show a correlation coefficient of .62. These items can be conceptualized as "problem solving." Similarly, the items, mobilizing support and changing ways of thinking, hang together. They are more highly correlated with each other ($r = .59$) than with any of the other items, and represent the function of "coalition building." For all three functions, the correlation between the items of the pair is significantly greater ($p < .05$, $df = 302$) than the correlation of either item with any other. Planning new research shows no outstandingly high or low correlation with any of the other items, suggesting some distinctiveness from all.

Another approach to studying the similarities and differences among decision makers' assessments of appropriate use is to use factor analysis. Since factor analysis builds on the basic correlation matrix, we do not expect the results to diverge from those in hand, but it adds a bit of insight.

Principal components factoring shows that one factor explains most of the variance (57 percent) in the set of ratings. By the standard rule-of-thumb, which disregards factors with eigenvalues of less than 1.00 (Rummel 1970:362–64), this common factor is the only one of interest. What it represents is an absorbing question. If we were playing "name the factor," we would search for a name that suggests that studies high on the factor were interesting studies, studies with something to say, studies broad-gauged enough to add to the contemporary discussion, or perhaps simply studies that respondents like. To put it more graphically, studies low on the factor were judged not good for anything.

Despite the power of the first factor, there are reasons to look at the next three as well. With a set of seven items it is unlikely that four factors would have eigenvalues greater than 1.00 if the items shared any common variance. The eigenvalues evidence a "discontinuity" between the fourth and fifth factors, another rule-of-thumb in choosing the dimensionality of a solution (Rummel 1970:364–65). Further, the four-factor solution presents us with substantively interesting information about the different purposes for which research may be used.

Table 8.2 presents the loadings of each of the items on the four unrotated factors from the initial factor matrix. (The unrotated matrix shows more directly than would a rotated matrix the similarities and contrasts among the items.)

Loadings on the first factor emphasize again how much the different purposes have in common. This factor not only explains 57 percent of the total variance, it explains over 49 percent of the variance in every item. This shows that decision makers are likely to rate a study as pretty much equally appropriate for each of the purposes. It is probably worthwhile to recall that while they were rating real studies, they were rating them for hypothetical situations. Usefulness, at least under these conditions, is a fairly generalized phenomenon.

Once we go beyond what the purposes have in common, the

Table 8.2. **First Four Unrotated Principal Components of Appropriateness Ratings**

Purpose	Factor 1	Factor 2	Factor 3	Factor 4
Raising an issue	.75	−.57	.07	−.06
Formulating new policies or programs	.81	−.43	−.01	−.18
Evaluating alternatives	.76	.22	−.44	.07
Improving existing programs	.77	.18	−.42	−.10
Mobilizing support	.73	.28	.35	−.34
Changing ways of thinking	.75	.36	.31	−.01
Planning new research	.70	−.01	.17	.66

second, third, and fourth factors tell us something about how use for different purposes differs. In particular, the second and third factors are what Rummel calls "bi-polar" (1970:373, 380–81); they set up contrasts between sets of items. The second factor contrasts the agenda-setting items to the other items, and the third factor distinguishes the problem-solving items from those related to coalition building. "Planning new research," whose loadings are insubstantial on the second and third factors, stands virtually alone on the fourth factor.

These data underscore the lessons of table 8.1. Ratings on appropriateness of research studies for different purposes show marked similarity. Superimposed upon the broad band of commonality, there are discernible wobbles. These small variations correspond to functions which we can characterize as agenda setting, problem solving, and coalition building, plus whatever functions are served by planning new research.

Characteristics of Studies
Appropriate for Different Functions

The next issue we turn to is whether certain characteristics of studies make them appropriate for particular purposes. Is Research Quality, Conformity to User Expectations, Action Orientation, or Challenge to the Status Quo especially important for some specific purpose or phase of decision making? (We do not consider relevance, because the wording of the question takes relevance for granted.)

To examine this question, we regressed the ratings of the appropriateness of studies for the seven purposes on the characteristics factors that describe the research. (See table 8.3.) This analysis shows the now-familiar pattern of general similarity with modest variations. The descriptive factors have similar effects on all the purposes for which studies can be used. In general, the strength of the factors shows this ordering: Challenge, Action Orientation, Research Quality, Conformity. Occasionally, the order changes for a specific purpose, but in no case does it change by more than one position.

That the two descriptive factors of the truth test, Research

Table 8.3. Effects of Research Characteristics on Appropriateness for Different Uses
(Standardized Regression Coefficients for Appropriateness Regressed on Research Characteristics)

Purpose	Research Quality	Conformity	Action Orientation	Challenge	R^2
Raising an issue	.06	.10	.23**	.34**	.26**
Formulating new policies or programs	.06	.18**	.21**	.39**	.32**
Evaluating alternatives	.14*	.10*	.27**	.29**	.30**
Improving existing programs	.06	.16**	.34**	.33**	.38**
Mobilizing support	.25**	.09	.20**	.28**	.30**
Changing ways of thinking	.25**	-.01	.18**	.40**	.36**
Planning new research	.16**	-.06	.16**	.31**	.20**

N (for inference) = 275.
*Significant at .05 level.
**Significant at .01 level.

Quality and Conformity, are relatively low in affecting appropriateness of use for different purposes is due to the structure of the question about purpose. The question was worded "assuming these study results were used." Previous analyses demonstrated that Research Quality and Conformity were important for deciding whether or not to rely on and use a study, but once use is assumed, they apparently become less salient.

Nevertheless, there are purposes for which the truth test factors are important. The most striking surge is the effect of Research Quality on "mobilizing support" and "changing ways of thinking." The standardized regression coefficient for Research Quality on both these purposes is .25, making Quality a close second behind Challenge in influencing a study's appropriateness. The implication is that to change people's minds and gain support for a point of view, it is necessary to have sound research that can withstand criticism. As observers have long remarked, opponents of a study's conclusions can suddenly become methodological pundits and raise technical objections to findings that they actually disagree with on political grounds (Rossi 1969). Our respondents' ratings indicate that they are well aware of such phenomena. For coalition-building purposes, they want research studies that can resist discrediting on the basis of methodological flaws. They may also be responding to an intuitive sense of the truth test: to convince doubters (for whom Conformity is low) and mobilize their support, it is crucial to have information of high scientific merit. For a study to serve well in building and maintaining support, it needs to be technically competent.

Conformity to User Expectations has its largest effects, although even these are not striking, on two purposes: formulating new policies and programs ($\beta = .18$) and improving existing programs ($\beta = .16$). Studies that support the understandings and beliefs of potential users add an extra dollop of certainty to such activities.

But it is the factors that provide direction for action, Action Orientation and Challenge to the Status Quo, that most clearly make a study appropriate for decisional purposes. Of the two, Challenge is considerably more salient. Studies that show shortcomings in current modes of programming or highlight courses of action not presently in practice are judged to be appropriate for every purpose. They are particularly valuable for changing ways of thinking about issues ($\beta = .40$) and formulating new policies ($\beta = .39$). By presenting results that challenge the premises on which current programs depend, they can appropriately be used at every stage of the decision-making process.

Action Orientation is less important than Challenge for every function except problem-solving. For the two problem-solving items, evaluating alternatives for action and improving existing programs, Action Orientation is just about on a par with Challenge, and it has its strongest impact on improving existing programs ($\beta = .34$). Since Action Orientation describes studies that give clear direction for practical action, its good showing on the problem-solving items makes intuitive sense.

What is perhaps most intriguing about these data is that even when we asked questions in terms of a rational sequence of decision-making activities, our respondents managed to suggest the overarching importance of Challenge. Whatever the specific decisional activity, studies that question current practices and concepts are judged to make a contribution.

Types of Research Appropriate
for Different Functions

It seems reasonable to expect that different types of research are more appropriate for one purpose than for others. In an effort to examine this supposition, we coded the 50 studies into four classes—descriptive studies, which provided data about a situation; causal analyses, which analyzed the origins of problems or conditions; implementation studies, which examined the processes of program operation; outcome evaluations, which investigated the effectiveness of programs for client groups.

It would be easy to develop hypotheses about the relevance of each type of study for specific decisional activities. For example, descriptive studies, which display the extent of a problem (such as repeated readmissions to mental hospitals) should be appropriate for raising an issue to attention. Causal analyses, which, for example, attempt to isolate the predisposing and precipitating conditions that lead to mental illness, should be appropriate for formulating new programs. Studies of implementation might be especially appropriate for improving existing programs. Evaluations of program outcome might be valuable for evaluating alternative proposals for programming and for improving existing programs.

We already know that decision makers do not make sharp distinctions among decision-making activities; as previous data in this chapter indicate, their ratings suggest that studies that are good for one purpose tend to be good for others as well. Nevertheless, without high hopes for dramatic breakthrough, let us look at the appropriateness of the four categories of studies for each decisional activity.

Table 8.4 presents the mean ratings on appropriateness. It shows that the type of research does not make a great deal of difference in appropriateness for different uses. All the ratings fall between 2.9 (appropriateness of descriptive studies for formulating new policies or programs) and 3.8 (appropriateness of studies of program implementation for raising an issue to attention). Since appropriateness was scored on a scale of 1 to 5, there is a potential maximum spread of 4 points, but the highest observed spread for any given purpose is 0.6 point (for raising an issue to attention).

The last column, eta squared, presents the percentage of vari-

Table 8.4. **Mean Appropriateness Ratings by Type of Research**

| Purpose | Mean Rating for Type of Study | | | | Eta Squared |
	Descriptive	Causal	Implementation	Evaluation	
Raising an issue	3.2	3.4	3.8	3.4	.02
Formulating new policies or programs	2.9	3.0	3.4	3.2	.02
Evaluating alternatives	3.0	3.1	3.2	3.4	.02
Improving existing programs	3.1	3.3	3.5	3.6	.03*
Mobilizing support	3.3	3.4	3.4	3.6	.01
Changing thinking	3.1	3.4	3.2	3.3	.01
Further research	3.7	3.4	3.4	3.6	.01
(N of studies)	11	14	8	17	
(N of ratings)	70	83	51	106	

NOTE: Ratings have been transformed so that higher values represent greater appropriateness.
N (for inference) = 303.
*Significant at the .05 level.

ance explained by type of study. The data show that type of study explains very little. For only one purpose, improving existing programs, is the eta squared significant ($p < .05$), and even there only 3 percent of the variance is explained.

We can sum the ratings across the rows to see which purposes are best served by research of any type. As some skeptics have long contended, research is seen as most appropriate for planning further research. Next in order come raising an issue to attention, mobilizing support for a position, and improving existing programs. At the other extreme, research is considered least suitable for formulating new policies or programs, evaluating alternatives, changing ways of thinking. It is tempting to embroider on these data, but the differences are too slight to support heavy interpretation.

Why So Little Difference?

All the analyses have suggested that there is a general model that makes studies appropriate for use, and that distinctions about appropriateness for specific uses are a second-order phenomenon.

We can detect small differences that correspond to the use of studies for the distinctive functions of agenda setting, problem-solving, and coalition building, but the distinctions are dwarfed by the common underlying model of usefulness.

This pattern leads us to consider why the use of research studies for what would appear to be very different purposes is not more clearly differentiated in respondents' ratings. We can suggest two explanations that are compatible with the data. One derives from the process by which decision makers consider and judge the usefulness of research for different purposes, and the other arises out of the nature of the decision-making process.

Decision makers who are presented with a report of research, not only under the simulated conditions of our interview but in the normal course of their work, are likely to think: Is this study any good to me? What can I do with it? Once they decide that the study is worth paying attention to (a judgment strongly influenced by its credibility, as we noted in discussing the "truth test" that they apply), they are likely to rotate its conclusions through a series of potential uses: Does it identify a need? Does it suggest action? Does it provide grounds for favoring one action over others? Will it help make the case for that action? and so on. If they do not regard it as appropriate for any of these decisional activities, it is not useful. But if it is useful for one of them, then they are apt to see ways in which it can be useful for other purposes as well. Take a study that demonstrates a lack of coordination between residential mental hospitals and outpatient community mental health facilities and recommends better continuity between them in arranging care for released patients. Decision makers might perceive such a study as useful for problem solving, but once they make that assessment, they may realize that it can also be used to make the problem visible (agenda setting) and to collect support for its implementation (coalition building). The thought processes by which they judge the appropriateness of a study may take off from one obvious and discrete mode of use (it can help improve existing programs), but once they make that judgment, they are likely to generalize the judgment to a range of other potential uses.

The special conditions of our interviewing procedure may

have heightened the generalizing tendency. For one thing, the question we asked called for consideration of a list of possible purposes for use, and respondents were in a sense forced to play the study through the list. Furthermore, the hypothetical nature of the question removed time constraints. In an actual situation, decision makers might well focus only on that particular purpose or phase of the decision process with which they were currently occupied, but without time restrictions, they were encouraged to range further afield. These circumstances could have contributed to the blurring of distinctions among uses.

The second explanation is that the process by which policy and program decisions are made is not nearly so segmental as our analytical constructs imply. Scholars find it handy to disaggregate decision-making into a series of discrete and logically ordered components. But inside the bureaucratic organizations in which our respondents work, the process of decision-making is continuous and iterative. The phases do not separate out into neatly labeled compartments; the people who work on particular programs may find themselves almost simultaneously identifying needs, mobilizing support, planning research, considering alternative policy proposals, and so on.

Not even the time order of decision-making is apt to follow the sequence that analysts and academics like to impose. A possible solution often surfaces before a problem has been established. In fact, the existence of a proposed solution may be a prerequisite for the identification of a problem. If there were no possible solution, then it would not be a problem; it would be a condition that had to be endured. New England winter weather is not a "problem" because there is no known solution; for many generations, poverty in the United States was not a "problem" because no possible solutions were politically acceptable. The mobilization of constituencies, too, may precede problem identification or problem solving. Before the emergence of the women's movement, domestic violence was neither recognized as a public issue nor considered an appropriate area for public intervention.

Thus, despite the analytic utility of distinguishing purposes and stages, decision-making may be too complexly interconnected a process to lend itself to the kinds of distinctions we have attempted to make. If the phases of decision-making are not sharply demarcated, particularly for the middle-level bureaucrats with whom we are dealing, then it would be surprising indeed if they could associate particular kinds of studies with particular uses. It is not only that any one research report can be harnessed to a multiplicity of purposes. It is also that the purposes themselves slide out of their analytic pigeonholes. If decision makers cannot say with assurance on any specific occasion (say, a staff meeting to plan next year's activities) whether their activity at that moment is developing new proposals, justifying existing programs, or building alliances, then it is unrealistic to expect that they can discriminate among studies that are discretely suitable for each purpose.

Summary

Studies that are appropriate for one purpose tend to be viewed as appropriate for other purposes as well. There are small distinctions among the kinds of studies that decision makers regard as suitable for different purposes, and we have detected differences associated with the functions of agenda setting, problem solving, and coalition building. But the distinctions are muted by the wide common band that underlies the model of usefulness. Just as a study was seen as appropriate for different users (see chapter 6), it is seen as appropriate for different kinds of uses. In explanation we have suggested that judgments of appropriate use tend to generalize from one purpose to another. We have also noted that the process of organizational decision-making itself is so iterative and composite that it often defies disaggregation into units with which particular kinds of research can be uniquely associated.

Chapter Nine

DECISION MAKERS' REPORTS
OF ACTUAL USE
OF RESEARCH

MENTAL HEALTH DECISION MAKERS not only have opinions, judgments, and expectations about social science research. They also have a history of experience. During our interviews we asked them to tell us about their past use of social science research in connection with their work.

Two sets of questions inquired about their explicit reliance on social science research. One set asked about the extent of their *conscious use* of social science research in reaching decisions on their jobs and the ways in which they used the research. The other set asked about the extent to which they sought out research when they were considering policy or program alternatives. Here the emphasis was not only conscious use but also *active search*, and further questions inquired about the circumstances and frequency of search and the sources they used to learn about and locate research information.

The often lengthy answers were transcribed verbatim from the tape recordings of the interviews. They not only give explicit illustrations of how decision makers have used social science research in the past; they also help to elucidate the meaning of the ratings of usefulness discussed in chapters 4 through 8. When decision makers rated studies in terms of their "likelihood of taking study results into account," their past experience with research provided the referents for the ratings.

Extent of Research Use

The overall impression is that decision makers in mental health are remarkably receptive to social science research. Although there is an outspoken minority that rejects its utility, the overwhelming majority reports prior use, often extensive use, and they sketch a wide variety of ways in which research informs their work. Given the dismal literature about neglect of social science research in public decision-making, these reports of frequent reliance upon its results and generalizations appear surprising at first view, but the detailed descriptions provide sufficient illumination to reconcile the previous sense that social science is ignored with these reports of widespread use. The key is that research *is* used but usually not in the ways to which observers have been attentive.

We asked respondents, "Do you consciously use the results of social science research on your job?" and "In what ways do you use social research on your job?" Their responses were coded into five categories:

No, never	11 percent
Not consciously	22 percent
Yes, but did not describe any ways used	10 percent
Yes, gave "general" uses	50 percent
Yes, gave specific uses	7 percent

There are those who reject social science research out of hand. The 11 percent who said that they had not used research usually referred to its worthlessness on grounds of irrelevance to their concerns or poor methodology or both. Illustrations of this type of answer are:

I think it's garbage. Consequently I have not developed much of an interest in it. I haven't seen many ways where it's used in mental health activities, at least developing mental health programs, that has been useful to those programs that I've been around. I think it's an academic pursuit mainly for academicians to fool around with. (290)*

No, because it's worthless. I've never seen anything useful in coming to decision or policy. It's skewed by being small specialized select populations. The questions they ask and the answers they get are so broad as to be totally worthless in coming to any decisions in areas that need attention. I've never seen any good research, social or otherwise, perhaps because they are too hard to do neatly in a university. (285)

*Numbers in parentheses are identification numbers of respondents. The 100s are federal, the 200s state, and the 300s local decision makers.

I know something about what research is available from psychology and sociology and anthropology. And many useful things have been turned up by those disci-plines. But they have contributed very little that will enable the director of a program like this to make a better rather than a worse decision. In my view . . . management makes use of whatever talents the incumbent has got and there is no body of knowledge or doctrine or dogma that is going to tell him how to do his job. . . . You can't rely on the results of anybody else's research to tell you what kinds of choices you should make. (136)

Another 22 percent boggled at the words "conscious use," but indicated that they believed research entered into their thinking and acting. The process by which they assimilated social science research was indirect, and its impact on their behavior was undirected, but they had a sense that it made a difference. Some of these responses are:

Consciously, no. What has been absorbed through readings play a part sometimes. There are times when you use statistics and findings. We're bogged down in day-to-day operations and don't have time to hunt up materials just to prove a point. You absorb a lot through reviews that come across the desk from time to time. (204)

Consciously, I don't think so. I think perhaps when you keep abreast of the field through reading I guess it becomes a part of your experience and it's not really a conscious thing. (261)

Seldom consciously. More often just the way things get absorbed. Essentially by filtering readings and presentations through my own consciousness and particular conditions here. (312)

I feel that my behavior has been influenced by a body of knowledge. I have been exposed and influenced. (321)

A skeptic might dismiss these answers as courteous but meaningless pap to satisfy the demands of the interview. However, given the rest of the information in the interviews, we are convinced that they represent an honest attempt to communicate the process by which social science research often plays a part in people's work activities. Much of the difficulty that respondents faced in answering the question obviously arose from the word "consciously." They are seeking to express the point that we noted in chapter 1: research is seldom used to affect decisions deliberately. Rather it fills in the background, it supplies the context, from which ideas, concepts, and choices derive. Ideas are slippery things. Even scientists, who work in a tradition that requires the citation of sources, find it difficult to trace the genealogy of their ideas. Decision makers, who are less attuned to footnoting their references, are probably less aware of the origins of many of the concepts with which they make sense of the world. It is hardly surprising that they balk at the word "conscious" to describe the process by which research concepts filter into their awareness and help them to structure reality.

A third group of decision makers faced the difficulty of articulating their use of research with a different set of answers. This group, 10 percent of the decision makers, said that they used research "constantly," "all the time," but they could not describe how they used it or provide an example. They, too, were fumbling for a way of expressing their awareness that they absorbed research information into their stock of knowledge but could not isolate its unique contribution.

Fifty-seven percent of decision makers reported that they used social science research and gave illustrations of use. But only 7 percent gave relatively concrete descriptions of the application of research to their work. The other 50 percent talked in general terms about using research to gain general direction and background, to keep up with the developments in the field, and to reduce uncertainties about their policies and programs. They discussed broad purposes, not specific decisions, specific aims, or specific content of research studies.

The most specific illustrations of research use recounted both the particular *research conclusions* that were influential and the particular *decisions* that the conclusions affected. But few responses tied down both the *research* and *decision* ends of the use process, despite probing (verging on nagging) by the interviewers. The most explicit example was provided by a federal official:

The Institute has data now which indicates most alcoholics can be served in outpatient services, and that is the major treatment modality, coupled with intermediate care, across the country. That data has affected our emphasis on out- as opposed to inpatient services. . . . Some of the evaluation material now is showing that aftercare and follow-up services are vital ingredients in a good program. A great deal of treatment can be undone without it. That's a mandatory element in accreditation of hospitals now. Research shows that certain groups—black, Indian, Hispanic—will enter treatment sooner if counselors "speak their language." We are encouraging the development of counselor characteristics in close relationship to the kinds of population they serve. This is another way we use data. (186)

The director of a local clinic also gave an illustration of concrete use. Although he did not describe the research results that gave direction, he indicated the purpose that they served:

We're always looking for ways to improve and enhance the effectiveness of our service and administration. So we're regularly, if not continually, scrutinizing the literature to see if it can give us help in this regard. ... For instance, an example would be a problem that most clinics suffer from. ... [About] 35 percent of the patients who apply for service continue. ... We, then, being concerned about this and wanting to improve the function of the agency ... began to look in the literature to find ways that we could have of maximizing the impact of the initial encounters with patients. ... And sure enough there were some valuable papers in the literature which assisted us in maximizing the impact of the initial contact with the patient. (304)

Few responses gave this degree of specificity. Even though most respondents reported that they used research, they found it hard to cite direct applications of research results to specific decisions. That concrete instances of use were mentioned so rarely suggests that the longtime laments of observers about the neglect of research have some basis in fact. But 50 percent of respondents discussed what we have labeled "general" uses of research, and before we conclude that research is actually neglected, let us look closely at these answers.

Reports of general uses of research included statements with considerable indeterminacy. Respondents indicated that they used a flow of research as an aid in formulating policy and setting direction. Some examples:

To the extent that the Administration looks to me for advice on policy issues as they come up, for example in the planning phase of budget formulation, we will make decisions on identifying priorities to be stressed in the budget development process, or later on, making decisions about allocations of funds within ceilings that are set. There the research and social science is taken into account. (101)

To enable us to get a better handle on the state of the art and the science. To sensitize us to what's going on and to help us formulate policy and establish new directions. (126)

Some comments were more concrete in identifying the kinds

of research that were used. A number referred to research about needs for service and the distribution of need. Respondents implied that information of this sort was helpful for developing programs and for targeting services to high-risk areas or special populations.

We use a great deal of socioeconomic and demographic information which will give us basic information on the area which will potentially be served by the mental health center. (254)

An example I can think of is an effort I'm doing currently, a short-term project in _____ county to assist their staff . . . to identify broad health needs, patterns of utilization of health services. (207)

The objective of the department is to meld the community programs and the hospital programs into a unified system of services. . . . When somebody gives me some kind of information . . . that has to do with the types of population which are in centers and which are in hospitals, I have to try to use this as a basis for planning for the kinds of change we would like to bring about. (253)

Another type of research reported as useful was evaluation research that indicated "what works." A number of people at all levels talked about using data about successful program strategies as models for their own efforts.

Largely we look at studies that are being conducted in this state and other states and on a national scope to see . . . what sorts of treatment modalities and methods and techniques have been effective . . . and we try to aim our programming along the lines that have proven successful in this state and elsewhere. (223)

We're looking for hard data to show something is or isn't useful. (161)

In terms of identifying new and improved methods by which to accomplish the goals and objectives of the division. (215)

Many people discussed the use of research to "keep up with the field." High-ranking officials in federal, state, and local agencies are experts in a substantive area, and they report using research to stay current with developments. To them social science research is a medium of communication about what is happening. They rely on it to tell them about the needs of people, about problems that are being encountered in providing service, and about emerging issues. These people gave answers that suggest social science research is a form of continuing education. It provides information that helps them maintain their claims to professional leadership.

[Research] has been used mainly for additional information for use in keeping up with what's being done, what's happening. (350)

[I use research] in reading and making myself aware of what is going on, what are the new things we know regarding people and the effects of the environment and the way they live on people. . . . Regarding social research, I'm interested in knowledge, all that's known about people and how they relate to the world and their surroundings and their needs. . . . (176)

I do it [use research] as a routine. It's part of being a professional. I feel the only constant thing is change. It's important to provide responsible service, and to be a responsible professional you must know what's going on. (357)

Another kind of research use is ritualistic. It satisfies the demands of the job, but its impact on action is problematic. Its major function seems to be to overlay the documents that wend their way through an organization with scientific patina, as for example in writing plans. One respondent talked about this type of use:

It was very important for me to have extensive studies . . . in writing my comprehensive plan. . . . That [writing plans] was the single primary objective of the office, and writing those plans you really have to utilize research, and that's what I did. (240)

This was a rare species of use, or at least rarely mentioned. If research is used, it usually serves more than a decorative function; it is expected to convince other people of the credibility and legitimacy of one's position.

Several people spoke about using research to support their point of view and persuade other participants in the decision-making process to accept their stand. They cite the use of research as ammunition in the political wars.

We would need the type of data that would not only outline the extent of the problem but also we need data that we could use to demonstrate to those people who review our budgets that there was in fact a demonstrable social and economic pay-off in investing money in this area. (111)

Primarily because any decision one makes in the public sector must be backed up. Other people's opinions unsupported by data aren't usually as valid for documentation of a position. (288)

This theme, the use of research to legitimate a position, comes up again in answers to the question about circumstances under which people seek research (see below). The answers suggest that research is used for legitimation because it has a special standing in organizational debate and bargaining.

Research is used not only to legitimate a prefabricated position. It is also used to help shape the fabrication before the position hardens. For example, one person said:

[I use research] to clarify my own thinking. Before I take a position, I want to see what others have said on a topic and studied. . . . If I'm going to prepare something, I want to be able to document it. . . . When I'm trying to push a particular position, I am going to scurry around and find all the articles for it. The assumption is if you can cite somebody who has done a careful study, it carries more weight than just another study. (174)

This statement starts with the use of research to clarify and inform the taking of a position, proceeds to documentation of the rationale for the position, and only then goes on to justification and promotion of the position. Research, it seems, has a part to play at each stage.

Other people talk explicitly about the internal as well as the external support that research provides. Research not only makes their advice more persuasive to others; it helps assure them in their own minds that they are right. Its contribution is to reduce the inevitable uncertainties that surround any policy issue.

It [research] is used to give us some confidence and assurance; what we're encouraging people to do is based upon these findings passed on to us from this research. (146)

A number of people discussed conceptual uses of social science research. They talked not so much about using research findings for particular purposes as about gaining insights into social processes as a foundation for understanding. Some of the social science concepts that were mentioned were:

Sensitivity to minority representation and minority issues generally as we try to formulate and implement policy. What we know of minorities comes from social science research. (102)

. . . a better understanding and perception of what is happening to the family system as a social institution—what are the impacts of the stresses associated with divorce, separation, alternative life-styles, changing mores, changing value systems. It's extremely broad. I don't know how to tie it down. (121)

For example, if someone says we need to build more institutions, I'm saying research has indicated that these kids don't need institutions. We have to develop alternative programs. (205)

The article in *Science* regarding issues of diagnosis and labeling as used in psychiatry . . . the issue then was what kinds of consequences were the result of labeling. That issue was important to me primarily because, although I'm a psychiatrist and essentially very interested in the medical model, I am aware that there are times when the process of labeling is not in the best interest of the patient. (371)

In this type of use, people view the intellectual perspectives gained from social science research as helping to shape their models of social reality. Social science research helps them make sense of the world and gain new or better insight into the complex issues with which they deal.

Many people underscored the point that social science research was not their only source of information and ideas. It was one source of many, and not usually powerful enough to drive the decision process. They read social science research, but it was auxiliary to their own firsthand experience. They were exposed as well to information from colleagues, program records, meetings and conferences, books and television, and the conversation of friends.

As one person said, "I read it [research] all . . . listen to a number of people, throw it all up in the air, and see what makes sense." Those social scientists who expect research to be authoritative enough to *determine* policy choices are giving insufficient weight to the many and varied sources from which people derive their understandings and policy preferences—some of which are far more vivid and direct in their impact than bloodless, statistic-ridden research reports.

Probably even more important for understanding these reports of research use, people in official positions often do not catalog research separately in their minds. They interpret it as they read it in light of their other knowledge, and they *merge* it with all the information and generalizations in their stock. Therefore, they find it difficult to identify the unique contribution that one study, or even a group of studies, has made to their actions.

One of the questions in the interview asked for reference to a specific study that the respondents had found useful for their work. With some effort, most of them produced a citation; 39 percent gave a full reference and 33 percent a partial reference. But many of them objected to the form of the question. They indicated that it was difficult, and sometimes meaningless, to disentangle one specific study out of the gestalt of knowledge that they had built up over the years. This pattern of response is identical to that reported by Caplan et al. (1975), who asked decision makers in a range of federal agencies to provide instances of the use of social science knowledge. They write:

Although a respondent may have given as an instance of his use of knowledge that he was influenced by an idea that he attributed to the social sciences—such as the belief that people's attitudes tend to follow their behavior rather than their behavior being governed by their attitudes—he cannot name a study or demonstrate the validity of that assertion. . . . Much of the importance of such an idea for the policy maker lies in its ultimate integration into his entire perspective on a problem. In asking him to cite instances of use, he is really being asked to atomize his conception of social reality, to take knowledge out of its context, a context without which the knowledge would not have been retained in the first place. (pp. 18–19)

Much of our data support this view of the integration of social science perspectives into people's understanding of how the world works. Because they amalgamate research with other sources of ideas as they develop understanding of issues, it is difficult for them to single out the specific sources. Several of our respondents explicitly tried to explain the complex process of assimilation:

It is a continuous awareness and stratification of several kinds of information—TV, newspapers, scientific articles, a book. All of these things overlap. It is very difficult for me to sort out where I got this information. (301)

I tend to integrate knowledge that's obtained in the articles into my own thinking. (370)

I don't think there is a specific way I take a piece of research and apply it in a precise manner. You build up a sequence of related pieces of research, you take it in, evaluating, assimilating, and at a later point, you use it. (150)

If the reports of research use that our respondents have given sound fuzzy and indistinct, this amalgamation of research with knowledge derived from variegated sources is part of the reason. They do not always know the provenance of the ideas and models that form their basic intellectual capital or which of them originally came, through direct or roundabout channels, from the studies of social science.

Another reason for the paucity of clear-cut instances of research use, and we will return to this, is that they are often unclear about the consequences of their daily activities. When asked how they use social science research in reaching decisions, we are in effect asking them not only to specify the social science *input* but also the decision *output*. And many of them do not believe that they make anything so crisp and clear as a decision on their jobs. They recommend, advise, confer, draw up budgets, testify, develop plans, write guidelines, report, supervise, propose legislation, assist, meet, argue, train, consult—but *decide?* It is not a concept that seems to aptly describe the flux of activities that engage officials even at the upper rungs of complex organizations.

Seeking Out
Social Science Research

We asked our respondents whether they *sought out* social science research when they were considering policy or program alternatives. As in the responses about using research, a minority of respondents disavowed any such activity. Twenty-one percent said that they never or almost never sought out research. The reasons that they offered were similar to those given to the question about use—irrelevance, untrustworthiness of the findings—and in addition, lack of time. The remaining 79 percent said that there were occasions on which they or their staff looked for research related to the issues with which they were dealing. But the search was usually less focused and crisp than our question implied. One respondent tried to explain the context in which seeking research took place:

Do I seek? It depends on how much I already know. (221)

Others elaborated on the interaction between ongoing perusal of research and their actions on policy or program:

A lot of it is informal. . . . We don't sit down and say, "All right, we're going into this program, let's find out everything we can about it." Because quite often it's an ongoing thing. It's sort of compiled somewhat informally, but conclusions are based on that sort of thing. (223)

If there is a clear-cut planning thing developing, it usually develops out of our needs here. Then we would turn to relevant literature I know is there from reading over the years and use it to support the plan and to give direction. (312)

It's ongoing. With regard to all the variety of functions, we're constantly seeking research and development input. (173)

Again, despite our attempt to set the question in a traditional decision-making context ("considering policy or program alternatives"), officials pushed against the limits of the language to make room for the more complex realities of their experience.

When it came to describing the occasions on which they turned to social science research, they were somewhat more explicit than they were in the answers about research use. In part, the greater specificity may be a result of the placement of the question in the interview. The questions on research use hit them right at the start, introducing a topic on which few of them had reflected before, whereas the questions about seeking out research followed approximately two hours of discussion of the subject. In part, too, the focus on directed search for research may have evoked more concrete imagery.

The conditions they reported for seeking research fell mainly into four categories: new situations, decisions that entailed important or expensive consequences, requests for consultant help on matters on which they lacked sufficient expertise, and situations where their judgment could be challenged and they wanted authoritative support.

When the agency was moving into new fields of policy or programming, many people reported that they looked to research for background and guidance. In response to the question about circumstances when they seek research, respondents said:

Any time we have a new area to deal with or a controversial area to deal with or where we feel the lack of personal background. (161)

If we get into newer areas, I ask staff to find out what there is on this and make a report and recommendations. Starting a new program or facing a problem if we don't know how to handle it. (232)

If we're going into a totally new endeavor. When we are looking at a new program area or when we are looking at a new way of doing something. (254)

The big decision is another trigger of search. If misjudgment would have serious consequences, officials canvas many people's opinions and experience and look for facts and judgments in many places, including social science research.

When we're faced with a policy or program change that would have long-range implications. (261)

When we need to make a significant program or policy decision, or where there is a great deal of staff ambivalence, a lot of diversified opinion, and we have to make a decision. (353)

The ones that involve enormous commitments of resources, manpower, and dollars. Those are the ones you lie awake nights on. (275)

Another prod to seeking out research is the request for consultation. Some federal respondents hold jobs that involve providing consultation and technical assistance to other federal agencies and to states, and many state officials are advisers to local agencies. When they are insufficiently knowledgeable about an area in which they are asked for advice, they seek research.

When I want to supply information as a result of a request. (176)

When asked to consult on a program issue that we need some backing on ourselves to help our consultees. (221)

Finally, a number of respondents (15 percent of the sample) mentioned seeking research for its credibility in documenting their arguments. When expert opinion alone will not do, or when an agency's position is suspect on grounds of self-servingness, research can serve as legitimation. Among the answers on this theme:

Primarily to make a point—to give evidence to support an argument or position. (180)

Most often when there is a need to support budgetary requests in Congressional hearings for appropriations for funding our programs. (160)

Generally to deal more effectively with the legislature. (299)

If I were trying to sell the hospital on certain programs. (350)

I seek research . . . in regard to mostly money and public support. When I'm going before the board of supervisors. When I'm trying to justify the amount of money it takes to run this place. (338)

At Congressional time, preparing testimony. . . . The one time where I give a damn about references is Congressional. (175)

The verbs that respondents used are graphic: "support," "back up," "sell," "justify," "document," "counter." We quote so many responses about the use of research as legitimation not because they outnumber other types of response, but because this is the only place in our study where they appear so explicitly. As observers have long commented, one function of research is to serve as a tool in bureaucratic politics—particularly, some of our respondents aver, in confrontation with legislatures over budgets.

Implicit in these responses is the suggestion that research has become an essential mode of communication and persuasion in the public arena. Other actors in the policy-making process expect officials to make their case in terms of data, facts, evidence, statistics, studies. They look for documentation from objective scientific sources. In this sense, social science research has become a necessary language of discourse in the public forum. Whether or not it changes officials' own minds, they use it as a new lingua franca for talking across the boundaries of interests, organizations, and content areas. Participants in decision-making, wherever they are located, have to be able to speak the language of social science if they are to communicate effectively.

Policy making is largely a process of persuading others and striking bargains. Proof of a *need* for programs and appropriations, and demonstration of a social *pay-off* from policies and services whether current or proposed, are critical components of the negotiating game. To be convincing, much of the argument these days has to be phrased in research terminology. It is noteworthy in our respondents' remarks that testimony before the legislature, which is not commonly regarded as a bastion of research support, calls for review of the research literature, that it is for the Congress that they "give a damn about references." Through the language of social science research, they seek to transform what might be seen as special pleading into something more akin to dispassionate review and support for policy.

It is instructive to note that respondents' answers to neither the use-of-research nor the seeking-out-research question parallel the "purposes for using research" that we asked about (and reported in chapter 8). They did not structure their replies about uses of research in terms of phases in the decision-making cycle (raising an issue to attention, formulating new policies, evaluating alternatives, etc.). As we noted in chapter 8, those distinctions are not particularly germane to the use of research. Studies that are useful for one stage of decision making are likely to be useful for other stages as well, because the analytical categories do not parallel with much exactness the gritty experience of bureaucratic life.

Varieties of Research Use

Respondents' reports demonstrate that social science research serves many functions for holders of upper-level bureaucratic positions. They use it on occasion as a direct input to decisions to help them make thorny choices. Particularly when the decisions are momentous in scope or consequence, they may attend to research results. Somewhat more often, they use research as general guidance, finding evidence of needs and problems and gaps or shortcomings in existing services, and identifying successful strategies as a model for future efforts. Some research use is ritualistic, a ceremony to satisfy requirements for rational procedure or scientific gloss. They are engaged by the concepts of social science, which contribute to their understanding of the nature of social problems, the range of possible options for addressing problems, and the context in which remedies must be applied. In new program areas, where officials lack firsthand experience, such orienting perspectives are particularly valuable. They use research ideas, too, to rethink old program assumptions and as scaffolding for building new formulations.

Another major use of social science research is as continuing education to enable officials to maintain their professional expertise. Research is, among other things, a medium of news about needs, services, promising approaches, obstacles and pitfalls, and the most up-to-date knowledge about human behavior. It offers information about the issues and ideas that are engaging the attention of social scientists and about current directions in intellectual thought. Even when they are not consciously using research, the perspectives that they have absorbed from the social science literature influence which features of the environment they accept as "given" and unchangeable, which aspects become candidates for intervention, and their understanding of the interconnections among social phenomena.

There are times when officials use these insights to challenge and clarify their own thinking. Sometimes they derive the warm comfort of reassurance that their judgments are sound and have support and reinforcement in systematic investigation. They use research, too, to buttress their position and promote their case in dealing with colleagues and superiors and to convince others to accept their standpoints, programs, and budgets. They speak the language of social science research to make their arguments convincing. By adopting its symbols and its grammar, they may find their positions subtly influenced by the structure of its rules.

Our research, like other recent empirical studies of the use of social science research in organizations, reaches the conclusion that public officials use research more widely than previous dirges on the subject have suggested. But they do not often use it by considering the findings of one study in the context of a specific pending decision and adopting the course of action recommended by (or derived directly from) the research. That kind of instrumental "utilization" is what many observers have expected and looked for in vain. Failing to find it, they have concluded that research is ignored. Instrumental use seems in fact to be rare, particularly when the issues are complex, the consequences are uncertain, and a multitude of actors are engaged in the decision-making process. The further restriction that many observers have imposed on their definition of research utilization—that the research *change* the decision from what it would have been in the absence of research— makes the frequency of "utilization instances" in policy-making rarer still. But when we recognize the many and diverse ways in which research contributes to organizational action, we get a much more positive view of the influence of research.

Processes of Acquiring
Social Science Research

We asked several questions about sources of research information. The best summary of respondents' views came in answers to the question: "Over all, what are the best sources of research information that is useful to your work?" Table 9.1 presents the responses, and provides a comparison with the responses of social science researchers and research review committee members to the same question.

As these data indicate, the means by which decision makers hear about relevant research are not dramatically different from

Table 9.1. Best Sources of Research Information

Source	Decision Makers (n = 147)	Researchers and Panel Members (n = 98)
Academic, scientific, professional journals	54%	74%
Literature, library, papers unspecified	20	29
Mass media, mass circulation magazines	11	7
Intramural staff, internal colleagues	16	0
Researchers outside own institution	7	13
Word of mouth, people generally	22	30
Meetings, conferences	7	17
Other	13	9

NOTE: Percentages total to more than 100 because of multiple responses.

those used by social science researchers. Over half of them rely particularly on academic, scientific, and professional journals. This is a strong endorsement of traditional scientific communications as the "best" source, though it is noticeably lower than that reported by social scientists. Decision makers also mention with some regularity the importance of word-of-mouth communication, and one-sixth of them credit their organizational colleagues with being particularly good sources. Part of the reason for the mention of intramural colleagues is the dependence on staff aides. A number of decision makers turn to assistants for general and specific research information.

Officials thus read a great deal and dip widely into reports of and about research in disciplinary, professional, and popular periodicals. They talk to colleagues and attend meetings, and many of them, particularly at the federal level, work in environments that are attuned to the social sciences. As one federal official said, knowledge about research seeps into their consciousness almost "by osmosis." Which of the research reports that they read are dismissed out of hand and which deposit some residue in their minds is the subject that the previous chapters have addressed; there we explored the "tests" that decision makers apply to the incoming streams of research information. Here we note that their net is cast wide, and they are exposed to quantities of social science research.

Why then are the responses about uses of research so overwhelmingly general and diffuse? Why are there so few examples of direct application of research results to specific decisions? In the final section of this chapter, we summarize the major themes that emerged from decision makers' responses to questions about their history of research use.

Rarity of Instrumental Use:
New Understandings

If concrete illustrations of decision-determining uses of social science research are sparse, ready explanations abound. As we noted in chapter 1, observers have compiled a catalog of reasons for the disjunction between research and decisions: research does not examine all the relevant variables, research rarely fits the exact circumstances within which decisions are made, research is not ready on time for decisions, research conclusions are not clear or authoritative enough to provide trustworthy guidance, research reports do not reach the right audience, decision makers do not understand or trust research findings or understand how to interpret and apply them, the lessons from research are outweighed by competing considerations of agency self-interest and individual career advancement.

Decision makers in our study agree on occasion with many of these explanations. But the substratum of their responses adds more basic insights into the nature of the use/nonuse paradox. When we listen to them carefully, we can recognize two pervasive conditions that limit both their ability to itemize instances of research use (even when they are convinced that research makes a difference in what they do) and, more basically, their opportunity to "apply research" in direct problem-solving ways. These conditions are (a) the auxiliary character of social science research to other forms of knowledge and (b) the relative rarity of crisp clear-cut decisions.

The first understanding is that social science research does not enter a benighted world that is bereft of understanding and direction. It is not a beam of light in a dark room. It is more like a candle in a lighted room (well- or ill-lighted, depending on the agency), adding some extra illumination, sometimes on topics that were previously shrouded in shadow.

Decision makers are professionals in their fields, with a body of knowledge derived from professional education and years of experience. They have spent their working lives providing services and running programs, and they have vivid firsthand experience upon which to draw. Their direct involvement gives them a long familiarity with the substantive issues of the field—and also with organizational history, accepted modes of operation, feasible options, and decision rules. Their experience has a directness and immediacy that research reports frequently lack.

For them, research enhances but does not substitute for experience. It supplements what they already know, on occasion offering unexpected insights or calling into question previously unexamined assumptions. But it does not and can not replace "ordinary knowledge" (Lindblom and Cohen 1979).

Because of the existing expertise of decision makers, the unique contribution of any one study—or even a group of studies—is usually hard to detect. If the research is compatible with their prior understanding, its conclusions or perspectives are likely to be assimilated without leaving discernible markers. If it is not compatible, it may be discounted (because it does not Conform to User Expectations), distorted to fit in with prior knowledge, put on "hold" until more evidence is in, compartmentalized (i.e., accepted but segregated from other knowledge), or accepted and used as a sensitizing perspective by which earlier knowledge is gradually reinterpreted to make sense of the world. A single study is unlikely to lead to an abrupt shift in beliefs. As Kuhn (1970) wrote about scientific research, even when it disconfirms prevailing theories, more research must be done, more evidence accumulated, and a plausible alternative theory offered, before the community accepts a change in paradigms.

Most of the time, research makes incremental, marginal additions to what decision makers already know. As Patton et al. (1977) discovered in their interviews with evaluation researchers, government project officers, and program officials:

... none of the impacts described was of the type where new findings from an evaluation led directly and immediately to the making of major, concrete program decisions. *The more typical impact was one where evaluation findings provided additional pieces of information in the difficult puzzle of program action.* (p. 145, italics in original)

Because of the gradual assimilation of social science research into officials' preexisting stock of knowledge, research only occasionally has discernible effects one study at a time. Rather, it is the accumulation of evidence from a body of studies that tends to make a difference. Decision makers absorb the general thrust of social science research through reading, listening, meeting-going, and the routines of their jobs. When many pieces of research converge on a major theme (e.g., the release of mental patients to the community is leaving many of them adrift and helpless, even with current modes of community care), decision makers begin to review their other information in the light of this perspective. If it helps to explain previous anomalies, they may reorient their prior views and come to reconceptualize the nature of the problem and the range of solutions for dealing with it. Even then, their reorientation is likely to be incremental (e.g., existing community care needs to be better linked to hospital release) rather than involve fundamental rethinking of the essentials of the problem.

Only on small operational issues does social science research seem to have a chance to affect outcomes directly, and then only if it fits within a larger consensual framework. Thus, a body of evidence that shows the superiority of a certain technique may have direct impact as long as the technique is within the repertoire of agencies as currently structured and is consonant with their other procedures and resources. But on larger issues, research is used less to help solve immediate problems than it is to conceptualize problems and think about appropriate actions.

The supplementary character of research knowledge thus tends to blur the use of research. Decision makers often absorb research information without clear marking of its origins. They merge what they learn from research with information derived from a variety of other sources. When they take action, they draw upon their general fund of knowledge, of which research has provided only some small part—a part which is neither clearly identified nor measurable. By virtue of these processes of assimilation, the "knowledge" that social science research supplies to potential users has indistinct and hazy borders.

The second insight that we gain from respondents' accounts is that "decisions," too, lack crisp definition. If the intake of research knowledge is a diffuse process, so too is the output of decisions. In fact, one of the most unexpected findings from the narrative reports of research use is the frequency with which holders of high-ranking organizational positions claim that *they do not make decisions.* Although their titles and statutory responsibilities suggest considerable authority and their reports of their jobs indicate deep involvement in deliberations over program direction and allocation of resources, many of them state that decision-making is an inappropriate concept for their work.

In our pretest interviews, we asked respondents to describe the kinds of decisions that they made on their jobs. As we reported in chapter 2, many respondents were so uncomfortable with the question that we discarded the "decision" wording in every question except one. We retained the word "decision" only in asking about the conscious use of social science research "in reaching decisions on your job." Even this scaled-down version drew frequent disclaimers. For example, one highly placed federal official said:

I don't know what it means when you say "reaching decisions." I decide to answer or not answer various pieces of correspondence. . . . I haven't seen a decision made in some time. Let's leave decisions out and talk about action. (174)

The idea that they made decisions about policy, program, budgets, allocations, or services was widely disconcerting. If officials do not give the label "decision" to their actions, even the highly consequential actions that they take, if they do not perceive their acts as decisions or as part of the making of decisions, then they can hardly identify research that influences their decisions.

Review of the responses suggests that three conditions mainly account for the disavowal of decision-making authority: (a) the dispersion of responsibility over many offices and the participation of multiple actors in decision-making, so that no one individual feels that he/she has a major say; (b) division of authority among federal, state, and local levels in the federal system; (c) the series of gradual and amorphous steps through which many decisions take shape.

Obviously in large organizations, decisions on complex issues are almost never the province of one individual or one office. Many people in many offices have a say, and when the outcomes of a course of action are uncertain, many participants have opportunities to propose, plan, confer, deliberate, advise, argue, forward policy statements, reject, revise, veto, and rewrite. In addition, legislative action is often required for major shifts in direction, and legislative appropriations are needed for major increase in activities. The operational staffs in the agencies are sensitive to the preferences and expectations of the legislature. However influential their own proposals and actions turn out in fact to be, they are conscious of the recurrent approvals and sign-offs that must be maneuvered within the department and the modifications that can be introduced during the legislative process. In fact, they seem to be more conscious of the power of others—whether or not it is exercised—than they are of the influence of their own actions.

Given the slow and cumbersome process through which proposals often travel, many organizational members are not fully aware of the influence they have. They make a proposal and see nothing happen for months. Even if the proposal is eventually adopted with only minor modifications, they may lose sight of the connection between what they proposed and what eventually happens. And when a series of adaptations is made, they seem to conclude that they have little influence in the system.

Officials at the top echelon can be equally convinced that they do not make decisions. From the top of the hierarchy, it often looks as though they are presented with a fait accompli. Accommodations have been reached and a decision negotiated by people in the many offices below, and they have little option but to accept it. Only rarely, and with the expenditure of a considerable amount of their political capital, can they change or reject it. To them the job often looks like rubber stamping decisions already made. Thus, the division of authority leaves each participant largely unaware of the nature and extent of his contribution.

The federal system adds further indeterminacy. During the interviewing in our study, we were told by people at each governmental level that "real" decisions were made elsewhere. Federal officials said that the Congress passed the laws and determined the appropriations, and all they did was write guidelines to carry out Congressional intent and pass the money down to agencies who made real decisions about services. State officials said that they were a conduit. They received federal funds hedged about by Congressional requirements and HEW guidelines, along with state funds restricted by requirements of the state legislature. Their main job was not to decide but to do the paperwork to move the money to operating agencies. To local agencies, it looked as though funds came ringed around by tight constraints—legislative provisions, federal guidelines, state plans and regulations—and extra regulations for funds received from city, county, and third-party payors. They saw little latitude for local "decisions." They did what they were allowed to do under the weight of rules.

Thus, fragmentation of authority for decisions is not only horizontal but vertical. For a decision to take effect requires co-operation at every level. What the federal agency "decides" can be distorted or undone by action (or inaction) in state and local agencies (see Pressman and Wildavsky 1973). What the care-giving agency "decides" is so hemmed in by requirements of other bodies that it feels it has little discretion. Again, people at every point are more conscious of the limits to their authority than of the latitude available.

The final set of reasons for the inaptness of the concept of decisions derives from the nature of bureaucratic work. Many problems and issues are dealt with simultaneously, and consideration of each one goes on over a protracted period. Responsible officials only rarely convene at one time and one place to make a decision. The image of decision-making represented by President Kennedy and his group of advisers thrashing out the nation's response to the Cuban missile crisis is inappropriate to most of daily bureaucratic life. Much more commonly, each person takes some small step (writes a memo, answers an inquiry, edits the draft of a regulation) that has seemingly small consequences. But over a period of time, these many small steps foreclose alternative courses of action and limit the range of the possible. Almost imperceptibly a decision has come about, without anyone's awareness that he/she was deciding.

Many moves are improvisations. Faced with an event that calls for response, officials use their experience, judgment, and intuition to fashion a response for the issue at hand. That response becomes a precedent, and when similar—or not so similar—questions come up, the response is uncritically repeated. Consider the federal agency that receives a call from a local program asking how to deal with requests for service from people who are not explicitly eligible. A staff member responds with off-the-cuff advice. Within the next few weeks, programs in three more cities call with similar questions, and staff repeat the advice. Soon what began as improvisation has hardened into policy. Bauer (1963) writes of this type of decision-making:

. . . it is ordinarily assumed that *important* decisions are made most deliberately and ordinarily with the least constraint of other considerations. But this is not always the case. For example, it has long been a complaint of our State Department that the ordinary problems get explicit attention and overall policy is made by default. There is a familiar phrase used to describe this: "Policy is made on the wires," that is, in the cabled responses to specific problems arising in the field. (p. 59)

Bauer suggests a change in terminology:

. . . I would like to suggest to the reader that there are times when the word "commitment" is more appropriate to what goes on than is the phrase "decision making." As a result of all the activities in which the individual is involved, the activities of other people in the organization, and the unanticipated consequences of all these, the supposed decision maker may find that in reality the decision has been made for him. To recognize that this is the state of affairs is no trivial intellectual feat. (p. 59)

Kissinger (1979) recently explained how an action, taken for a considered purpose, can be repeated unthinkingly under conditions for which it was not designed. Writing about the "double-bookkeeping" that kept the bombing of Cambodia secret, he said:

The method of reporting was set up for the first (and we then thought only) strike on March 18, 1969. . . . What was originally conceived as a one-time response to the North Vietnamese offensive became a continuing practice about two and a half months later—after Hanoi had turned down a new peace offer. The double-bookkeeping set up for a single attack was then repeated by rote and without a special new decision. This may have been mindless. . . .

Repetition is only one route to the accretion of policy without decision. Some decisions take shape through a series of actions and reactions. An inside or outside event triggers a move, that sets off the next move, that leads to the next—until the unconcerted series of well-advised or bumbling moves has shifted the direction of policy. (Through such a series of disastrous moves, the great powers stumbled into the First World War.) The many independent accommodations and contests lead to a result that no one anticipated.

Orlans' (1972) description of the process—and the role of knowledge—is graphic:

> . . . countless proximate decisions are reached in many offices, each with a different brew of fermenting knowledge—and, of course, much else, besides knowledge—until, like Moscow starting to burn, an hour comes and goes in which, we later say, the matter was consummated. (p. 20)

Probably even more common is the decision that "happens" as a side effect of other decisions. Nobody is paying explicit attention to the issue at hand, but the unintended consequences of action taken for other purposes effectively set policy. A town that adopts strict environmental regulations to preserve open spaces, coastline, and water in effect limits the influx of new residents. Without conscious consideration, it "decides" to keep out lower income and minority families. Or a state agency with insufficient office space moves to an available suburban location that happens to be poorly served by public transit. In so doing, it in effect "decides" to reduce the number of inner-city employees, even while its equal opportunity office is trying to increase minority representation on staff.

A recent report on the international arms race points to similar accretion of policy through the daily technical activities of military engineers and managers. These staff people are not making decisions; they are doing their ordinary work to improve the weapons systems in their charge. Yet these "routine" activities have far-reaching implications. Shapley (1978), in a section subtitled "Real Decisions Are Rare," writes:

> . . . what seems to happen is that the ebb and flow of technical development goes largely unwatched by policymakers. . . . So the conventional view of how military policy is made seems incomplete. Only rarely are political leaders handed genuine choices as to whether to escalate or deescalate the arms race, such as the ABM issue of the late 1960s. And even then, their options are determined by trends in military technology that have already been guided by lower level engineers and project managers. (p. 292)

Much of the literature on organizational decision-making assumes that a set of officials with authority for an issue-arena exists, that it becomes aware of a problem or opportunity within its jurisdiction that requires action, that it generates options for dealing with the situation, considers the advantages and disadvantages of each option, and makes a conscious choice. In such a process, research and analysis (as well as other information) can be formally taken into account. But under many conditions, each one of the assumptions breaks down. Many decisions "happen" without the (a) acknowledged responsibility, (b) boundedness of time and events, (c) purposiveness, (d) calculation, or (e) perceived significance that are subsumed in this image of decisions.

The respondents in our study tended to view their work as a stream of ongoing activities. They rarely thought of it as making discrete decisions but rather as "doing their job." They planned and recommended and administered, but these were not time-specific, choice-determining events. As Barnard (1962, 1st ed. 1938) wrote about an order to move two telephone poles across the street:

> . . . it can, I think, be approximately demonstrated that carrying out that order involves perhaps 10,000 decisions of 100 men located at 15 points, requiring successive analyses of several environments, including social, moral, legal, economic, and physical facts of the environment, and requiring 9000 redefinitions and refinements of purpose, and 1000 changes of purpose. If inquiry be made of those responsible, probably not more than half-a-dozen decisions will be recalled or deemed worthy of mention. . . . The others will be "taken for granted," all a part of the business of knowing one's business. (p. 198)

People in high organizational positions similarly compress dozens of large and small decisions into the category of knowing their business and doing their work. They concentrate on the ongoing flow rather than the policy outcomes of what they do. Even when their activities contribute to a shift in agency direction, they are not always aware of their contribution. The steps that lead to change often take place in uneven iterations. Their plans, proposals, and advice feed into the hopper, but the hopper leads not into a streamlined decision-manufacturing machine but into a Rube Goldberg contraption—with unexpected delays, reverse backflows, and unmarked disposal exits. It is often hard for them to know when, even whether, their advice has influenced agency policy.

Even more fundamentally, the point at which incremental shifts can be defined as "a decision" is shrouded in ambiguity. When decisions accrete through a series of small unorchestrated steps, it is sometimes possible only in retrospect to recognize that a decision has been made. In such cases, the conscious use of research to guide decision-making is a relatively uncommon event.

In specialized analytic offices (Aaron 1978; Meltsner 1976b; Menges 1978), the application of research can and should be the order of the day, and analysts draw upon research evidence in developing position papers and recommendations to policy makers for the resolution of specific issues. But in the normal course of events within the middle levels of bureaucracies (from which our respondents were largely drawn), social science research does not commonly drive the organizational machinery.

On the other hand, officials engage in a busy variety of activities. Drawing upon the knowledge that they have absorbed from social science research (as well as other sources) is highly compatible with the manner in which they conceptualize and perform their jobs. What they do is conditioned by what they know. The integration of research generalizations and concepts into their weltanschauung can have pervasive—if ultimately unmeasureable—effects. To the extent that their viewpoints are shaped by information, misinformation, and ideas from the social sciences, their policies bear the imprint.

Chapter Ten

DECISION MAKERS' REPORTED CRITERIA FOR USEFUL RESEARCH

THIS CHAPTER, unlike the preceding chapters, is based on what decision makers *say* are the characteristics that make research studies useful to them. It examines their stated reports of the characteristics that are important to them in selecting studies for use. It then compares these *reports* of desired characteristics with the *effects* of the same characteristics on the usefulness of the specific studies that they rated during the interview (as discussed in chapter 5). In effect, it examines whether decision makers can articulate the criteria that they actually employ in practice.

The practical question we are addressing is whether a social science investigator can find out which attributes of a study will make the study more useful by asking decision makers. The applied social research literature abounds in injunctions to consult early and often with potential users. Although there are several reasons for this advice, one of the reasons is to find out what specific features the research should incorporate if it is to be useful. Our aim in this chapter is to examine whether decision makers can in fact tell ahead of time which characteristics of a study will increase its usefulness to them.

Very early in the interview, before we presented abstracts of research or rating forms, we asked respondents a set of open-ended questions about the kinds of social science research that they would like to have available for their work, what made them favor the findings of one study over another study on the same topic, and what made some studies more useful than others.

In response to the question on the kinds of research they would like to have, most decision makers described the topics that they would like to see investigated. Since that was not our primary interest,[1] we followed up with a question that aimed to neutralize the salience of research topic: "Assuming that you had several studies on one topic, what would make you favor the findings of one study over another?" The spontaneous answers to this question piled up in the category that we classified as "research quality." See the first column in table 10.1. The most frequently given answers referred to the methodology of the study and to its conceptualization, or to a surrogate indicator of research quality—the reputation of the researcher, her institutional affiliation, and/or the journal in which the study appeared. Other than research quality, the only response offered by more than 10 percent of the decision makers was the match of the population studied to the population with which the respondent was concerned. Relatively small numbers of people gave answers that had to do with agreement with user's beliefs, implementability, report presentation, or usable information.

Table 10.1. Attributes of Research Volunteered by Decision Makers as Criteria for Useful Studies

Attribute	Reason to Favor One Study Over Another (N = 147)	Generally Makes Research Useful (N = 133)
Research quality		
Good methodology (other than conceptualization and sampling, q.v.)	39%	5%
Reputation of researcher, institution, or journal	33	6
Good conceptualization of study	31	9
Sample well-drawn, representative, adequate response rate	20	8
Validity (general)	18	11
Conclusions supported by the data	6	2
Good analysis or interpretation of data	2	2
Other	13	8
Fit to user's needs		
Population studied fits user's concern	19	18
Relevant to work	3	28
High priority of issue, socially significant	3	5
Timeliness	2	13
Other	4	3

Table 10.1. *(Continued)*

Attribute	Reason to Favor One Study Over Another (N = 147)	Generally Makes Research Useful (N = 133)
Dissemination—widely known, etc.	1	8
Presentation of report		
Clearly written	9	12
Presents adequate information about methods, concepts, definitions	3	—
Relates findings to other research	2	1
Other	6	3
Usable information		
Manipulable variables, points out problem, users involved in study	7	25
Takes costs into account	3	2
Explicit recommendations	3	8
Other	3	11
Implementability		
Confirms previous research	3	2
Administratively feasible to implement	3	3
Inexpensive to implement	3	3
Suggests original action approaches	2	1
Other	6	3
Agreement with user's beliefs		
Agrees with user's experience	10	2
Supports user's ideology	5	5
Provides political support for agency, programs	2	2
Other	7	3
Other		
Useful, practical (general)	5	8
Other	5	6

NOTE: Percentages total to more than 100 because of multiple responses.

The next question asked was what they thought, in general, made some social science research studies more useful than others for decision makers in mental health. Responses to this question were more broadly distributed, with the largest number classified under "fit to user's needs"—which included the relevance of the topic, the nature of the population studied, and the timeliness of the report. Respondents also mentioned items having to do with research quality with some frequency, particularly the validity of findings, but not nearly as often as they mentioned quality when discussing their own criteria for favoring a study. The intrinsic usability of the information, notably the item that included manipulability of study variables, identification of specific problems, explicit attention to usefulness, and involvement of potential users in the study, was next in order of frequency. The second column in table 10.1 lists all the responses and their frequency of mention.

The final question in the group was a structured question, designed to obtain a set of responses that were comparable to each other and to other data in the inquiry. The structured question asked: "How important are each of these characteristics to you when you choose to use a research study?" The form listed 29 characteristics and asked for a rating on each item from 1 to 5, where 1 was "essential," 2 "highly desirable," 3 "desirable," 4 "unnecessary," and 5 "undesirable." The items on the list were identical to the items on which respondents later rated the research abstracts they read.[2]

Decision Makers' Stated Criteria
for Using a Study

Table 10.2 presents decision makers' answers. The first column shows the percentage of decision makers rating each item essential, and the following columns show the percentage rating each item highly desirable, desirable, unnecessary, and undesirable. Items are ordered by their mean importance score. To distinguish these ratings from decision makers' ratings of the "characteristics" of the specific studies that they read (see chapters 4 and 5), we call these data "criteria." They are the criteria stated by respondents as important to them.

There are obvious and inevitable differences between the spontaneous responses (table 10.1) and the structured ratings (table 10.2). When volunteering a response to an open-ended question, people single out the things that appear most significant in terms of the wording of the question, and they take many other things for granted. When confronted with a structured question, they have to run all the items through their calibrating procedure and make judgments about each of them (Gorden 1975:350–57). Thus,

Table 10.2. Ratings of Criteria for Useful Studies

Criteria	Essential	Highly Desirable	Desirable	Unnecessary	Undesirable
Recommendations are supported by the data	66%	23%	10%	1%	0%
Understandably written	57	32	11	0	0
Objective, unbiased	45	37	15	3	0
Deals with a high priority issue	33	47	15	5	0
Adds to practical knowledge about the operation of policies or programs	33	43	22	2	0
Findings are internally consistent and unambiguous	30	43	21	5	1
Technical quality of the research is high	23	50	23	4	0
Has direct implications for a course of action	29	39	25	7	0
Analyzes the effects of factors that decision makers can do something about	26	42	28	4	1
On time for pending decision	26	34	31	8	1
Generalizable to equivalent populations	15	53	26	6	0
Adds to descriptive, causal, or theoretical knowledge in the field	18	40	38	3	0
Raises new issues or offers new perspectives	9	50	33	8	0
Provides quantitative data	12	40	42	6	0
Comprehensive, i.e., includes most potentially explanatory variables in analysis	11	44	33	10	1
Findings can be applied within existing agencies and programs	14	32	36	18	1
Contains explicit recommendations	12	32	35	18	2
Grounded in a theoretical framework	10	30	42	17	1
Inexpensive to implement	5	31	44	20	1
Not overly technical in presentation	6	29	44	20	1
Statistically sophisticated	9	28	32	27	4

Targeted, i.e., focuses on a narrow set of dependent, or outcome, variables	7	23	39	27	5
Implies the need for major change in philosophy, organization, or services	6	24	28	39	3
Compatible with the ideas and values of the potential user	13	12	25	44	5
Challenges existing assumptions and institutional arrangements	3	23	28	45	1
Implications of the findings are politically acceptable	3	12	31	46	8
Consistent with a body of previous knowledge	3	17	30	50	1
Findings are unexpected or novel	0	12	15	72	1
Supports a position already held by the user	0	5	12	75	8

185

the items that lead the pack in importance on the structured question did not appear with much frequency in the open questions probably because most respondents took them for granted or believed that they did not make apt distinctions in the context of the questions.

On the structured question, two criteria are named by more than half of the decision makers as essential: recommendations supported by the data and understandable writing. The next most frequently cited criterion is objectivity and lack of bias. What seems most striking about this pattern of response is the emphasis (in two of the top three items) on keeping the researcher's opinions and predilections out of the research. Decision makers in mental health want research to be data-based and objective, and they object to the intrusion of researchers' values in interpreting the evidence.

The other top criterion, understandable writing, seems a reasonable requirement for a research report. But the extent to which decision makers support it over such other items as high technical quality, direct implications for action, and generalizability is surprising. Decision makers evidently want to understand what they read. Only then can they judge how competent, authoritative, and implementable a study may be.

Very low on the list of criteria are what we originally thought of as the political items: supports a position already held by the user, implications of the findings are politically acceptable, compatible with the ideas and values of the potential user, challenges existing assumptions and institutional arrangements, implies the need for major change in philosophy, organization, or services. Fewer than a third of decision makers cite these items as either essential or highly desirable, and these are the only items that received more than one or two ratings as "undesirable." The highest percentage of undesirable ratings on any criterion is 8 percent, and this frequency appears for "politically acceptable" and "supports user position." "Unnecessary" ratings go to these items in much greater proportion: 75 percent say that supporting user position is unnecessary, 46 percent say political acceptability is unnecessary, and 44 percent say compatibility with user ideas and values is unnecessary.[3]

The array of responses suggests that decision makers in mental

health are interested in using research that is objective, understandable, and adds to practical knowledge on important issues.
Considerations of authoritativeness and technical merit occupy the
middle range of their concern, as do issues of feasibility and practicality (e.g., manipulable variables, direct implications). At the
bottom of the list is interest in research that is politically acceptable and confirms their existing beliefs and values, but down near
the bottom, too, is research that has unexpected findings, challenges existing arrangements, or points to a need for major change.

If we were to transform these responses into the language of the
factors, we would conclude that Research Quality and Action
Orientation were the primary criteria, followed at a considerable
remove by Challenge to the Status Quo and Conformity to User
Expectations.[4] This, of course, is not exactly what the analysis of
the ratings of the 50 studies indicated as decision makers' priorities.
Having the two parallel sets of ratings will enable us to compare,
item by item, what decision makers *say* their criteria are for useful research with the criteria that are "revealed" as actually predicting their judgments of the usefulness of real studies.

How Well Do Decision Makers Predict
the Characteristics that Make Studies Useful?

Can decision makers identify those attributes of a research
study that actually influence the likelihood that they will take the
study into account? We have to develop a measure of correspondence between their reports of the importance of the criteria and
the "revealed effects" of the same items on their likelihood of use.[5]
Table 10.3 presents the data with which we are working. The first
column shows decision makers' mean ratings of each criterion
for useful research. The second column shows the simple correlation coefficients between the ratings of the descriptive characteristics of a study and the ratings of likelihood of use of the study;
this measure is the effect of the characteristic on likelihood of use.

The next step is to compute a measure of correspondence between the two columns. We use the Pearson correlation coefficient
between the two columns for the 26 items. This new correlation
indicates the association between the stated importance of an item
and its revealed effect on likelihood of use.

Table 10.3. Aggregate Correspondence Between Reported Importance of
Criteria and Revealed Effects

Characteristic	Criterion Rating[a]	Revealed Effect[b]
Recommendations supported by data	1.46	.46
Objective, unbiased	1.75	.35
High priority issue	1.91	.28
Adds to practical knowledge	1.93	.46
Findings consistent/unambiguous	2.02	.45
Technical quality high	2.07	.49
Direct implications	2.10	.49
Manipulable variables	2.11	.43
On time for decision	2.23	.39
Generalizable	2.24	.39
Adds to theory	2.27	.48
Raises new issues	2.40	.29
Quantitative data	2.43	.31
Comprehensive	2.45	.45
Applicable within existing programs	2.61	.47
Explicit recommendations	2.65	.24
Inexpensive	2.80	.08
Statistically sophisticated	2.88	.26
Targeted	2.99	.22
Implies need for major change	3.09	.28
Compatible with user ideas	3.16	.26
Challenges assumptions	3.18	.19
Politically acceptable	3.23	.18
Consistent with previous knowledge	3.29	.29
Findings unexpected/novel	3.63	.13
Supports user position	3.86	.28

[a]The score for the criterion rating is the mean rating by decision makers on the criterion, where
1 = "essential" and 5 = "undesirable."
[b]The revealed effect score is the Pearson correlation coefficient between the descriptor rating
of the characteristic and the usefulness rating of the research study.

The analysis now has 26 "cases," the 26 characteristics items.
The unit of analysis is the characteristic, and values are aggregated
across individuals. When we compute the correlation coefficient
between stated importance and revealed effect, the correlation is
.69.[6] Even with only 26 cases, a correlation of this magnitude is
significant at the .001 level. Almost half the variance in the total
observed correlation between characteristics ratings and likelihood
of use is explained by what decision makers *in the aggregate* say
about the importance of the items. The criteria ratings *of the group*
have explanatory power.

Although the correlation is very high, some of the variance remains unexplained. If one were to use the criteria ratings of the decision makers to predict which characteristics would influence use, some errors would be made. For instance, the aggregate responses of decision makers overestimate the importance of high priority issue and objectivity, and underestimate applicability within existing programs and consistency with previous knowledge. The misestimation does not follow any intelligible pattern; it does not correspond to our categorization of the characteristics into factors. This suggests that error in prediction from criteria ratings to revealed effects would have to be accounted for item by item. But over all, the errors are not substantial and prediction is good. Responses of the group of decision makers about the importance of research characteristics for the usefulness of studies are relatively accurate.

Ability of Individuals to Predict
Their Own Usefulness Ratings

A logical next question is how good are decision makers *as individuals* in describing their preferences. If they are able to report the attributes that make studies useful to them as individuals, then a researcher conducting a study for a particular client or an identifiable user group could gain a great deal of help by consulting with the users in advance. They could indicate what kind of study would have the best chance of getting their attention.

Another happy fallout would be the ability to segment the audience. If decision makers are capable of describing not only their espoused criteria for useful research but also their criteria-in-use (Argyris 1976), then it might become possible to identify groups of potential users who will respond to special research features or modes of presentation. Even when research is destined for a large audience rather than a relative handful of clients, the researcher would be able to tailor the study—or at least the format, detail, and emphases in the study report—to satisfy the expressed standards of specified audiences. Much as market researchers aim to segment the audience for products, identifying different groups who will respond to considerations of quality, price, and style, social researchers could identify segments of *their* audience who would respond to, say, criteria of research quality, administrative applicability, and challenge to organizational operations.

We can see in table 10.2 that although there is considerable agreement on the relative desirability of the criteria, some respondents deviate markedly in the importance that they assign to a criterion. For example, almost half the decision makers rate "compatible with ideas and values of the potential user" either unnecessary or undesirable, but 13 percent rate it essential. Similarly, almost a third regard statistical sophistication as unnecessary or undesirable, but for 9 percent it is essential. If these judgments of decision makers represent behavioral differences, researchers can gain valuable information by canvassing their potential audience about their standards of judgment.

To investigate the degree to which a person's stated preferences agree with revealed effects on the individual level, we constructed two regression equations for each research characteristic. In the first one, we regressed usefulness on the characteristic rating alone. In the second equation, we took the person's criterion ratings into account by adding an interaction term; the interaction term was the product of the characteristic rating and a dummy variable which took the value of 1 if the respondent rated the characteristic "essential" or "highly desirable" and 0 otherwise. If the criterion ratings represent working standards, then the second equation should increase the power of explanation.

An example may make the procedure clear. Let us take two respondents who rate the same research study. One believes it essential, if a study is to be useful to her, that it have high technical quality and quantitative data. The second respondent states that his essential criteria for useful research are explicit recommendations and direct implications for action. They both rate the study and agree that it is low in technical quality and quantitative data but high in explicit recommendations and direct implications. Therefore, we would expect that the first respondent will find the study not useful whereas the second respondent will find it very useful. By weighting their characteristic ratings by the importance they ascribe to the characteristic (1 for essential or highly desirable and 0 for desirable, unnecessary, or undesirable), we would expect to improve the prediction of the usefulness rating that they give the study.

Table 10.4. Effects of Research Characteristics on Likelihood of Use, by Ratings of Importance of Criteria

| Criteria | Unstandardized Regression Coefficients | | |
	When Rated Highly Important	When Rated Less Important	Difference
Recommendations supported by data	.49	.52	−.03
Objective, unbiased	.41	.38	.03
High priority issue	.27	.33	−.05
Adds to practical knowledge	.42	.42	−.00
Findings consistent/unambiguous	.48	.48	−.01
Technical quality high	.53	.51	.02
Direct implications	.43	.44	−.01
Generalizable	.41	.39	.03
Manipulable variables	.40	.46	−.06
On time for decision	.27	.43	−.16
Raises new issues	.29	.34	−.05
Adds to descriptive, causal, theoretical knowledge	.54	.46	.08
Comprehensive	.51	.51	−.00
Quantitative data	.35	.34	.00
Applicable within existing programs	.50	.47	.03
Explicit recommendations	.18	.23	−.05
Statistically sophisticated	.33	.25	.08
Inexpensive	.08	.05	.03
Targeted	.23	.20	.03
Implies need for major change	.23	.26	−.03
Challenges assumptions	.21	.17	.04
Compatible with user ideas	.35	.29	.06
Consistent with previous knowledge	.39	.33	.06
Politically acceptable	.14	.21	−.07
Findings unexpected/novel	.15	.18	−.04
Supports user position	.22	.30	−.08

NOTE: The statistics in the table are derived from two regression equations:

1. $U = b_{3i}D_i + a_{1i}$

2. $U = b_{4i}D_i + b_{5i}(D_i \cdot C_i) + a_{2i}$, where

b's are unstandardized regression coefficients; i represents a characteristic; U = Usefulness rating; D_i = Descriptor rating; and C_i = Criteria rating, dichotomized as $C_i = 1$ if the characteristic is highly important ("essential" or "highly desirable") and $C_i = 0$ otherwise.
   The statistics in each column are:
   First column = $b_{4i} + b_{5i}$ = the effect of characteristic i on usefulness among those rating it as highly important;
   Second column = b_{4i} = the effect of characteristic i on usefulness among those not rating it as highly important;
   Third column = b_{5i} = the difference between the two groups in the effects of characteristic i on usefulness.
   The sum of second and third columns does not always equal first column because of rounding.

Table 10.4 shows the unstandardized regression coefficient for each characteristic when it is rated essential or highly desirable (first column) and when it is rated less important (second column). The third column presents the difference in slopes, i.e., in the unstandardized regression coefficients. A comparison of the columns indicates that a characteristic does *not* have more effect on usefulness when the respondents say that it is important. Of the 26 characteristics, 11 have higher unstandardized regression coefficients when the item is rated essential or highly desirable; 12 have lower unstandardized regression coefficients; on 3 items there is essentially no difference. The negative differences are, in fact, slightly larger in magnitude than the differences in a positive direction, indicating, if anything, a slight misprediction of the importance of the characteristics when respondents' reports of their criteria are taken into account.

The conclusion from table 10.4 is that self-reported criteria ratings do not identify those decision makers for whom particular characteristics are more or less important. As individuals, decision makers are not good guides to which characteristics make a study useful to them. Although in the aggregate, they can identify the attributes that make studies useful, they do not do well at predicting the importance of study characteristics for their own judgments of a study's usefulness.

We conducted a number of analyses to test this conclusion further (Bucuvalas 1978). Basically, we constructed analogs to table 10.3 for each respondent and calculated the degree of correspondence between the criterion rating and revealed effects. Since we could not use a Pearson correlation for revealed effects at the individual level, we calculated measures of distance between criterion ratings and usefulness ratings. Then we computed correlations across all characteristics for each individual.

The results of these analyses are consistent in showing that individuals are not successful in predicting which research characteristics affect usefulness in particular cases. The highest correspondence between criteria ratings and any of the measures of revealed effects, averaged across individuals, was $r = .10$—not very impressive. Some decision makers did well for the studies they rated, as high as $r = .74$; others did poorly, as low as $r = -.45$. Large differences occurred even between the two studies rated by the individual. For one respondent, the correspondence between criteria ratings and revealed effects was $r = -.40$ for one study and $r = .50$ for the other. In fact, respondents tended to be inconsistent on the two studies. Over all the analyses we did, the correlation between correspondence on one study and on the other was uniformly slightly negative, on the order of $r = -.06$. In all, it appears that decision makers' criteria ratings do not predict the effects of research characteristics on usefulness at levels much better than might be expected by chance.

A Paradox: Aggregate Responses Good, Individual Responses Bad

How do we explain the greater accuracy of decision makers in the aggregate than of decision makers as individuals in representing their criteria-in-action for useful research? There are a number of possible explanations, and although some of them can be disposed of fairly readily, we will not (fair warning) reach any one authoritative answer. The possibilities are intriguing, taking us into realms of decision theory and cognitive psychology, and for those readers who want to come along for the ride, we will state the alternative cases as fairly as we can.

One possibility is that respondents are misreporting their criteria. Working in professional fields that expect allegiance to the norms of science, they may tend to overstate their adherence to such norms and underestimate the counternorms based on political values. However, this is not a persuasive explanation on several grounds. First, their responses to the question about criteria, where the motivation to dissemble was probably most direct, are not obviously biased in the direction of social desirability. As table 10.2 shows, their answers do not reflect an inordinately scientific bias; their ratings of the importance of research methodology (technical quality, comprehensiveness, statistical sophistication, etc.) fall in the middle range of importance. Second, as table 10.3 shows, their ratings of the importance of research methodology items are not obviously overestimated compared to the revealed effects of these items on their judgment of specific studies. Third, and perhaps most telling, conscious misreporting would not explain the relative accuracy of responses at the aggregate level.

Another possible explanation refers to the decision rules that respondents use in assessing the usefulness of a study.[7] Our method of calculating the revealed effects of research characteristics on a study's usefulness assumes that respondents combine the characteristics additively, that a moderate score on all the characteristics yields a moderate rating on usefulness. But this linear model may be inappropriate. There are other decision rules that are nonlinear (Dawes 1964; Einhorn 1970, 1971). Some outstandingly high (or low) feature of a study may swamp consideration of other features. For example, if a study rates very high on the importance and timeliness of its subject matter, then concern about its technical quality may be muted—even though the decision maker is usually finicky about quality. If a study is very low on technical quality, concern about clarity and feasibility of recommendations (which ordinarily would weigh heavily) may become unimportant. It may be the pattern of characteristics, rather than their presence one at a time, that determines usefulness.

Respondents may use a conjunctive decision rule, in which a study has to have a minimal level of all of the important characteristics to be judged useful; a study with moderate scores on *all* characteristics would probably score high on usefulness under such a rule. Or they may use a disjunctive rule, where a study has to have "flying colors" on at least one of the set to be judged useful; in this case, a study with all moderate scores would be low in usefulness. One characteristic could be the deciding factor, either because it was too low under a conjunctive rule or had "flying colors" under a disjunctive rule. If decision makers used such rules, revealed effects, as we have calculated them, would appear to change from an individual's rating of one study to another (as the data show they do). The aggregate scores could still be good predictors of usefulness because the most important characteristics would play the critical role most often. Thus, even though nonlinear models are not generally as good as linear models in predicting behavior, this explanation seems to explain the paradox in our data.

However, it does not appear to accord with table 10.4. When we split the respondents into two groups on the basis of their reported criteria, there should be some gain in explanatory power. There is none. The observed results suggest that their criteria ratings are meaningless—but then how do aggregate responses on criteria manage to correlate so well with the usefulness ratings?

A third explanation is that respondents lack insight into their own motives and cognitive processes (Bem 1972; Nisbett and Valins 1972; Nisbett and Wilson 1977). Cognitive psychologists report that people are frequently faulty in explaining their own behavior. People report reasons for behavior that laboratory tests show were obviously inoperative and fail to report reasons that were observed to be influential. This kind of "self-insight error" may be afflicting respondents in our study. Respondents are not purposely misreporting but actually are not cognizant of the criteria they use or the weights they assign to different factors in making judgments (Slovic and Lichtenstein 1971; Slovic, Fischhoff, and Lichtenstein 1977).

Studies of attribution processes often reveal that people are as accurate in explaining the behavior of others as they are in accounting for their own behavior. One interpretation is that in developing explanations they draw *not* on introspection and private knowledge about their own mental processes but on culturally supplied rules or theories. They give reasons for behavior—their own as well as other people's—that are available as plausible explanations in the culture or subculture (Nisbett and Wilson 1977) and salient in the situation (Taylor and Fiske 1978). By doing so, they report reasons that are as accurate or inaccurate for explaining why other people act as they do as for explaining their own actions. Thus, if respondents in our study are drawing on "a priori theories" about which criteria influence research usefulness, the aggregate responses may be generally accurate, even though the reports about their own judgments lack special self-insight and are relatively poor.

The final explanation that we consider here is based on the fact that the criterion question asked for judgments in general, whereas the characteristics and usefulness ratings were tied to specific research reports.[8] In reporting their general criteria, respondents are averaging out their experiences with many different studies. In rating the particular studies provided in the interview, they are dealing with the one case in hand. Had we given them 40 or 50 studies to rate instead of 2, their ratings over the series might have approximated their criteria. (Actually, averaging even their two ratings marginally improves the accuracy of the ratings.) If the decision makers apply generally similar criteria in assessing research usefulness, the aggregate responses would gain in accuracy because of the cross-sample averaging procedure.

Implications for Researchers

Whatever the constellation of reasons, the data suggest that researchers are likely to receive helpful general guidance from a *group* of potential users, but that tailoring a study to the preferences of a specific client will not improve its usefulness—even for that client. Rich's (1977) follow-up of the Continuous National Survey shows a parallel result. His research found that officials in seven federal agencies who actively participated in framing the questions they wanted answered rarely used the information in the ways they had originally intended. Although changes in circumstances may have contributed to the erosion of their predictions of use, much of the slippage was apparently due to inability to express their intentions and needs in accurate terms.

Does this imply that social scientists who want their work to be used need not consult in advance with potential users? We certainly would not make that leap from our data. There are many good reasons for social scientists, particularly those performing research for specific clients, to maintain early and close contact (although the prescription has perhaps been uncritically oversold). There is the matter of substantive focus. Researchers who learn about an agency's issues and concerns will have better insight into relevant subject matter and will at the same time be able to help the agency clarify its own questions and options. There is the matter of trust. Close collaboration may help to engender understanding and confidence between users and researchers (although it sometimes exacerbates differences). There is the matter of commitment. Involvement in the origin and process of a study often leads to official commitment to take the results seriously (unless a close-up view discloses serious flaws in the conduct of the research). Finally, there is the matter of interpretation. Social scientists sometimes lack operational or clinical experience in the workaday routines that are the stuff of agency life. When their research collects data about this world, they can often profit from insiders' knowledge to make sense of the data and draw conclusions that are meaningful and realistic. Thus, there are reasons above and beyond decision makers' specifications for the research that argue for consultation and contact. But social scientists should be aware that collaboration is not likely to yield sure-fire formulas for the kinds of studies that will make an impact. Clients are not apt to be good judges of what their criteria actually will be when they confront a piece of research.

Of course, most social science research, even of quite applied intent, is undertaken without specific clients in mind. And most social science research in the human service fields, even when funded by federal agencies, will be primarily used—if it is used at all—by people scattered across federal, state, and local agencies who make the daily choices about operational policy and practice (NAS 1978). Our analysis suggests that lack of direct contact with potential users is not necessarily a significant disadvantage. Knowing the general configuration of decision makers' criteria for useful research is likely to be good enough. (Of course, the criteria of officials in mental health may or may not be relevant for understanding the criteria of officials in criminal justice, education, health services, employment and training, or any other field.)

That decision makers' pooled responses are highly associated with the usefulness of research is by no means unimportant. Decision-making in public agencies is largely a group process. If a research study is to affect the course of events, it has to appeal to more than the one decision maker who commissioned it or read it. It has to pass the standards of a heterogeneous group of people who are involved in proposing, advocating, criticizing, negotiating, deciding, implementing, acting. Therefore, the fact that aggregate responses about criteria are a good reflection of criteria-in-use suggests that asking groups of officials what they want in research can still be a fruitful endeavor.

NOTES

1. For our purposes, the most interesting feature of the responses to this question was that only 2 respondents said that they wanted no research and 6 could not say what kind of research they wanted. The other 147 decision makers gave a rich catalog of answers.

2. Three of the items that appear on this criteria list were not included in the list of characteristics on which respondents rated studies. These items were omitted because of the procedure we used for abstracting studies. We wrote the abstracts in identical format and therefore believed that we had eliminated most of the variation in "understandably written," "theoretical framework," and "technical presentation." In retrospect, despite the homogenization, we would include at least the item on understandable writing in order to learn the respondents' perceptions of the clarity of writing and detect the relation of these perceptions to the usefulness ratings. The results presented in table 10.2 indicate the importance that decision makers attribute to good writing.

3. A rating of "essential" can be construed as a prescribed feature of social research, "highly desirable" and "desirable" ratings translate as preferred, "unnecessary" as permitted, and "undesirable" as proscribed (Merton 1961). Items on the authoritativeness of research and its technical merit tend to be prescribed or preferred. Interestingly, it is the items relating to the authoritativeness of a study that are more likely to be prescribed than are items on technical competence (such as technical quality, generalizability, comprehensiveness of analysis, and quantitative data). Implementability items are generally preferred. Only the plausibility and political acceptability items tend to fall in the permitted zone, with a scattering of proscriptions.

4. When we tried to identify groups of decision makers who emphasized each of the characteristics factors, we found that the data did not cluster in these ways. Very rare were respondents who highlighted one type of criterion at the expense of others. Much more frequent were mixed patterns of ratings, with individuals giving high criteria ratings to a few items from several factors. No clear-cut groupings of decision makers emerged that stressed the same constellation of criteria.

5. We use the term "revealed effects" in analogy with the economic usage of "revealed preferences," in which consumers' actual purchases represent revealed preferences for goods.

6. Rank-order statistics give much the same result as the Pearson correction coefficient that is presented here.

7. We thank Paul Slovic for calling this interpretation to our attention.

8. For further discussion of explanations for the data, see Bucuvalas (1978).

Chapter Eleven
VIEWS OF SOCIAL SCIENCE RESEARCHERS

W HERE THE LAST CHAPTER explored the feasibility of asking decision makers what kinds of research they want, this chapter is concerned with the likelihood that social scientists will respond by suiting their research to decision makers' needs. It looks at the intentions of social science researchers in undertaking government-funded research.

An apparent way to increase the utility of social science research for policy and program decisions is to enlist social scientists in the cause of usefulness. If more social scientists took pains to plan their research, analyze their data, and communicate their results in terms that matched the interests of decision makers, perhaps their efforts would improve the fit between social science and agency operations. This is a theme with a venerable history in the applied social science literature (Sadofsky 1966; Sherwood 1967; Suchman 1967; Caro 1971; Longood and Simmel 1972; Lazarsfeld and Reitz 1975).

For generations, "applied" social science research was a stepchild within the university (Rossi, Wright, and Wright 1978), viewed as several notches below "basic" research in importance and prestige.[1] While there were for-profit and nonprofit research institutions that specialized in user-oriented studies, many academic social scientists viewed their competence as suspect. Those social scientists who aimed at career mobility and disciplinary recognition within the academy tended to shy away from work that bore the "applied" stigma.

Of course, there were exceptions even in earlier periods, and one can make a parlor game out of naming social science luminaries who trafficked in real-world issues. (Yes, Comte, Marx, and Keynes count.) In the last quarter of the twentieth century, the old prestige distinctions between basic and applied are fading under the pressure of declining enrollments, fewer tenure slots, and the growth in government funding for mission-oriented research. Even in high-ranking universities, many social scientists—and not only in the practice-oriented professional schools—are engaged in research that would once have been called applied, now often carrying the more respectable label of "policy research." More than a half-dozen academic journals have been launched with the word "policy" in the title to publish the results of such research. To what extent the greater acceptance of the applied orientation within university social science departments connotes a change in intent, and a serious commitment to be useful to decision makers, remains to be seen. How long the traditional denigration of applied work will maintain its hold even under changing conditions, and tempt social scientists to use applied research funds for discipline-oriented investigations, is still an open question (Useem 1976).

The changing external environment and the rising academic interest in policy-oriented research suggest that the times may be suited to developments in the social sciences that favor attention to decision makers' concerns. Such attention need not involve acceptance of the values of decision makers nor limitation of the research to the constricted set of options that decision makers perceive as feasible. It need not foreclose criticism or controversy nor turn the researcher into a technician to serve the interests of the bureaucracy. As we have shown, and perhaps belabored, in previous chapters, agency decision makers themselves believe that research that challenges current premises and modes of operation makes a contribution to their work. What attention to the concerns of decision makers can mean is that social science researchers address issues that are relevant to policy and program and communicate the results of that research in terms and through channels that reach people in positions of responsibility.

For social scientists who want their work to have an impact on practical affairs, one of the common prescriptions is to conduct studies to fit user needs. Who should define those needs and how closely the formulation of research should match users' definition of the question are issues that have long been discussed and contested.

The discussion becomes particularly heated when the users are officials of a government with which social scientists are out of sympathy. In this chapter we present data on social scientists' views of government-funded research. Their responses shed light on the feasibility of expecting researchers to plan and conduct their research with an eye to increasing its practical utility.

We interviewed 50 social scientists who had conducted research under funding from NIMH, NIDA, or NIAAA. From these interviews, we have four sets of data that give indications of their attitudes and behavior regarding useful research. First we asked them the extent to which they had *intended* their last completed study to be useful for decision-making, and the extent to which its results *had* practical implications. Questions also asked what, if anything, they had done to ensure the study's usefulness. From these responses we can see how earnestly a group of social scientists who have received government funding take the matter of making their research relevant. Since they have received support from one of the ADAMHA institutes, and since about 40 percent of them work outside of university settings, it can be expected that they are more attuned to relevance than are researchers within universities who receive funding from a basic research granting agency, like the National Science Foundation, or receive no outside funding. However, NIMH in particular has long had a tradition of supporting basic as well as applied research, and a large majority of the researchers we interviewed performed their research under long-term grants.

Second, a number of questions inquired about researchers' perceptions of decision makers' use of social science research—whether and how they use it and what the constraints are on its use. These data give indications of their expectations from decision makers. To the extent that they believe decision makers disregard research, they probably will view attention to usefulness as meaningless ritual. On the other hand, if they expect decision makers to take research seriously, they may devote greater care to matters of relevance.

Third, since they rated the same research reports in the same ways as did decision makers, we can analyze the extent to which research characteristics affected their judgments of the studies' usefulness to relevant decision makers. From the analysis we can discern which research characteristics (Research Quality, Conformity, Action Orientation, Challenge) influence their ratings of decision makers' likelihood of using the studies. These data show which factors they believe matter to decision makers.

Finally, we can compare their ratings of the usefulness of research reports, study by study, with decision makers' ratings. This comparison gives clues about their ability to discern useful studies when they see them. If researchers are going to be in charge of the "usefulness business," it is a matter of some moment whether they view studies in the same terms as do potential users.

Usefulness of Their Own Research

Researchers were asked about the last study that they had completed in mental health or related fields: "When you started this study, to what extent did you intend the results to be useful for decision-making about social policy or programs?" They gave answers on a 5-point scale, ranging from "to a great extent" to "not at all." Over half of them said "to a great extent," the highest point on the scale. Following is the distribution of responses:

To a great extent	1	55 percent
	2	20
	3	8
	4	14
Not at all	5	2

(N = 49)

Only one person indicated that his interest in the usefulness of his study was solely a tactical maneuver. This researcher, who rated his intentions regarding usefulness as "2" on the scale, said:

It would be pro forma, relating your work to significant social issues in order to get a grant. (534)*

When asked if they did anything in planning, designing, or

---

*Numbers in parentheses are the identification numbers of respondents. All 500 numbers are researchers.

conducting the study intentionally to assure its usefulness, most of them indicated that they did nothing special. For example:

At the start of the study, no, because how could you know how to promulgate it until you knew what your research was going to show? Beyond expecting to write it up for professional journals and going to professional meetings, we made no specific kinds of plans. (570).

A few researchers talked about making their research as technically competent as possible in order to increase its authoritativeness. An example:

Only that it was well done and that the results whatever they might be would be reasonably conclusive. (540)

About a quarter of the social scientists indicated that they did take special steps during the planning and performance of their research to increase its potential utility. Their responses fell into three categories: concentrating on policy-relevant issues, using measures that had practical meaning, and establishing contact with action-oriented user groups. A few people gave responses in each of these categories.

On the issues addressed:

First of all, the types of issues we address ourselves to rose out of our knowledge of the field and of the pressing problems that need solution. . . . (583)

On measurement:

The variables that are concentrated on are those which would be pertinent to the actions of government officials and agencies. (528)

In the use of instruments that had clinical meaning. (533)

On contact with decision-oriented groups:

By involving agencies right from the beginning. (530)

We set up a community advisory committee. It became a steering committee for the project. We gave feedback to community groups as part of the methodology. (509)

If a minority of the social scientists concentrated on usefulness issues during the planning and conduct of the study, many more were concerned with usefulness once their study was completed. They reported that the point at which they focused on research application was in the reporting and dissemination of the study's results. It appears that most of the attention to usefulness occurs when the results are in hand.

In the final drafting we attempted to get it written in extremely lay language. . . . Essentially it was in the cleaning up of the report more than in the design and methodology. (593)

We try to relate the findings to implications. We believe that researchers ought to be willing to say something about the implications of what they are doing. (583)

We spent a lot of time with the intended users of the study showing them options. . . . (514)

[I tried to assure usefulness through] dissemination of the report. Though I'm not sure I've sent it to many key scholars in the field, most are James Q. Wilson-types that policy makers listen to. Also to government decision makers. (588)

Some of the responses showed evidence of earnest and prolonged effort to plan, conduct, and report studies in ways that fitted the decision environment. Many others seemed to involve less sustained attempts to get the results a hearing. So despite their articulated concern with the utility of their work, even this group of largely application-oriented researchers did not often take steps that were significantly different from those that discipline-oriented researchers are accustomed to. By and large, the main difference was to focus their dissemination efforts on a user audience, not instead of, but usually along with, a disciplinary audience.

We asked them how their study had come out. Did it prove to be useful to decision makers? Most of them believed that it had. In their narrative responses, about 80 percent reported that at least some of their findings had the potential of contributing to the work of people in mental health agencies.

They were also asked a structured question: "Would you say the research has applied, practical, or policy implications which are (a) clear, immediate implications, (b) fairly clear, long-range implications, (c) potential but not clear implications, or (d) no presently discernible implications for action?" This question was replicated from the 1969–70 Carnegie Commission National Survey of Higher Education. We retained the original wording exactly in order to allow comparison with that extensive questionnaire study of over 60,000 academic men and women at some 300 American colleges and universities (Fulton and Trow 1972). Of the 49 respondents who

Table 11.1.   Applied Implications of Social Scientists' Own Research

	Social Science Researchers		
		Carnegie Commission Respondents	
Applied Implications	Our Respondents (N = 49)	Funded in Whole or Part by HEW (N = 104)	All Social Science Researchers (N = 252)
Clear, immediate	49	26%	32%
Fairly clear, long-range	29	34	34
Potential but not clear	20	38	28
No discernible implication	2	2	5

replied, almost half (49 percent) reported that their most recent study had clear and immediate implications for action. Over a quarter (29 percent) reported fairly clear, long-range implications. Only 22 percent believed that their results fell into the foggier two categories. The pattern of response is not markedly different from the responses on *intent*. There is only a minor fall-away from the top category.

To allow comparison with the Carnegie Commission data, the staff that conducted the Carnegie Commission study prepared for us special runs of their data, singling out only social scientists who had recently conducted research.[2] Table 11.1 shows the responses of our respondents and the relevant Carnegie Commission respondents. Clearly the social scientists in the field of mental health whom we interviewed were much more likely to see their research as relevant and practical. One reason is that our respondents included a sizable number (21) who worked outside of universities, mainly in nonprofit research institutions and service-provider agencies, whereas the Carnegie Commission respondents were all in academic institutions. Another possible explanation may be the passage of time. Our study, coming six years later, may also reflect a changing emphasis in government-funded research. In any event, most of the mental health researchers in our study are convinced of the utility of their work.

Perceptions of Decision Makers'
Use of Research

Social science researchers, even those as use-oriented as these, are skeptical about decision makers' use of research. Fewer than one in ten believe that decision makers make *frequent* use of research for any purpose—policy, program, operational decisions, planning, advising, etc. Just over 30 percent think that decision makers use it occasionally, perhaps for a special need or under special circumstances. But 60 percent believe that research use is haphazard or unlikely. Here are some representative answers to the question on the extent to which mental health decision makers use social science research:

My first response to that is: God only knows! (590)

Not at all. . . . They don't respect it . . . they don't read it. (568)

They're remarkably immune to social research. Because of the politics of it all, they are strongly opposed to its use. (533)

It's a running battle all the time to have policy makers address themselves to research findings. . . . The average policy person in city government and maybe even state and federal . . . doesn't *think* research. (583)

It depends upon the decision maker, upon the mental health research, upon the politics of the situation. (546)

Most people in those positions are very sincere, dedicated people who really do think very deeply about these kinds of problems, but my view of it is that they use social science research opportunistically. . . . (595)

Spotty, uneven. It depends to some extent on the research itself, on how well it is tuned in on the problems that concern decision makers or practitioners . . . the extent to which persons designing and funding social science research in mental health understand the nature of the problems these people are concerned with. After that, it depends on the steps that are taken to make the material—especially significant findings—available to persons occupying these positions. (577)

I think they try to make use of it. But it seems to me that in mental health, in general, the findings still have many ambiguities about them. It is such a difficult and complex problem that many findings appear antithetical to each other and lawmakers and policy decision makers have a good deal of difficulty in sorting out these ambiguities and doing what is called for. (570)

When asked *how* they believe decision makers used research, most of the researchers disclaimed knowledge. Some thought it such an unusual event that they were unwilling to guess what form use would take. Of the 41 who offered responses, about half referred to inputs into planning, developing, or operating programs or policies, although these were phrased in very general terms. About two-fifths discussed the use of research as justification for programs or support for positions already taken. Most of the rest talked about "background," "keeping up," general information. The researchers were much more likely than were the decision makers themselves to emphasize the political uses of research—ammunition, vindication, legitimation. They were not as likely to offer the "keeping up with the field" mode of use that many decision makers stressed.

You can see a lot of it [use] in the areas of drugs, alcoholism, behavior modification in general, where people are attempting to use findings to restructure social policy. (555)

The long-range sifting process, yes. In day-to-day decisions, not very much. . . . When it gives practical advice as to techniques and maneuvers, [they listen]. They listen very closely to anything connected with the distribution of funds. . . . If it [research] . . . relates to a funding area, it will have maximum impact. (533)

My impression generally is that studies of immediate problems that focus on immediate issues confronting decision makers are those that are most useful. I think, personally, that studies which have a broader perspective could provide some kind of understanding either of general trends or theoretical explanations for human behavior and should be more influential than they are (567).

My impression is that people tend to use it if it agrees with their stance and are reluctant to use it and won't use it if it doesn't. (549)

They select from the research those findings which can justify the programs. (545)

Explanations of the reasons for low levels of use usually referred to decision makers' lack of awareness of the research that has been done, their disinterest in it, the competing demands placed upon them, and the often unclear or conflicting nature of the evidence. One person spoke at some length about the pressures that lead to oversimplification of issues in the policy area. Once an issue has become "sloganized," people tend to resist research that points out distinctions, qualifications, complexities. This researcher said, in part:

People tend to oversimplify the problem so they can make policy. . . . Take researchers. They are not pure, objective, abstract scientists who set up a critical study, test the theory, and tabulate results. Researchers have their own biases. . . . It's hard enough for a researcher to say what he found. Take all the researchers and they disagree violently. . . . They can't agree on some of the most elemental things. . . . Take policy makers. They have their own biases, political pressure, friends. They tend to react in terms of what will be expedient. In my opinion slogans tend to dominate the field and become the order of the day. . . . If you had clear-cut results and unanimous agreement, you'd still have the problem of getting others who are subject to political pressures and their own cognitive biases to incorporate it and use it. . . . In order to get change you've got to capture the slogans. . . . More important than presenting evidence is to put it in the right slogans to catch people's imagination. (560)

Relationship of Research Characteristics
to Likelihood of Use

Social scientists' ratings of the 50 research studies presented during the interview suggest which characteristics of research they believe influence decision makers' likelihood of taking account of a study. Regression of their ratings of likelihood of use by the "most appropriate user" on the research characteristics factors shows several things. First, the data indicate that, in the view of researchers, the qualities of the study play a modest part in whether decision makers choose to pay attention to it. All the research characteristics combined account for 23 percent of the variance in likelihood of use. (For decision makers rating studies for their own use, the comparable figure is 42 percent. For decision makers rating likelihood of use by other appropriate users, the variance accounted for is the same—23 percent.)

Second, analysis of their ratings shows that the research characteristics that are by far the most important are Action Orientation (standardized regression coefficient is .34) and Conformity to User Expectations (standardized regression coefficient is .26). Research Quality ($\beta = .06$) and Challenge to the Status Quo ($\beta = .03$) show very little relation to likelihood of use.[3] Thus, their ratings suggest that decision makers are engaged by studies that give clear guidance for implementation and that agree with their prior knowledge and values. It is a fairly jaundiced view: decision makers will use research that tells them how to do what they want to do.

The other usefulness measure, the substantive contribution that a study can make, is much better predicted by the characteristics factors. Analysis of researchers' ratings on the intrinsic usefulness of studies shows that the factors explain 50 percent of the variance. By far the most important single factor in the regression is Action

Orientation ($\beta = .51$), suggesting that explicit direction for feasible action represents the best contribution to decision makers. Next in importance for substantive usefulness is Challenge to the Status Quo ($\beta = .26$), followed by Research Quality ($\beta = .15$) and Conformity to User Expectations ($\beta = .14$). From the social scientists' perspective, research can make the most significant contribution to decision makers' work primarily when it gives direction and secondarily when it suggests change.

Table 11.2 presents a comparison of the data derived from researchers' ratings with those from decision makers and research review committee members. This table gives the *unstandardized* regression coefficients, because these data are appropriate for comparison *across* groups. The most striking feature of the data from researchers is the overwhelming emphasis on Action Orientation. Their ratings ascribe much greater weight to Action Orientation than do decision makers, more even than do review committee members. They apparently believe that Action Orientation not only increases likelihood of use but also represents the most important contribution that a study *can* make. In their view, it is the outstanding predictor of the substantive usefulness of a study's information and ideas. They seem to subscribe to the problem-solving model of research use. The data imply that from their perspective, practical prescriptions for feasible action represent the essential ingredient of useful research.

Their ratings assign considerably less importance to Research Quality. They indicate that Research Quality is unlikely to make a difference to decision makers. Their ratings also show that Quality adds a relatively modest amount to the substantive usefulness of studies. In comparison, research review committee members' ratings give much greater weight to Research Quality in increasing a study's substantive contribution.

Congruence with Decision Makers on Which Studies Are Useful

Researchers try to make their studies useful. To what extent do their perceptions of what is a useful study agree with the perception of decision makers? To answer this question, we computed correla-

Table 11.2. Effects of Research Characteristics on Usefulness for Appropriate Users, as Rated by Researchers, Review Committee Members, and Decision Makers

(Unstandardized Regression Coefficients for Usefulness Measures Regressed on Research Characteristics)

Unstandardized Regression Coefficients

Research Characteristics Factors	Likelihood of Use				Substantive Usefulness			
	Researchers	Panel Members	Decision Makers for Others	Decision Makers for Self	Researchers	Panel Members	Decision Makers for Others	Decision Makers for Self
Research Quality	.08	.06	.17	.54	.21	.40	.22	.31
Conformity to User Expectations	.40	.30	.25	.28	.23	.12	.22	.15
Action Orientation	.38	.11	.28	.19	.62	.49	.27	.22
Challenge to the Status Quo	.04	.26	.24	.31	.32	.31	.37	.28
Relevance[a]	—	—	—	.14	—	—	—	.16
Variance Explained	23%	15%	23%	42%	50%	60%	38%	35%

[a] Relevance does not apply to most appropriate users; they are appropriate users precisely because the research is relevant to them.

**Table 11.3.   Agreement Between Researchers and Decision Makers on
Usefulness of 50 Studies**
(*Intraclass Correlations Between Mean Scores*)

	Researchers	
Decision Makers	Likelihood of Use by Most Appropriate User	Substantive Usefulness for Most Appropriate User
Own likelihood of use	−.01	.03
Substantive usefulness for self	.13	.27*
Likelihood of use by most appropriate user	.13	.09
Substantive usefulness for most appropriate user	.01	.00

*Significant at .05 level.
N = 50.

tions between the mean usefulness ratings of researchers and of
decision makers for the fifty studies.

The intraclass correlations in Table 11.3 show that researchers'
ratings do not match decision makers' ratings very closely. Only
their ratings of a study's substantive usefulness are significantly
associated with decision makers' ratings of the study's substantive
usefulness for themselves. Correlations on the other measures are
not significant. Members of research review committees do considerably better in terms of agreement with decision makers. (See
table 12.2.) Part of the reason may well be that, as we have just seen,
researchers' conceptualization of "usefulness" is more instrumental
than is decision makers'. They apparently think of use more in
problem-solving, social engineering terms than do decision makers
—or even review committee members. In their ratings they apparently do not make much allowance for the conceptual uses that
constitute much of what decision makers describe in reporting their
research use.

Conclusion

Most social science researchers in our sample (all of whom have
received funding from NIMH, NIDA, or NIAAA) try to make their

own studies relevant and practical. Their efforts go less into conceptualization, planning, or conduct of studies in useful ways than into dissemination of results to people who can apply them. Most of them believe they have succeeded in producing useful work. But they have little faith that decision makers pay attention to research. Analysis of their ratings of studies suggests a belief that the qualities of research studies have only a modest relationship to decision makers' willingness to give them a hearing.

The studies that they rate as best contributing ideas and information to decision makers are characterized primarily by Action Orientation, with some additional support from Challenge, Research Quality, and Conformity. Much more than decision makers, they apparently view research use in terms of specific inputs to specific decisions. Perhaps for this reason, their ability to match decision makers' ratings of which particular studies are useful is relatively low.

NOTES

1. In the standard terminology, "applied" means "meant for application" and has little connotation of actual application by users.

2. Disciplines represented were anthropology, economics, political science, psychology, sociology, social work, education, public health, and other.

3. No table presents the standardized regression coefficients. Table 11.2 presents unstandardized regression coefficients.

Chapter Twelve

MEMBERS OF RESEARCH
REVIEW COMMITTEES

MEMBERS OF RESEARCH REVIEW COMMITTEES have a considerable say about which mental health research is done. They are
influential gatekeepers in the research process, because their review
of proposals helps to determine which proposals receive federal
grant support. Although there are other sources of research funding,
and some research can be done by investigators without external
support, in practice the approval or disapproval of grant applications by research review committees is often the key decision for
whether or not a proposed study is conducted.

In the mental health fields, contract research represents a small
fraction of government research support. According to the extensive
review of mental health research by the Research Task Force of the
National Institute of Mental Health (1975), federal contracts for
research and "research-related activities" amounted to $10.2 million
in 1972, compared with $82.5 million for federal research grants,
and the $10.2 contract figure is inflated by the inclusion of activities
like "preparation of handbooks," "information campaigns," and
"conferences" that are peripheral to research per se (NIMH 1975:
44–47). Most social science research on mental health is dependent
upon grants, and grants are dependent upon the actions of research
review committees.

In our inquiry we interviewed 50 members of the research
review committees of NIMH, NIDA, and NIAAA. We asked about
the criteria that they and their committees use in assessing grant
applications, and we learned how important the usefulness of
proposed research is for the decision to approve, how important
they believe it should be, and why. We also investigated the degree
to which review committee members recognize research usefulness

213

when they see it. We analyzed their judgments of the usefulness of the same 50 social science research studies that decision makers rated and compared their ratings with decision makers' ratings. With these data, we can see the extent of correspondence or discrepancy between their judgments of useful research and those of decision makers.

Review of Grant Applications

The primary review of proposals for research grants in NIMH, NIDA, and NIAAA is performed by research review committees composed of qualified, nongovernmental experts.[1] They are chosen because of their substantive knowledge of a field of study and of research, and they are considered the applicants' "peers." They generally serve for four-year terms, and meet three times a year to review all the grant applications submitted within their specialty (mental health services, crime and delinquency, epidemiology, etc.). There were 17 research review committees attached to the three institutes at the time of our study, 12 of which reviewed applications for social scientific research.

The action taken by research review committees is a recommendation for approval, disapproval, or deferral. (On deferred applications, further information is collected by mail or through site visit, and approval or disapproval is recommended at a subsequent meeting.) Members also rate approved applications on a scale of 1 to 5, and a composite priority score is calculated for the committee as a whole.

A statutory Advisory Council for each of the institutes performs a second review. The Advisory Council is also composed of experts from outside government, at least half of them authorities in relevant scientific and professional areas and the rest lay members noted for their activity and interest in the field. The expertise of the Advisory Council thus extends beyond research to broader issues of policy and practice. Advisory Councils meet three times a year to review the recommendations from all of the research review committees, and they have the authority "to modify the recommendation" of the review committee in light of their responsibilities to consider "the missions of the Institutes, the total pattern of research in universities and other institutions, the need for the initiation of research in new areas, and matters of policy" (National Institutes of Health 1976:9). They make the final determination of approval. Then, staff of the institutes decide which of the approved projects will actually be funded.[2]

In practice, the action of the initial review committee is key. Experience indicates that neither the Advisory Councils nor institute staff deviate much from the initial recommendation. Advisory Councils in practice almost never overturn initial committee recommendations, in large part because they do not have time for thorough review of the large numbers of proposals that come to them from the several review committees. In effect they entrust the detailed analysis of the quality of proposals to the more specialized, more research-oriented initial review committees. In determining which of the approved studies will be funded, staff tend to abide fairly closely by the priority ratings of the committees. On occasion, they do select on the basis of current concerns and priorities. But some staff believe that they do not have the responsibility to overrule committee decisions (Davis and Salasin 1978:116), and since review by impartial outside experts provides insulation from political pressures, others are reluctant to jeopardize the insulation by failing to follow committee priority ratings. In the event, the research review committees dominate the funding process. What Grace M. Carter concluded about NIH grants holds in large measure for the ADAMHA institutes:

Although the Advisory Councils influence decisions about the funding level of programs within the Institute, they only rarely disagree with the priority scores assigned by the IRG [initial review group] to particular grants. The administrators within NIH are not bound by law to follow the priority order of those applications recommended for approval by Advisory Councils, but in practice most of them do so. Thus, the IRG plays a very large role in determining which grants will be funded. (Carter 1974:80)[3]

Because of this central role, it becomes important to understand the extent to which research review committees take the potential usefulness of research into account. Usefulness is not an explicit criterion for review committees' approval of research proposals, but to the extent that the Advisory Councils and the institute staffs forego independent judgment, they are the place where—if anywhere—the usefulness of research to decision makers is considered. If they do not take account of the potential for practical application, then it largely goes by default.

The formal charge to research review committees within NIMH, NIDA, and NIAAA does not include mention of usefulness, except in terms of importance to the field of knowledge. The National Institutes of Health (NIH) *Orientation Handbook for New Members of Study Sections* (NIH 1973) applies to members of ADAMHA study sections and sets out the central criteria for proposal review. The basic theme is scientific merit, but other criteria are indicated as well. Thus, the handbook states:

> The primary responsibility of each Study Section is to select . . . those proposals which appear most likely to make significant contributions to understanding in the medical, biological, physical, or behavioral sciences. (p. 2)

> Study Sections review applications on the basis of scientific merit, which includes an assessment of the importance of the proposed research problem; the novelty and originality of the approach; the training, experience, and research competence or promise of the investigator(s); the adequacy of the experimental design; the suitability of the facilities; and the appropriateness of the requested budget relative to the work proposed. (p. 5)

> The ratings should be based on an evaluation of the merit of a proposal in relation to the "state of the art" of its particular area. (p. 6)

As these passages suggest, the rationale for peer review is that highly capable researchers in the applicant's substantive field are the people best qualified to assess a proposal's merit. They are expected to use their substantive and methodological knowledge to assess the formulation of the research question (its importance, the aptness of its conceptualization, the "ripeness" of the field for inquiry), the design, measurement, and analytic strategies proposed for studying the question, and the potential contributions to scientific knowledge. Originality is given some weight. The track record of the investigator is to be considered, largely as assurance that the person can do what is being promised. Feasibility (the state of the art, appropriate facilities, a reasonable budget) is also to be taken into account. But clearly it is the quality of the research, and not its potential usefulness for practitioners, managers, or policy makers, to which review committee members are expected to respond.

Our question is whether, despite its formal absence, usefulness gets any consideration at this critical stage of research management. We interviewed 50 members who were then serving, or had served in the immediately preceeding year, on the 12 NIMH, NIDA, and NIAAA research review committees that considered proposals for social science research. The twelve committees represented are the same ones that provided funding for the grant-supported studies that we used in our inquiry (except that we interviewed members of the Mental Health Small Grants Review Committee although none of its studies was included). Most of the twelve review committees had purview over both "basic" and "applied" research; only one was considered responsible exclusively for basic social science research.

We began the interview with a set of open-ended questions about review criteria and followed with a structured question asking specifically about usefulness as a criterion. The three opening questions asked:

As a member of a research review committee, now or in the recent past, you have helped to make decisions about which social science research to fund in the broad field of mental health. What are the main criteria that your review committee used for approving applications for social research grants?

What do you think the main criteria *should be* for approving applications for social research grants in the broad field of mental health?

Which criteria are most important to *you* as you make judgments about whether or not to fund a study?

After review of the responses, nine categories were constructed to accommodate committee members' remarks as completely as possible. Table 12.1 lists the categories in the order of frequency of mention and presents the percentage of review committee members offering each response. A brief description gives the flavor of answers in each category.

The "research quality" category includes unelaborated as well as specific comments about "scientific merit," "good experimental design," and "methodological rigor." Under "logic and presentation," the prevailing theme was conceptualization. Comments had to do with formulation of the research question, its theoretical premises, clarity and logic of development, quality of thought. Classified as "contribution to scientific knowledge" were responses about the potential to "contribute to understanding," to add to

Table 12.1.   Criteria for Judging Research Proposals

Criteria	Used by Committee (N = 50)	"Should be Used" (N = 50)	Used by Self (N = 50)	Mentioned in Any Category (N = 50)
Research quality	82%	66%	72%	88%
Logic, presentation	64	52	56	76
Contribution to scientific knowledge	42	48	44	64
Social significance	42	36	34	52
Usefulness for policy or program	36	36	36	52
Capability of investigator	28	18	28	44
New, disadvantaged researcher	24	12	14	32
Originality	16	12	16	28
Generalizability	4	8	6	12

NOTE: Percentages total to more than 100 because of multiple responses.

knowledge in the field of mental health or other scientific disciplines, to "advance the state of the art."

Answers in the "social significance" category referred to the importance of the research questions addressed in terms of societal need. Most of the responses were phrased in global terms and mentioned the relevance of the research to significant social problems. "Usefulness for policy and program" was more specific. Answers were placed in this category only if they referred to potential impact on practice or program. Typically they mentioned a contribution to improvement of mental health programs or agencies.

"Capability of the investigator" included comments about researchers' education, experience, and past record of research accomplishment. Answers about "new or disadvantaged researchers" reflected a concern with giving consideration to new investigators, those who are professionally young, members of minority groups, or women. The Small Grants Program in NIMH is specifically set up to give research opportunities to less experienced investigators (*Behavior Today* 1976:6–8), and some, but by no means all, of the answers in this category came from members of its review committee. Representative answers in the "originality" category were "a new way of tackling the problem," "particularly imaginative," "elements of creativity." "Generalizability" responses referred to the extent to which the proposed research would be generalizable to populations, institutions, or locations beyond those studied directly. They have to do with external validity. Although implicit may be a concern with the applicability of results to decisions, it is also possible that the concern is with theoretical generalization.

As table 12.1 indicates, the three responses most often given are criteria that have official sanction—research quality, logic and presentation, and contribution to scientific knowledge. Since review of grant applications for scientific merit is the basic function of peer review, the only surprise was that research quality was not mentioned more frequently. The reason is that some respondents separated out elements of research quality in ways that led to their classification as logic and presentation or contribution to scientific knowledge. The pattern of responses suggests that the premises on which peer review is based are in fact operative: review committee members screen on the basis of the official criteria.

However, social significance and usefulness for policy and program, which are not officially endorsed, receive only slightly less support. Over a third of the review committee members believe that each of these criteria is used by their committee, is important to them, and should be used. Each is mentioned more often than two of the criteria with official imprimatur: capability of the investigator and originality. Research review committees attached to these mission-oriented agencies are not unconcerned with the possible contribution that research can make to coping with important mental health problems. Their spontaneously offered comments give usefulness a place of unexpected visibility.

Even if we restrict our attention to the category that most directly links research to action, usefulness for policy or program, we see a significant degree of interest. The 36 percent of review committee members recorded as citing usefulness in response to each of the three questions are not always the same people. Over all, 52 percent of the committee members mentioned usefulness at least once (and only one respondent said that his *committee* considered the usefulness of a proposal and did not say that it was one of his own criteria or one that he believed should be used). There is substantial support, even if not majority support, for invoking considerations of practical utility in the review of research applications.

Ratings of the Importance
of Usefulness

We also asked a structured question about usefulness as a review criterion. The question was:

When you are deciding whether to approve a research application, how important a factor is the probable usefulness of the research for policy or program decisions? Please rate from 1 to 5 where 1 means this is a highly important factor and 5 means not important at all.

Forty-six of the 50 panel members responded, and almost half of them gave it either a 1 or 2, the top categories on the 5-point scale:

Highly important	1	20 percent
	2	28
	3	30
	4	15
Not important at all	5	7

Only 22 percent of the respondents rated it 4 or 5 in importance. The responses indicate that usefulness for decisions receives at least some consideration from most review committee members.

A check of the twelve committees from which review committee members were drawn indicated that consideration of usefulness occurred on all committees. On no committee was there unanimity on the degree of attention that the panel accorded it. On committees more oriented to basic research, it was cited less often. But despite the differences among committees in their relative concentration on basic or applied research, some members of all committees reported that usefulness was used as a criterion in evaluating research proposals.

Review committee members gave extensive explanations of their responses. A few dismissed usefulness as a criterion out of hand. One basis was its uncertainty. Whereas they believed that scientific merit was real and measurable, some people saw usefulness as difficult to define.

[Review panel criteria] should exclude social relevance, which is very personal, very "iffy," very uncertain, a very dangerous way to go. (419)*

Several more indicated that their mandate as panel members was to concentrate on scientific merit and leave consideration of usefulness to others.

As I understand the charge of the grant review committee that I'm on, that's our charge, to ignore the overall usefulness of the thing in terms of the mental health field. . . . [P]olicy decisions as I understand it are made by the Mental Health [Advisory] Council. (426).

At the other extreme, some members of research review committees were committed to research that had the potential for practical application. For several, it was a matter of social concern. Given the pervasive needs for effective services, research was justifiable to the extent that it helped meet societal needs.

I believe in pursuit of knowledge for its own sake, but I wouldn't put more than a small percentage of money there. The state of society is such, the needs are so great, that unless knowledge can be applied . . . then we are failing in our responsibility to society. (454)

As of today, with the scarcity of money, the decision-making process must be made on what money is available to fund any project, and therefore usefulness becomes an extremely important thing. (451).

Others believed that usefulness deserved high priority because of their own and their committees' responsibilities. In their role as panel members, they were public servants with a public trust.

Science is funded by Congress in mental health areas in order to produce knowledge which will be useful in mental health areas. (437)

The mandate of the committee is: how will it help improve services to people in need? (467)

I am working with a center funded with taxpayers' money with a mission to solve a specific problem, and it's a matter of integrity and responsibility to use the money for that specific mission. (481)

*The number in parentheses is the identification number of the respondent. All panel members have 400 numbers.

But the potential applicability of the research is only one criterion. Several panel members were outspoken about the necessity of keeping it in perspective. Usefulness, they indicated, was important only if the research also passed muster on methodological grounds. Attention to issues that are programmatically relevant is not sufficient; the study must also be done competently.

It's highly important, but only if the application is good in other respects. It's the most important thing: are you doing something worthwhile? But that's only achieved when the other criteria are met. (480)

It would have to pass research muster first, which would be higher [in importance]. . . . If, in fact, it wasn't a good research proposal, that [usefulness] wouldn't be enough. (416)

If there were a matter of two proposals of equal merit, and one had possible application, and I had to choose one to approve, then I guess I'd choose that one because it's important. (469)

Obviously it would be desirable to have proposals that satisfied criteria of both usefulness and research quality, and most of our respondents would be happy to approve them. But many of them phrased their responses in terms of a *trade-off* between usefulness and research quality. Not that useful research is intrinsically of lower technical quality; rather the point is that the troublesome decisions in research review arise when one or the other attribute is weak. Some review committee members come down on the side of usefulness.

Personally, I'm more responsive to applicability . . . less fascinated by the beauties of the investigation, and I imagine more kind to something that is more applicable but the research structure isn't as good than vice versa. (467)

I'm not as rigorous about methodology. Although I don't think I'm, well, into that sloppy stuff that goes by, I think sometimes that rigor can be sacrificed if the problem is of sufficient interest. (405)

Now the ——— committee, as contrasted with other committees, is more likely to relax those criteria—good problem in a theoretical sense, well-designed, originality. Under what conditions? One condition would be the importance of the social problem area, in the broad sense not only of mental health relevance, but also the broader specific importance on the agenda of society. (418)

On the particular committee on which I served, the likelihood of having mental impact was a more important issue and *should* have been a more important issue since the committee was deemed in part an educationally oriented committee. . . . The criteria relating to impact on the clinician or on the general mental health field were more important than methodological soundness. (455)

Others are less willing to sacrifice technical merit to the demands of practicality. Their responses emphasize the necessity of sound methodology if the research is to have value for any purpose, scientific *or* practical. Research whose findings are flawed or erroneous is not a reliable basis for decision-making. John H. Noble, Jr., who was on the staff of the Assistant Secretary for Planning and Evaluation at HEW, has put this case as strongly as anyone, and some of the panel members echoed his statement:

No matter how relevant is the research to government policy, it cannot provide answers unless it is properly designed and executed. . . . [S]tudies that mislead because of error in design, procedure, or inference are a menace to policy-makers and the commonweal. (Noble 1974:916)

But there is more to the argument that relegates usefulness to a subordinate position. A number of panel members forcefully took the position that it is difficult, often impossible, to foretell which research studies will prove to be useful. They claimed that if review committees invested too much of their funds in attending to issues of immediate practicality, they would foreclose opportunities for research that had longer range but more fundamental use.

We really don't understand what the questions *are* thoroughly until we have the answers. If we limit research to mission-oriented research it will cut us off from asking important questions. It's the old commitment to basic research, which doesn't say, do research for its own sake, but says if you really want to understand, don't limit yourself to something that says this will help you tomorrow. (478)

Research which does not seem to have policy implications at one period of time may in fact have quite definite policy implications later. (433)

Nobody can really evaluate usefulness before the fact. So if you put all your weight on that, you're potentially throwing out the stuff that will be useful in the future, like penicillin. (471)

I want things to make a difference, but things lead to policy directly or indirectly. . . . If you want to design research to lead to *immediate* policy outcomes, you wouldn't do much research, you wouldn't ask any of the questions that are interesting. (485)

Sometimes the most applied research really isn't the most useful to other people and more basic research really would be. (469)

The intrinsic unpredictability of which research will in fact inform mental health policy and practice leads some panel members to come down foursquare on the side of knowledge-building as the primary test. Usefulness is not irrelevant, but if it cannot be foreseen, then the best course is to approve rigorous research that will add to the stock of scientific knowledge. In the long term, some say, this course may yield consequences of great social benefit.

The needs of society as we interpret them are extremely transient, faddish, and not formulatable in a fashion that is amenable to scientific test, and I think the most important thing is to acquire knowledge. . . . Knowledge is forever as far as I'm concerned, and it's got to be—its development has got to be to some extent independent of the whimsey of the society and culture. (423)

I am much more inclined to look at a piece of research myself in terms of its scientific merit, perhaps initially, that this is the important thing. And then secondarily, whether or not it may immediately or in some future date influence policy. . . . I think that first of all it has to be done. Once it's done, then it is always there and can be used to influence policy and programs. If it's not done, then it can't do anything. (438)

There is value in building knowledge over time. As knowledge builds it enters the thinking of policy makers. . . . Knowledge for its own sake has value which can have indirect impact by entering their thinking. (484)

It seems to me that if a study is well conceptualized, it probably has some potential use in policy or program design even though the investigator may not think of it as primarily applied research. (452)

The assumption is, the more knowledge there is, the more likely something good will happen. (420)

The discussions of review committee members evidence considerable sophistication about the uses of social science research. They recognize that social science research can be useful to decision makers not only when it has immediate relevance "for policy or program decisions" (as our question asked); several of them call attention to the more basic conceptual contributions that can also make research "useful."

The tilt in their answers is toward the cumulation of scientific knowledge. For a few members, this is the overriding consideration, and the potential usefulness of research is considered too capricious a phenomenon to provide a sensible guide for proposal review. For others, the development and growth of knowledge in the committee's area of jurisdiction is expected to generate understandings that will almost automatically be useful, sooner or later, for decision-making. Their subject matter, after all, is mental health, a field of practice. Supporting sound research in mental health is enough; when the results of sound research come into currency, they will raise the level of program and policy discussion. Other panel members wrestle with the issue with less assurance that usefulness is preordained. They want research to make a difference in policy matters, but they are aware of the uncertainties and trade-offs that invoking a criterion of usefulness introduces. If proposal review comes down to a choice between a study with high scientific merit and little applicability on the one hand or a study with high practical relevance but only adequate methodology on the other, panel members are divided in their choices.

For very few panel members is the usefulness of research irrelevant. Half of them *spontaneously* mention usefulness as a relevant criterion for proposal review, and three-quarters give it at least moderate endorsement when asked to rate its importance. Without explicit formulation in regulation or guidelines, usefulness gains their attention because of their formal role as advisers to mission-oriented agencies, because of their professional interests in program improvement, and because of their human concerns about people in anguish. Nevertheless, they were appointed to review committees because of their scientific expertise, and their basic charge is to pass on the scientific merit of the proposals that come before them. Therefore, most of them try to reconcile considerations of usefulness with requirements for research quality. Their resolutions of the trade-off span the spectrum, but rarely are they inattentive to the possible usefulness of the research proposals they review.

Panel Members' Ability to
Judge Usefulness

Discovering that research review panels give a measure of attention to the probable usefulness of research in the review process is noteworthy. The important next question is: how good are they at judging the usefulness of specific studies? If their perceptions of which research studies are useful is discordant with the *actual* usefulness of the studies, then their efforts to take usefulness into account will yield little benefit.

We cannot make a direct test of their ability to identify studies of greater or lesser usefulness, but our data do enable us to compare their ratings of the usefulness of studies with the ratings given those same studies by federal, state, and local decision makers. Clearly we make no claim that the decision makers are "right" on any absolute basis, but they hold positions that require them to take action on policy and program, and they have had more of the grit of experience in coping with operational problems than have the research-oriented review committee members. A comparison between their ratings and the ratings of review committee members will shed some light on panel members' capacity to assess usefulness on a study-by-study basis.

Decision makers rated each study in terms of the likelihood that they would take its results into account in their work and the extent to which it contained ideas or information that could contribute to their work. They also rated it on both measures for other decision makers whom they named as "most appropriate users" of the study. Members of research review committees rated the same studies on the same measures in terms of the decision makers whom they deemed the most appropriate users of the study results. Each study was rated by about six decision makers (two federal, two state, two local) and two research review committee members.

Over all, there was considerable agreement between decision makers and review committee members on who the most appropriate users of the studies were deemed to be. For example, decision makers designated staff in local care-giving agencies as appropriate users in 54 percent of the cases, compared with 55 percent of the mentions by review committee members. Although neither set of respondents showed high internal consistency in designating the most appropriate user for a particular study, the distribution of their responses was similar. (See chapter 6.)

Table 12.2 presents the intraclass correlations between the mean scores of review committee members and decision makers for the usefulness of the fifty studies. As the data show, review committee members' ratings of likelihood of use do not match decision makers' ratings of their own likelihood of using a study. During the interviews, many review committee members told us that they had little understanding of the factors that motivated decision makers to turn to particular studies. They tended to consider outside events as critical, and their ratings of likelihood of use were not

Table 12.2.   Agreement Between Review Committee Members and Decision
Makers on Usefulness of 50 Studies
(*Intraclass Correlations Between Mean Scores*)

Decision Makers	Panel Members	
	Likelihood of Use by Most Appropriate User	Substantive Usefulness for Most Appropriate User
Own likelihood of use	.01	.27*
Substantive usefulness for self	−.06	.26*
Likelihood of use by most appropriate user	.27*	.19
Substantive usefulness for most appropriate user	.03	.18

*Significant at .05 level.
N = 50.

highly associated with the characteristics of the study. (See table 11.2) Their ratings of likelihood of use do correlate significantly with decision makers' ratings of the likelihood that *other* users will take the study into account. When both sets of respondents are talking about other people's use, they are in fair agreement.

Review committee members are relatively good at matching decision makers' ratings for the substantive usefulness of studies. Their ratings of the contribution that a study can make in terms of ideas and information correlates significantly ($p < .05$) with decision makers' ratings of both their own likelihood of using a study and the substantive contribution they believe it can make to their work. Thus, while the associations are not powerful, the data suggest that panel members have a measure of awareness of the kinds of studies that are likely to make a contribution to users.

We compared the ratings of those panel members who said that they did take usefulness into account in proposal review with those who said they did not. There was essentially no difference between the two groups in matching decision makers' ratings of usefulness.

One of the reasons that panel members do not approximate decision makers' ratings of a study's usefulness more closely appears to be their emphasis on Action Orientation. As table 11.2 indicated, their ratings of substantive usefulness are more highly related to the Action Orientation of a study than are decision makers' ratings. But they are better than social science researchers in judging usefulness in decision makers' terms (see tables 11.2 and 11.3). Since they have a fair fix on the substantive usefulness of specific social science research studies, the attention they give to usefulness in grant review is likely to advance the cause of useful studies.

When we look at the agreement between the two panel members rating each study, we find that the intraclass correlation between the pairs' ratings on likelihood of use, a situation on which they feel ill informed, is low (.06, n.s.). On substantive usefulness, agreement between the pairs' ratings is better $(r_i = .27, p < .05)$. The relationship, although significant, is not overpowering. But it turns out that it is just about as good as their agreement on Research Quality. Despite the fact that they are experts on Research Quality and serve on review committees because of their competence to make quality assessments, the agreement between the pairs of review committee raters on the Research Quality of a study is only .25 (p $< .05$). As we noted in chapter 5, other investigators have also found modest levels of agreement among social scientists rating the same studies on quality, and these data fall within the usual band of agreement. For our discussion, the relevant point is that review committee members evidence as much agreement among themselves on the substantive usefulness of specific studies as they do about their specialty, the rating of Research Quality.

In sum, members of research review committees in NIMH, NIDA, and NIAAA give some consideration to the potential usefulness of social science studies in review of grant applications. It is not the paramount criterion; research quality is their primary focus. Nevertheless, many of them are attentive to the probable usefulness of the proposed research for policy and program development. When they rate the contribution that the ideas and information from a study are likely to make, they are fairly good at predicting the studies that decision makers say are substantively useful and that they themselves are likely to use. Their internal agreement on substantive usefulness is about as high as their agreement on the Research Quality of completed studies.

NOTES

1. Research review committees are also called "study sections," "review panels," "peer review committees," in some official documents "initial review groups" (IRGs), and other permutations of these terms. We will use the terms "research review committees" and for brevity "panels."

2. This simplified sketch covers the basic elements of the process (NIH 1976). For a more detailed picture, and comparison with other federal agencies, see Wirt, Lieberman, and Levien (1974).

3. Essentially the same situation, but without second-tier review, holds for staff decisions at the National Science Foundation (Cole and Cole 1978). At the National Center for Health Services Research, staff are expected to exercise more independent judgment. "Approved health services research applications continue to be priority-ranked by the Study Section, but funding depends more on the relationship of a project's objectives to Center program priorities than on priority scores" (McFall 1978:211).

Chapter Thirteen

PERCEPTIONS OF OBSTACLES TO THE USE OF RESEARCH

THIS CHAPTER PRESENTS respondents' *opinions* about the relationship between social science research and agency decision-making. At the end of the interview, we presented them with a set of hypotheses about obstacles that arise in the creation, diffusion, and use of appropriate research, a list that we developed after extensive review of the literature on the subject. We asked them to rate each item on a four-point scale from agree strongly to disagree strongly. The opinions that they register indicate their perceptions of the weak links in the process from research initiation to research application. In addition, items were included about their own orientation to research use.

The opinion data presented in this chapter refer to the whole process of research use. Where earlier chapters have focused on one stage in the process, here we open up the series of events and problematic linkages that lead from research to action. In chapter 1, we laid out the map. We conceptualized the research-to-policy process as a loosely coupled system with three comments: research production, research application, and the institutions and arrangements that link the two.

In the production of research, factors that can limit the usability of research derive from researchers and from the institutions in which they work. Some specific hypotheses are that able social scientists are uninterested in policy-oriented research, that those who engage in it allow their own political values to intrude, and that the reward structures in universities and other research institutions discourage interdisciplinary work and work responsive to government needs. Such factors can undermine the intrinsic usability of social science research.

In the world of agency action, problems can arise from the attitudes and behavior of decision makers and from the constraints that their institutional milieus impose on the use of even that research which is usable. Hypotheses refer to the political nature of the processes that determine policy and which allow little or no attention to research, the rapid change in policy issues, decision makers' tendency to use research only to justify their policy predilections or legitimate their programs, and the aversion of both individuals and agencies to research findings that challenge their assumptions or contravene their philosophies.

The third component is the linkage between research and action settings. Government research offices are generally expected to fill the linking role—soliciting, reviewing, funding, monitoring, and disseminating appropriate research. Research review committees are auxiliaries in one phase of the process. Weaknesses hypothesized in this component were various: research offices do not anticipate knowledge needs far enough in advance to plan research that can be completed in time to affect decisions; decision makers cannot articulate the specific questions that need to be studied; there is little direct communication between researchers and decision makers; those who support research by grant or contract are out of touch with the real needs of decision makers; they fund irrelevant projects; they fail to disseminate research findings to appropriate decision-maker audiences.

Since our respondents included people active in all three components, their views should provide insiders' perspectives on operative failings and give some explanation for disjunctions in the research-to-policy nexus. One of our expectations was that members of each sector would tend to blame the other sectors for existing shortcomings—decision makers being particularly negative toward factors within the research component that lead to irrelevant or impractical research, researchers complaining about decision makers and their agencies for failure to accord research the attention it deserves, and both perhaps being sensitive to the faults of linkage structures in failing to bridge the gap. If researchers and decision makers are "two communities" with differing expectations and values, as Caplan (1975), Berg et al. (1978), and others have stated, such buck-passing might be a natural response.

The Data

Table 13.1 presents the responses of decision makers, research review committee members, and social science researchers to the 27 opinion items. Responses are divided into four categories: receptivity to research use, constraints on use arising within the decision-making process, constraints arising from the research process, and flaws in the link between research and decision-making.[1] Within each category, items relating to individuals are listed first, followed by the items about their institutions. (In the interview, the items were interspersed.)

Over all, the most striking pattern in the responses is the high level of agreement among the respondent groups. Their opinions about the potential of social science research and about the sources of problems in connecting research to policy show a surprising degree of congruence. On only three items do any of the groups differ by 25 percentage points or more, and all three of these relate to linkage constraints. In general, decision makers, research review committee members, and researchers perceive the same obstacles to the use of research. They are about as sensitive to the constraints in their own institutions as to the constraints operating on their counterparts. Furthermore, all groups tend to discount some of the hypotheses presented, and they concur in their denials.

Receptivity

The six items in this category, unlike those that follow, deal with the respondents' own beliefs. All three groups articulate resounding endorsement of research as an input into policy. They disagree with the statement that "The social sciences are too limited in methodology to be able to make substantial contributions to government policy," and they believe that there is such a thing as "research in the public interest." There is overwhelming support for the idea that social science research *should* be used in decision-making. Seventy-nine percent or more of each group agree that "An agency should implement the conclusions of good, relevant research even when this would reduce its budget or influence," and "Good research *should* be used whether or not its conclusions are politically acceptable to high policy-makers." All groups agree on the need for

Table 13.1. Views of Decision Makers, Review Committee Members, and Researchers on Barriers to Use of Research

	Percent Agreeing		
Barriers to Use	Decision Makers (*N* = 155)	Research Review Committee Members (*N* = 50)	Researchers (*N* = 50)

Receptivity

The social sciences are too limited in methodology to be able to make significant contributions to government policy.	32	26	22
There is no such thing as research in the public interest because different people want different things.	17	10	10
Good research *should* be used whether or not its conclusions are politically acaptable to high policy makers.	83	83	79
There is nothing as practical for decisions as a good theory.	38	59	52
One or two research studies, however cogent, are not enough to base an important decision on; there needs to be a body of consistent evidence.	72	73	76
An agency should implement the conclusions of good, relevant research even when this would reduce its budget or influence.	82	83	87

Decision-making constraints

Many decision makers tend to ignore social science information that is not consistent with their own beliefs.	75	85	92
Most government decision makers believe that social science research contributes to intelligent program decisions.	54	34	32
Policy issues change so rapidly that it is almost impossible to plan a two-year study that will still be relevant when it is completed.	39	18	20
Government policies are arrived at through political processes that pay little or no attention to research.	72	79	90
Government agencies tend to ignore research findings that are not in line with agency assumptions and philosophies.	67	75	88
Government agencies have a limited range of options for action, and research findings that fall outside that range are of little use.	61	55	74

Table 13.1. (*Continued*)

	Percent Agreeing		
Barriers to Use	Decision Makers (*N* = 155)	Research Review Committee Members (*N* = 50)	Researchers (*N* = 50)

Research constraints

Most researchers are reluctant to engage in decision-relevant research because they do not want to get involved in controversy.	31	31	43
The most able social science researchers are not interested in doing research that is oriented to government needs.	29	29	39
The political values of social science researchers inevitably interfere with their research.	38	31	36
Interdisciplinary research, which is desirable for studying many policy issues, is discouraged by the organization of the university along departmental lines.	74	65	63
The academic reward system, with its emphasis on publishing in disciplinary journals, discourages social science researchers from doing decision-oriented research.	68	69	74
Research institutions do not provide incentives or professional rewards to social scientists for doing research that is responsive to government needs.	54	45	63
Many research groups that conduct contract research under competitive bidding procedures tend to slant their findings to please the client agency.	65	57	73

Linkage constraints

Research program officers in government, who influence the kind of research that is initiated and funded, are poorly informed about the informational needs of decision makers.	69	42	50
Most decision makers are not able to adequately define or specify their research needs.	68	72	77
Most government research program officers fail to disseminate research results to decision makers who could use them.	64	58	60

Table 13.1. *(Continued)*

Barriers to Use	*Percent Agreeing*		
	Decision Makers (N = 155)	*Research Review Committee Members* (N = 50)	*Researchers* (N = 50)
The government research officers, who decide on which kinds of research to support, have few incentives to select issues of major importance to decision makers.	51	34	33
The lack of direct communication between researchers and decision makers is a major obstacle to making social science research useful.	83	84	86
Few government research offices try to forecast emerging issues for research, so that they are usually supporting research on "last year's problems."	67	49	80
Government offices that acquire research through contracts often sacrifice research quality for speed of reporting.	51	76	70
Review of research proposals by outside panels tends to neglect considerations of relevance to decision.	48	31	44

a consistent body of evidence rather than one or two studies as a basis for decision, which seems a responsible position to take. The only qualification on receptivity is the reservation, strongest among decision makers, about the practicality of good theory.

Such high rates of support for the application of social science research, particularly from decision makers, are likely to evoke some skepticism. Research use begins to look like a "motherhood" issue, and what with the decline in zest for motherhood may even be overtaking it in popularity. There is probably some exaggeration in these responses. But the important thing is that decision makers assert this as a norm. They say this is what *should* be done, whatever the actual practice may be. They make no claims that this is how things are actually working. On the contrary, the next area of agreement is that social science research is not being widely used.

Decision-making constraints

There is general consensus that research currently has little impact. Two-thirds or more of each group agree that research is ignored because "Government policies are arrived at through political processes that pay little or no attention to research," "Many decision makers tend to ignore social science information that is not consistent with their own beliefs," and "Government agencies tend to ignore research findings that are not in line with agency assumptions and philosophies." Most also believe that "Government agencies have a limited range of options for action, and research findings that fall outside that range are of little use." But most of them disagree that policy issues change so rapidly that timely research is impossible.

When we look at federal, state, and local decision makers separately, we find that it is the local people who are most likely to blame decision-making constraints for lack of research use. They are most apt to state that decision makers ignore research that is inconsistent with their beliefs, that agency options are limited and research outside those limits is irrelevant, and that policy is set through political processes. One local respondent was particularly articulate about the boundaries of his authority:

We are a system within a system. My service has to function within the hospital system, and that belongs to the larger state system, which has to function within the U.S. health system and with all the social and political implications. In the process of decision-making you have to keep in mind how many people are affected and how many variables are at play. There are many decisions I can't make because I'd be going beyond my capacity.

It appears that people administering local agencies perceive themselves as less autonomous, more hamstrung by political and organizational limits, than decision makers at other levels of government.

Researchers are somewhat more critical than either decision makers or review committee members of the "drag" on research use that is due to decision makers and their agencies. But as we shall see, they also tend to be more critical of researchers and research institutions. They generally evidence a tilt toward the negative.

All three groups perceive receptivity to research among decision makers as lower than their own receptivity. Even among decision makers, a bare majority agree with the statement, "Most government decision makers believe that social science research contributes to intelligent program decisions," although over 80 percent endorsed two much stronger formulations for themselves (research should be used whether or not politically acceptable, and even if use would reduce agency budget or influence). If researchers are skeptical about decision makers' commitment to social science research, the decision makers in our sample evidence only a little less skepticism about their colleagues. Some readers might look on this item as "projective," with respondents displacing their own opinions onto other decision makers. Later in the chapter we offer an alternative interpretation.

Research constraints

Decision makers, review committee members, and researchers also tend to agree on the constraints that occur in the research context. Three-fifths or more believe that the social science disciplines are part of the problem, at least in the university. The academic reward system with its emphasis on publication in disciplinary journals discourages social scientists from doing decision-oriented research, and the organization of universities by departments inhibits the interdisciplinary research that is often desirable for studying policy issues. There is somewhat less assent to the statement that "Research institutions do not provide incentives or professional rewards to social scientists for doing research that is responsive to government needs," but there may have been some disparities in which "research institutions" were the referent. In all events, researchers are most likely to agree with the statement. Majorities of all groups are also critical of research organizations that conduct contract research under competitive bidding procedures. They believe that such groups "tend to slant their findings to please the client agency." Again, researchers are a bit more critical.

On the other hand, all three groups tend to absolve researchers as individuals from major blame. They do not believe that researchers are unwilling or unable to produce usable research. Most respondents disagree that researchers are reluctant to engage in decision-relevant research because of potential controversy, that the most able researchers are uninterested in policy research, or that the political values of researchers inevitably interfere with their research. Rather, they indicate it is structural arrangements, particularly the system of professional recognition, that limit the contribution of social scientists.

Linkage constraints

The final set of items deals with the linkage of research and decision-making, both in terms of the specification and acquisition of relevant research and the dissemination of research results to appropriate users. Over 80 percent of all three groups say that "lack of direct communication between researchers and decision makers is a major obstacle. . . ." Better communication, too, seems to be something of a "motherhood" issue. With somewhat less unanimity, respondents criticize decision makers' contribution to the dialog. Over two-thirds of all groups say that decision makers are unable to define and specify their research needs, a factor that makes the performance of relevant research erratic.

Interestingly, in the course of our study, we had a perfect serendipitous example of the phenomenon. We asked the administrator of an alcoholism program what kinds of research he would like to have available to help him in his work. He said he'd like research on the "genetic and hereditary aspects of alcoholism." It just so happened that one of the research studies we gave him to rate dealt with exactly that topic. After he had read the abstract of the study, the interviewer asked him to what extent the study contained ideas or information that could contribute to his work. On a 5-point scale, he rated it 4—next to the bottom of the scale. When probed, he said, "The report says why some are alcoholics. The why is not so important to us . . . it is not relevant to the work of this agency. . . . We don't care here how they got here . . . we are the ambulance at the bottom of the cliff." Within half an hour, then, we watched a decision maker define his research needs, we provided what he specified, and we found out that it wasn't useful to his work, thus capsulizing a process that often takes two or three years, tens of thousands of dollars, and untold units of frustration.

Researchers and decision makers also agree that government offices that acquire research rarely try to forecast emerging research issues; two-thirds of both these groups (but not of review committee members) say that as a consequence, agencies usually support research on "last year's problems." Lower proportions—but still at least half of researchers and decision makers (but again not of review committee members)—say that government research program officers are poorly informed about the informational needs of decision makers. Over half of all three groups believe that "offices that acquire research through contracts often sacrifice research quality for speed of reporting." At the dissemination end, there is also majority agreement that "Most research program officers fail to disseminate research results to decision makers who could use them." On a positive note, over half of all groups *disagree* that "review of research proposals by outside panels tends to neglect considerations of relevance. . . ."

Review committee members are least likely to be critical of linkage offices and their staffs. They are considerably less likely than decision makers to say that research program officers are poorly informed about the informational needs of decision makers and significantly less likely than researchers to blame research program offices for failure to forecast emerging issues for research. In fact, on the eight linkage statements, they are most charitable of all the groups on four, partway between decision makers and the usually captious researchers on three, and hypercritical on only one: the sacrifice of research quality in contract research. Review committees deal with grants, and not contracts, and they evidently view grant procedures as superior for ensuring quality. They also believe somewhat more strongly than the other groups that their own review process gives attention to the relevance of research to decisions, although majorities of the other groups concur. (For elaboration of the criteria of review committees, see chapter 12.)

When we look at the whole pattern of review committee members' responses, we see that they tend to take a position intermediary between decision makers and researchers in assigning blame for failings in the research-to-policy connection. Almost all of them are themselves social science researchers, prestigious members of their fields, who were selected on the basis of their elite professional standing to advise government agencies on the studies they should sponsor. In taking on the role of committee member, they seem to become more sensitive to the needs and efforts of government staff and come to share some of their perceptions. Thus, they are more favorable than other researchers on all the items relating to decision makers and their institutions.

Although participation in a review committee is a very part-time commitment—three meetings a year, preceded by some days of reading proposals and writing critiques, plus occasional site visits to applicants[2]—it gives them a backstage view of certain agency operations and apparently allows them to see with a double eye. Like occupants of other boundary positions, their location at the intersect between research and government sensitizes them to the perspectives of both camps. It seems to evoke sympathetic under-standing of both government *and* research, so that they are consistently more sympathetic to both spheres—not only more positive toward government than other researchers but usually more positive toward research than either decision makers or researchers. And as we have seen, they are particular champions of research program offices, the groups with which they interact most fre-quently in the research review process. Their dual role relationships perhaps encourage them to mediate among the groups and seek to effect mutual tolerance.

On linkage constraints, there is greater diversity of opinion among the three respondent groups than on the other subjects we asked about. Nevertheless, the weight of opinion is that the "middleman" role between research and decision making is inade-quately performed. And in this case, it is the people as much as the organizational structures in which they work that receive the blame. Thus, for example, there is more agreement that research program officers are poorly informed about information needs than that there are "few incentives to select issues of major importance to decision makers."

Decision makers are particularly negative in their views about linkage agents. When we examine the differences among decision makers at federal, state, and local levels, we can pinpoint the dissatisfaction more precisely. It is state and local decision makers who indicate greater dissatisfaction, with special criticism of research program offices. They are substantially more critical of these offices than federal officials on all grounds. They are more likely to say that research offices do not try to forecast issues, are uninformed about decision-making needs, have little incentive to be relevant to decision makers, and fail to disseminate research results to people who can use them. They appear to be saying that federal research programs are largely ignoring the needs of the state and local decision makers whom they represent. While about half the federal respondents believe that research programs serve decision needs, only from a fifth to a third of state and local respondents believe they are responsive. The implication is that despite the substantial focus of ADAMHA research on issues relevant to local service providers (see chapter 6 on Most Appropriate Users), federal research funding programs may not be well equipped to understand the information needs of distant users in state mental health departments and local care-giving agencies.

Intervening variables

Position and location, as we have seen, make some difference— although overall it is a surprisingly modest difference—in respondents' perceptions of constraints on research use. Personal characteristics make almost none. Analysis of the responses by profession, length of time in position, previous experience, highest degree, field of degree, political orientation, and age shows that none of these characteristics accounts for significant differences in response.

Summary

In sum, there is substantial consistency among decision makers, research review committee members, and researchers about the research utilization process. By and large, they agree that:

1. social science research is useful for decision-making;
2. social science research *should* be used as a basis for making decisions; and
3. social science research is not being widely used by government agencies.

Among the more important obstacles to research use they see are:

1. decision makers' unwillingness to rely on research that is inconsistent with their own beliefs or their agency's philosophies;

2. the political nature of the decision-making process;
3. the institutional drag on social scientists' responsiveness to government research needs, particularly the disciplinary reward structure in the university;
4. inadequate communication between decision makers and researchers;
5. the inability of decision makers to define and specify their research needs; and
6. the inability of government research program officers to fill the communication gap, either from decision maker to researcher about knowledge needs or from researcher to decision maker about research results. State and local decision makers are particularly sensitive to defects in this communications channel. Research review committee members are less critical of their effectiveness.

Not perceived as serious limitations on research use are:

1. the state of social science methodology;
2. the inability or unwillingness of social researchers to do relevant research;
3. the value assumptions embedded in social research; or
4. the rapidity with which policy issues change.

All respondent groups tend to agree in the main that this is how things are. They are about as sensitive to the constraints in their own institutions as they are to those in counterpart institutions.

Comparison with Other Data

On several of the issues, the interviews provided parallel data derived from the ratings of specific studies and answers to questions about behavior with which we can compare the opinion responses. Such a comparison will indicate the extent to which the opinions that people express are actually operative when they get a few steps closer to real-life behavior.

With regard to decision-making constraints, people believe that decision makers' own beliefs set limits to their acceptance of social science research. Our previous analysis showed that Conformity with User Expectations does indeed contribute to the usefulness of specific studies. They also hold the opinion that agencies ignore research that is "not in line with agency assumptions and philosophies." But here our analysis indicated that Challenge to the Status

Quo is a feature that showed a *positive* relationship to the studies' usefulness ratings. The lead item in the Challenge factor was "challenges existing assumptions and institutional arrangements"; the item loading next highest was "implies the need for major change in philosophy, organization, or services." There seems to be a contradiction between respondents' perceptions and their ratings of actual studies.

As we noted earlier, the nature of the utility test helps us to understand the discrepancy. In the utility test, there is a trade-off between direct guidance for implementable, incremental action *and* challenge to existing philosophy and policy. A study can be useful if it gives clear direction or if it helps decision makers rethink current policy. In the latter case, the impact will be on the decision maker's conceptualization of future alternatives. When research has had such an effect, the impact of the research is largely unobservable. The effect has taken place within the user's mind, and if and when it results in external change, the connection to the research will be far from obvious—even to the user himself.

The truth test, too, suggests how the effect of research can be obscured. A study that does not Conform to User Expectations may be discounted, particularly if it is insufficiently strong on Research Quality. But if its Research Quality makes it at least moderately credible, it may move the decision maker's expectations slightly in its direction. It becomes part of the background knowledge and experience on which expectations are based. If several additional studies report convergent conclusions, especially if their Research Quality is good, expectations may change considerably. When observable action is eventually taken, it may seem to be associated with studies that Conformed to User Expectations, but only because there has been a gradual shift in expectations taking place underground and unobserved.

These kinds of processes also help to explain the sharp contrast between respondents' perceptions of their own receptivity to research and the disregard of research by others. What they are reporting is their failure to observe other decision makers use research. Like most observers, they are apparently talking about clear-cut applications of findings to decisions, the type of use associated with Action Orientation. While they are more sensitive to the indirect conceptual uses that they themselves make of research, they do not *see* these kinds of uses by other people. Therefore, they overlook both the cumulative effect of research on expectations and the diffuse effects of research on the ways that people think about the world.

This is not to suggest that powerful constraints do not limit research use in decision-making. They do. The "political processes" and "limited range of options for action" that respondents agree on represent some of them. It *is* to suggest that our existing framework and vocabulary for discussing research use needs modification.

Respondents' opinions about linkage constraints are generally consistent with other data in the study. For example, over two-thirds of decision makers and somewhat higher percentages of review committee members and researchers believe that decision makers are unable to define their research needs. Our analysis in chapter 10 indicated that this was largely true with respect to their criteria for useful research. Correspondence is low between the characteristics of research that decision makers *say* are important to them and the characteristics of the studies that they find useful. Only at the aggregate level are they at all accurate in identifying the criteria that influence their judgments of specific studies. While we do not have data on their ability to specify the substantive *topics* for research that would have greatest utility to them, we do have data on the kinds of research that they say they want. Review of these responses suggests that they rarely go beyond generalities ("evidence about programs that work," "studies on continuity of care," "research on populations like those we serve here"), and the one example that we happened to test (described earlier) indicates that even some of these responses are woefully misleading. Of course, responses to an interview are not the same as planning with a research staff. But we have no grounds on which to doubt the opinions about decision makers' inability to define their needs for research.

We have no data with which to compare the opinion item that collected the greatest consensus: "The lack of direct communication between researchers and decision makers is a major obstacle to making social science research useful." But if decision makers can not articulate their research needs, communication does not look like an all-purpose panacea. It does not appear to be an effective means for helping researchers to learn the kinds of studies that would be most serviceable. Decision makers cannot tell them. If direct communication is as valuable a mechanism as people believe, its value must lie elsewhere. It might increase decision makers' understanding of research, their comfort with its concepts, their trust in its validity, their ability to interpret and apply its results to the particular situation, their awareness of its limitations. But recent work (e.g., Berg et al. 1978) indicates that direct contact can have both positive and negative effects on research use. Contacts with researchers during the course of a study can reveal the shortcomings (as well as the strengths) of the research and make decision makers skeptical of its worth. And when findings of different studies are divergent or contradictory, communication may lead only to confusion—or to inappropriate acceptance of the results promoted by the most persuasive or charismatic communicator.

About the role of research review committees, the opinion data are largely consistent with the responses of review committee members themselves. As chapter 12 showed, most review committee members report that they give at least some attention to the usefulness of research in their review of research proposals (and they repeat that judgment in the opinion items; only 31 percent say that outside panels neglect considerations of relevance). A majority of decision makers and researchers agree. Although the percentages are somewhat lower than for panel members, they too perceive that panels attend to usefulness.

The last two items for which we have comparative data refer to contract research. A majority of all groups of respondents agree that research acquired under contract often sacrifices research quality for speed of reporting and that contract research groups tend to slant their findings to please the client agency. Analysis of the grant and contract studies in our sample showed that the patterns of association being posited do in fact hold—although not necessarily the causal links. Among the 50 studies that respondents rated, contract studies had lower scores on Research Quality than grant studies, although the difference was not statistically significant, and for-profit research organizations which tend to do contract research scored significantly lower on Research Quality than other research performers. These data lend credence to respondents' perceptions (particularly review committee members' and researchers') that contract research sacrifices quality. But it is not clear from the data whether the contract mechanism, the type of research organization conducting the study, or the kind of research these organizations typically do should bear the onus. Type of study also showed a relationship to Research Quality (not statistically significant, but stronger than the relationship between contracts and Quality), and the type of study that for-profit firms often do under contract— studies of program implementation—had lower ratings on Research Quality than descriptive studies, causal analyses, or outcome evaluations. Because of the small number of studies in our sample and the high intercorrelations among funding mechanism, type of research organization, and type of study, it was impossible to sort out the relative contribution of each variable.

Our data also showed that studies conducted under contract and studies performed by for-profit firms were more likely to Conform to User Expectations. The analysis of course does not indicate that contract researchers "slant their findings" to please the agency. The empirical association may result from the greater control that agencies exercise over the definition of the research problem in contract studies. Again, there is support for the pattern of association, but neither the shady intent nor the causal mechanism underlying the empirical relationship is clear.[3]

In sum, respondents have identified a series of constraints on the use of social science research. So far as our data allow us to tell, many of their opinions have a basis in fact. But they do not point toward ready solutions. Some of the prescriptions that they imply, such as more communication between researchers and decision makers, better planning of research agendas, and better dissemination of research reports, run aground on seemingly intractable obstacles that they also acknowledge. For example, respondents agree that decision makers cannot define their specific research needs, and if this is largely true, then better communication, planning, and dissemination become exceedingly difficult to accomplish. When decision makers cannot specify their research needs, they cannot seek out researchers who would be able to fulfill their informational needs, nor can they make their needs visible to staff in linkage positions who could plan targeted research or disseminate relevant reports to them.

Similarly, respondents recognize the problems that the academic reward system and the single-discipline structure of university research impose on the policy orientation of research, problems with the objectivity and quality of contract research, and the political processes and limited options that constrain agency operation. But no wholesale remedies have yet been devised.

Yet there are grounds for comfort in the data. Respondents in different positions perceive the situation in similar ways; they do not engage in mutual recriminations. If reforms can be developed—and they may have to be piecemeal, situation-specific, agency-by-agency reforms—there appears to be an underlying receptivity to mechanisms that would increase the flow of valid knowledge to people in positions of authority. There are few indications in these responses that research conclusions would carry the day, but as previous chapters have indicated, such knowledge may be able to contribute to better understanding of problems, programs, and environments, and upgrade the background assumptions and conceptual apparatus that decision makers bring to bear on their work.

NOTES

1. The categories are a priori groupings by topic. A factor analysis of the items revealed little empirical clustering. Ten factors with eigenvalues greater than 1.0 occur (in 27 items) accounting for only 60 percent of the variance. Only one or two items loaded highly on each factor.

2. Although review committee status is a part-time commitment, it was in their role as committee members that we interviewed them. Many of the questions in the interview focused on review committee functions, activities, and norms. It was the salient role in the interview.

3. It is only fair to mention that contracts, studies performed by for-profit organizations, and implementation studies were rated more likely to be used—although only the relationship between type of study and likelihood of use was significant.

Chapter Fourteen
CONCLUSIONS

IT IS TIME to take stock. What have we learned that we did not
know before? Our inquiry has yielded a collection of results,
some of which support previous observations and some of which
challenge them—and recast the discussion in altered perspective.
In fact, if we followed the convention of Szechuan Chinese res-
taurants and printed the "hot and spicy" items in red, we would
have a colorful book indeed.

Our inquiry has dealt with a limited number of respondents in a
single field, mental health, and we do not know how typical they are
of other fields or how far our conclusions will stretch. Nevertheless,
the findings help to make sense of anomalies that have long plagued
commentators on research-policy relationships. In this chapter we
summarize the major points that have emerged in our analysis. In
doing so, we forgo the necessary qualifiers ("in mental health,"
"among the respondents we interviewed," "in the United States," "in
1975," etc.), but they should be kept in mind. We hope that further
research with other groups at other locations will test the limits of
their generalizability. At the end of the chapter we speculate about
unanswered questions and further directions for research.

We began the study, in part, to learn something about the
characteristics of social science research studies that make them
useful to decision makers. By the end we had indeed found out much
about the characteristics of research studies that decision makers
judged more or less useful for their work, but along the way we
found that many preconceptions about the nature of research use
have been unduly simplistic. The circumstances under which social
science research enters the decision-making domain are more
complex, ambiguous, and elaborated than most previous observers
have perceived, and it seems premature to offer simple prescriptions

248

to policy-oriented researchers on how to make their work more useful. Much more important will be to understand the conditions and processes of research use.

Receptivity to Social Science
Research

Mental health decision makers at federal, state, and local levels believe that social science research can contribute to policy and that it should be used. A large majority express adherence to the view that good research should be used even if such use would reduce agency influence or budgets or would have unfavorable political repercussions. They also agree that research use is not now common among decision makers, but like the decision makers across federal departments interviewed by Caplan, Morrison, and Stambaugh (1975), they evince normative support for its extension.

They also report high levels of research use themselves. They read a good deal of research, and they consider that their knowledge of research affects their work. But the ways that they use it do not generally fit the analytical model of decision-making (in which one defines the problem, searches for alternative solutions, weighs the costs and benefits of alternatives, and selects the best option). They do not conceptualize their work in this fashion nor do they report their use of research in such crisply defined decision-oriented terms. Nevertheless, they believe that social science research should, and does, make a difference in what they do.

Decision Makers' Frames of Reference
for Research

Agency decision makers are bombarded with information, not only from social science research but from a host of other sources. They screen the research that they read or hear about through a series of implicit filters. If it fails to pass the filters, they tend to discard it. If it passes, it deposits a residue that becomes incorporated into their stock of knowledge, which they draw upon when action is called for.

An understanding of the frames of reference that decision makers use in screening research was derived from factor analysis of ratings of fifty actual research reports. The factors represent the criteria that decision makers employ to describe and judge studies. They are:

√ (a) relevance to their work;
√ (b) the technical quality, objectivity, and cogency of the study (Research Quality);
√ (c) its plausibility given their prior knowledge, values, and experience (Conformity with User Expectations);
√ (d) the explicit guidance it provides for feasible implementation (Action Orientation); and
√ (e) its challenge to existing assumptions, practice, and arrangements (Challenge to the Status Quo).

The major difference between these factors and the factors that we had initially hypothesized was the split between conformity with their own knowledge and beliefs *and* conformity with (or obversely, challenge to) the assumptions and practice of mental health institutions. We had expected conformity to constitute one dimension relating to the political acceptability of research studies. Instead factor analysis revealed that it had two separate components.

Separation of Own Knowledge and Values From Agency Practice

The distinction that decision makers made between their own knowledge and values and the current practices of mental health organizations was unexpected. When agency staff resist the acceptance of new information, their action is likely to be viewed as a device to protect their agency, their turf, their value dispositions, their accustomed styles of work, and their careers. The action is generally seen as "political." But the fact that respondents segregated their own beliefs from the philosophies and operations of mental health organizations suggests that the conventional view is mingling two distinct phenomena together under the "political" label. In their ratings respondents distinguish the two. They treat research that challenges their own understanding differently from research that challenges agency operations. They resist research that is incompatible with their own beliefs (counterintuitive research). They are receptive to research that is critical of mental health policy and practice. The suggestion is that their reaction to research that contradicts what they know and value is not so much a political response based on the potential threat to their positions and their *stake,* as a cognitive response: the research appears to be *wrong.* In contravening the knowledge and values that they have developed over the years, such research is suspect on intellectual grounds.

Moreover, the two factors that we call Conformity to User Expectations and Challenge to the Status Quo are not opposite ends of a continuum. They are not negatively correlated. It turns out that they are hardly correlated at all. Studies that challenge agency practice are just about as likely to conform with user expectations as to conflict with them. This fact suggests that, at least in these professionally staffed agencies in a field in flux, decision makers are not necessarily wedded to existing institutional ideology or practice.

Much of the discussion of "bureaucratic politics" in the political science tradition assumes an identity among agency policy, staff career interests, and staff viewpoints (Allison 1971; Halperin 1974). Our data show that people in decision-making positions in mental health agencies are as inclined to be critical of agency operations as to support them. There is a qualification to this statement: In the ratings from which these data derive, decision makers were reacting to research about policy and programs in many locations, not necessarily in their *own* agencies. Yet the current of support for practice at variance with existing practice is pronounced.

Effects of Research Characteristics
on Usefulness

All five of the factors describing social science research studies (relevance, Research Quality, Conformity to User Expectations, Action Orientation, and Challenge to the Status Quo) are positively related to judgments of the usefulness of studies. The data thus confirm two of the hypotheses that we began with. Decision makers view research studies as more useful to the extent that they meet technical standards of research competence, and they view studies as more useful to the extent that they suggest practical and administratively implementable action.

However, our expectation that political acceptability is a standard by which they judge the usefulness of studies was not supported. The data confirm that respondents judge studies more useful to the extent that they are compatible with their own knowledge and values. But they contradict the hypothesis that research studies are more useful to decision makers when they are congruent with organizational philosophy, program arrangements, and the political environment.

There are two surprises in these data. The main one is the positive relationship of the Challenge to the Status Quo factor to research usefulness. The second is the strength of the positive relationship of Research Quality. Let us look at Research Quality first.

Importance of Research Quality

We had expected that the technical competence of a study would be positively associated with usefulness, but we were unprepared for the strength of the association. Not unlike the social science researchers whom we interviewed in this study, we suspected that research quality would make only marginal increments to the usefulness of a study for decision makers. However, analysis reveals that Research Quality, as they rate it, is the single most significant factor for both measures of usefulness.

At the same time, they are less impressed by the salience of Research Quality for other decision makers' use of research. When they rate the usefulness of studies for the most appropriate users, analysis shows that while Research Quality is positively related to usefulness, it ranks last among the factors for both others' likelihood of use and substantive usefulness to them. The pattern of the data suggest that, whatever their own propensities to pay greater attention to more competent research, they do not see this as common practice. There are reasons why others' reliance on Research Quality may not be visible. They do not observe other decision makers making crisp and clear-cut uses of research, and they do not understand other people's criteria for the more diffuse kinds of research use that go on. The ratings of studies by mental health decision makers themselves at all levels of government demonstrate that Research Quality does in fact influence the attention that they give to studies.

Other data shed light on reasons for allegiance to scientific merit. In analysis of specific purposes that a study could serve if it was used, Research Quality emerges as a factor that is related to the appropriateness of a study mainly for two purposes: changing ways of thinking about an issue and mobilizing support for a position or point of view. The implication appears to be that Research Quality is of value not only because of adherence to the norms of science but perhaps more importantly because it increases the power of research as ammunition in intraorganizational argument. To change minds and mobilize support, it is valuable to have research evidence of sufficient merit to withstand methodological criticism and convince others of one's case.

Positive Effect of Challenging
Research

Research that is critical of agency practice, implies a need for major change, and is not politically feasible is associated with high ratings both on substantive usefulness and on likelihood of being taken into account. Challenge to the Status Quo is a factor that is positively related to both measures of usefulness. These data run counter to much that has been written and long taken for granted about the resistance of organizations to research that threatens their policies and modes of operation. How can we reconcile these findings with our own previous knowledge and beliefs?

Challenge can apparently serve two important functions. It reveals a need for action. All is not well. Programs are falling short of their goals. Previously taken-for-granted assumptions are thrown into doubt. Something should be done. Where studies that support current agency practice have a ho-hum quality about them, challenging studies create a sense of operational discomfort that can stimulate new thinking, new planning, and a motivation to act.

Another function served by Challenge is the conceptual function of providing alternative perspectives, alternative constructions of reality. If all is not well under existing premises, challenging research can offer a different map of the terrain. Or to change the metaphor, it provides a variant angle of vision which opens up not only a new range of possible activities but a new set of questions. A way of seeing is also a way of not seeing (Kuhn 1970:111–35), and once new sightlines are opened up, some old features of the landscape fade into shadow and previously unnoticed features leap into prominence. Challenging research can thus not only make decision makers ready to change but can also restructure the questions they ask, the evidence they seek, the analyses they respond to, and the range of options they consider.

In the analysis, Challenge is one of the two most vital factors for predicting usefulness. Decision makers' ratings of research studies show that Challenge is an asset to research usefulness both for decision makers themselves and for those whom they designate as most appropriate users of the studies. There is a receptivity to controversial findings, an openness to research that assails existing practice, that suggests that decision makers are willing to take account of research with perspectives at considerable variance with current policy.

Three conditions must be kept in mind in interpreting the results. First, Challenge to the Status Quo was not negatively correlated with User Expectations; it was essentially not correlated at all. So considerable support already existed for the perspectives proffered by research that challenged agency practice.

Second, the social science research studies that respondents rated were drawn from the existing pool of federally funded studies. While they exhibited varying degrees of Challenge to accepted mental health philosophies and programs, none raised fundamental questions about the social or economic order. We are dealing with Challenge to the Status Quo within a limited range.

Third, judgments that research studies were substantively useful or likely to be taken into account did not necessarily mean that decision makers were ready to take immediate action to implement them. In fact, the significance of Challenge emphasizes that using research does not always—or even usually—mean the instrumental application of specific findings to specific decisions in the short term. Decision makers are willing to take challenging studies into account and believe that they contribute useful ideas and information, but the contribution they make apparently lies more in directing attention to possibilities for fundamental change than in directing change itself.

The importance of Challenge to the Status Quo for the usefulness of research suggests that decision makers do not limit their attention to studies of immediate feasibility. They are receptive to a spectrum of research results and prize studies that are critical of the assumptions embedded in current policy.

Truth Tests and Utility Tests

The five factors—relevance to the content of one's work, Research Quality, Conformity to User Expectations, Action Orientation, and Challenge to the Status Quo—represent decision makers' frames of reference for evaluating the utility of social science research. When we look at Research Quality and Conformity to User Expectations, we realize that both of them provide grounds for *trusting* a study. Research Quality refers to the scientific merit and authoritativeness of research. Conformity to User Expectations represents the compatibility of research with people's prior knowledge, experience, and values. People can find a study trustworthy because its conduct accords with the canons of science, and they can trust it because its results conform with their previous knowledge and understanding. The two factors provide different and independent grounds for faith in research results. One depends on the competence of the *process* of research performance, the other on the plausibility and intuitive acceptability of research *conclusions*.

Social scientists tend to denigrate decision makers' concern for the validity of research. Both the published literature and the responses of social scientists in our inquiry allege that decision makers are predominantly interested in the political or ideological advantage they can derive from research. Analysis of decision makers' ratings of studies indicates that this is not necessarily the case. What it does suggest is that decision makers have two independent means of testing research for validity. They can rely on the conceptual and methodological rigor associated with the scientific method, or they can compare research results with the understandings they have developed from their education, direct experience, observation, personal contacts, and all the previous information they have amassed. These two separate bases for assessing the trustworthiness of research represent what we have called the "truth test."

Analysis demonstrated that the effects of each component of the truth test are contingent on the other. The more a study Conforms to Expectations, the less important is the effect of its Research Quality on decision makers' likelihood of using it. Conversely, the more it departs from User Expectations, the more important it is that it be high in Research Quality. When a study yields counterintuitive findings, Research Quality becomes more essential for decision makers' willingness to pay attention to it. Thus, the truth test is composed of interdependent components whose effects are contingent upon each other.

The other two frames of reference, Action Orientation and Challenge to the Status Quo, both provide direction for action. Action-oriented research gives explicit guidance and clear direction for feasible reform. Challenging research suggests more fundamental change. It points out shortcomings in current assumptions or practice, or it demonstrates the superiority of alternative policies that have greater promise than those currently in operation. These two factors represent alternative ways in which research can give guidance for change. They comprise a "utility test."

Analysis shows that the effects of Action Orientation and Challenge to the Status Quo on decision makers' likelihood of using a research study are contingent upon each other. Action Orientation is more important for usefulness when a study does not challenge existing practice, and a challenging study is more likely to be taken into account when it is not action-oriented. When a study provides feasible direction for incremental modifications, it does not add much to its likelihood of use to show fundamental deficiencies in current practice. Similarly, when a study implies a need for basic redirection of policy, decision makers may be receptive to its ideas but they get little added push to use it from clear instructions for implementation. There is a trade-off between the two types of utility.

The analysis has disclosed that potential users of social science research filter the stream of research to which they are exposed through two basic screens: a truth test and a utility test. Research that survives the dual review will receive a hearing. Of course, passing the review does not guarantee that research will affect decisions. Decision makers work in complex systems where many wheels squeak and the supplies of grease are limited. The evidence that research provides is only one source of information, and not usually the most important, with which they deal. Research that scores high on truth and utility may not prevail. But at the least it will receive respectful attention.

Effects of Decision Makers' Characteristics
on Likelihood of Research Use

Whereas characteristics of research studies are significant predictors of decision makers' ratings of the usefulness of the studies, the characteristics of decision makers themselves are less important. We analyzed the relationship of over a score of decision-maker characteristics with their ratings of likelihood of using the studies, and once the research characteristics factors had been taken into account, only a few items were related to ratings of research usefulness. Frequent prior use of research in their work and a belief that agencies have wide options for policy are associated with higher likelihood of using a research study. Long tenure in their positions and experience as practitioners are associated (at lower levels of significance) with reduced likelihood of use. These variables add only a modest (if statistically significant) amount to the variance explained.

We analyzed the interaction of decision-maker characteristics with the research characteristics factors to see whether there were identifiable categories of decision makers who emphasized one or another of the factors in judging research usefulness. We sought to identify "types" who placed particular stress on one factor in making judgments about usefulness. The search for a "scientific type," "a managerial type," and so on, was not successful. Within the range of variables available, we found few systematic differences among decision makers in the weight that they placed on given research characteristics factors in judging usefulness. Analysis showed that prior employment in a research organization is associated with greater reliance on Research Quality in assessing a study's usefulness; belief that agencies have wide options is associated with greater reliance on Action Orientation. These are the only interactions, out of over a score examined, that approached statistical significance.

This does not mean, of course, that individuals do not differ in the weight that they assign to different characteristics of research. But our data do not reveal identifiable categories of decision makers that weight research characteristics factors in similar ways. It may often be important to know what weighting scheme an individual decision maker employs in assessing the usefulness of a study, but our data give little help in prediction. Within the range of variables examined, decision makers appear to differ idiosyncratically rather than systematically.

Decision Makers' Capacity to Specify their Criteria for Useful Research

The data analyzed in our study came *not* from decision makers' opinions of which characteristics of research would increase a study's usefulness for them but from their ratings of specific research studies. They rated the studies on descriptive dimensions and on usefulness, and our analysis focused on the association between the two sets of ratings.

Early in the interview, they also indicated which characteristics of research they believed would increase the usefulness of a study to them. Therefore, we can compare what they *say* are their criteria with what the analysis of their ratings of specific studies revealed as their criteria-in-operation.

The results of this analysis are twofold. As individuals, decision makers are poor predictors of which research characteristics affect their likelihood of using research. The relationship between stated criteria (opinions) and revealed criteria (based on ratings of specific studies) is low. However, as a group, they are relatively accurate. Averaged across individuals, the correlation between stated criteria and revealed criteria is a respectable .69.

It is possible that decision makers lack insight into which research features actually affect their judgments of usefulness. Or it may be that they use complicated decision models that do not lead to straightforward linear relationships between research characteristics and usefulness. They may in fact take into account the research characteristics that they say are important to them but not in one-to-one correspondence with their usefulness ratings. Their general model may not apply uniformly to each particular case. In all events, at the individual level, their reports about their criteria for useful research do not have much explanatory power.

Nevertheless, the fact that aggregate reports of criteria correlate highly with revealed criteria is not unimportant. Most decisions in agencies are not the output of a single decision maker but are the consequences of the judgments of many people in many places, all of whose assessments of information influence the decision. The composite reports of the group as a whole are a good indicator of the operative criteria for the usefulness of research studies in the aggregate. Therefore, surveying decision makers' opinions about standards for useful research may be a productive device for providing guidance to research programs.

Research Review Committees
Consider Usefulness

The research review committees that pass on proposals for social science research at NIMH, NIDA, and NIAAA use scientific merit as the primary criterion in review, but a sizable proportion of committee members also gives some weight to the potential usefulness of proposed research for mental health policy and programming. In many cases, the issue is one of trade-off between usefulness and research merit. One of the problems that they have to contend with is the unpredictability of usefulness; until a study has been done, it is difficult to foresee what its implications will be and what kind of contribution it can make. Nevertheless, a substantial minority report that they pay attention to the probable usefulness of proposed research during the review process.

Do they know usefulness when they see it? In rating the usefulness of the fifty social science studies that our inquiry presented, review committee members evidence fair agreement with decision makers. They have a reasonably good estimate of which studies are likely to meet decision makers' standards of utility. Their agreement among themselves on a study's usefulness is not particularly high, but neither is their agreement on a study's research quality. There is about as much internal discrepancy on the latter ratings, which constitute their specialty, as there is on usefulness.

Social Scientists' Orientation to
Research Usefulness

The social scientists whom we interviewed had conducted mental health research under sponsorship from NIMH, NIAAA, or NIDA. Most of them reported that they intended their studies to be useful for policy or program decision making. To assure usefulness, they concentrated on dissemination of their results to appropriate users in terms that were clear and comprehensible. Only a minority took other steps in planning and carrying out the research to see that it matched the needs of user groups. Upon completion of the study, most of them were satisfied that their results had proved to be useful.

Yet few of them are sanguine that decision makers pay much attention to social science research. What use occurs, they are inclined to believe, is marginal, erratic, dependent upon the particular situation—or else it is an opportunistic effort to justify agency activities by recourse to congenial evidence. Their ratings of the research studies presented during the interview show only a modest relationship between features of research studies and the likelihood that decision makers will take them into account; they do not perceive that characteristics of studies have major effect on decision makers' likelihood of use. The factor that their ratings disclose as most highly related to both decision makers' likelihood of use and (even more) the substantive usefulness of studies is Action Orientation. The suggestion is that the usefulness of research, in their views, is dependent primarily upon the practical guidance it provides for problem solving. Their ratings assign a much greater importance to Action Orientation than do decision makers' ratings —greater even than research review committee members' ratings. Perhaps for this reason, their ratings of the usefulness of individual studies do not match decision makers' ratings as well as do review committee members' ratings. Researchers apparently have a simplistic view of the decision-making process inside large organizations, and because they conceptualize decision-making as a series of discrete problem-solving choices, they fail to appreciate the variegated contributions that research can make.

Use of Research for
Different Purposes

When we tried to isolate the specific decisional activities for which particular kinds of studies were most suitable, we found that studies appropriate for one purpose are generally considered appropriate for other purposes as well. There are high correlations among ratings of appropriateness for different functions, even though the functions listed were as diverse as raising an issue to attention, improving existing programs, and planning new research. Superimposed upon the broad common band of usefulness are small differences associated with functions of agenda setting, problem solving, and coalition building.

It seems probable that the processes of organizational decision-making, as much as the generalized utility or nonutility of research studies, are responsible for the pattern of results. Decision-making inside an organization does not readily disaggregate into discrete activities or stages. Staff is simultaneously and iteratively engaged in developing plans, improving programs, mobilizing support for policies. The interconnectedness of activities militates against the unique association of particular studies with particular decisional activities.

Appropriate Users of
Research Studies

Just as appropriate uses for a study are difficult for respondents to single out, so too are appropriate users. Respondents evidence only moderate agreement on the positions for which each study is best suited. On only 15 studies out of 50 did more than half the decision makers rating a study agree on the level of government at which the most appropriate user was located. Probably because responsibility for mental health programming is dispersed across the federal system, they believe that people at various locations can reasonably use the same information. That federal, state, and local decision makers tended to name positions at their own level of government as appropriate users somewhat more often than other respondents suggests that intimate knowledge of staff responsibilities reveals possibilities for use that outsiders are unaware of.

Over all, more than half the mentions of appropriate users for the 50 research studies were staff in local care-giving agencies. A substantial part of federally funded mental health research is evidently geared to local issues. Yet respondents' answers to opinion questions show that local decision makers are the group most critical of federal research offices for their inattention to decision makers' informational needs. They seem to be saying that despite the emphasis on local issues, research that federal agencies support is not thoroughly responsive to the concerns as local agencies define them. Federal control over research funding, both by grant and contract, combined with the concentration of research on issues related to local service provision, may not result in research of maximum relevance at either level.

Opinions on Obstacles to
Research Use

Decision makers, social science researchers, and members of research review committees tend to agree on the positive and negative features of the research-to-policy process. By and large, they believe that social science research should be used even when such use would have unfavorable consequences for an agency, but they also agree that research is not currently being widely used. They recognize that obstacles to use arise in the research sphere (particularly in the academic reward system which discourages decision-oriented research and interdisciplinary cooperation) and in the decision-making sphere (particularly because of political pressures, the tendency of agencies to ignore research that is incompatible with their interests, and decision makers' inability to specify their research needs). They also report, although with somewhat less unanimity, that government research offices fail to perform the communications function adequately, both in understanding and making known decision makers' research needs and in disseminating relevant research reports to them.

The congruity of perceptions among people in different positions indicates that they are not engaged in buck-passing or mutual recriminations. They are sensitive to the failings in their own institutions as well as in the institutions of others. And they evidence a measure of receptivity to reforms that could improve the contribution that research makes to decision-making.

The Meaning of Research Use

A major reinterpretation that emerges from the inquiry is the meaning of "use of research." The conventional interpretation is the direct application of the findings of a study to the solution of a problem: a decision is pending, research provides information that is lacking, and with the information in hand the decision maker makes a decision. Such uses occur, but they are rare. Particularly when social science research is done outside the agency, the likelihood is small that a study's results will match the problems, information gaps, and available options confronting a decision maker with sufficient exactness to be translatable directly into action.

As the decision makers whom we interviewed reported, a much more common mode of research use is the diffuse and undirected infiltration of research ideas into their understanding of the world. They reported few deliberate and targeted uses of the findings from individual studies. Rather they absorbed the concepts and general-izations from many studies over extended periods of time and they integrated research ideas, along with other information, into their interpretation of events. This gradual sensitization to the perspectives of social science, they believe, has important consequences. Over time it affects what they think and what they do. It is not planned and conscious use, not directed toward immediate applications, but the research information and ideas that percolate into their stock of knowledge represent a part of the intellectual capital upon which they draw in the regular course of their work.

Our inquiry was not the first to note the largely conceptual nature of research use. Observers have commented upon it before (e.g. Crawford and Biderman 1969; Janowitz 1970) and several recent research studies have come up with similar findings (Caplan, Morrison, and Stambaugh 1975; Rich 1975; Knorr 1977; Patton et al. 1977). As Albert B. Cherns has written:

Much of the trouble lies in our notions about the application of research. We tend to have sophisticated ideas about it when we discuss it in terms of "sociology of knowledge," but to revert to simplistic models when we are arguing about "application" and "applied research." . . . [W]e take over a model derived from a false reading of the translation of research in the natural sciences into technological developments. (Cherns 1972:18)

Respondents reported other types of research use as well. A few gave illustrations of clear and direct uses of research for particular decisions. Some use research as a form of continuing education to keep abreast of new developments in the field and maintain their expertise. Others rely on research to reduce uncertainty and increase their confidence in their own judgments. Still others use research as a source of legitimation—to convince the people with whom they deal of their viewpoints or to justify their programs and their budgets.

But the indirect and undirected use of research was a major theme. Because the link between their intake of social science research and their output of actions is so tenuous and ill defined, they find it difficult to cite particular studies that influence particular actions. The connection is underground, shielded even from their own awareness. Yet they have a firm sense that a link exists—that research does indeed influence action.

Outsiders may scoff. It sounds like a courteous tale told to fob off a visiting social scientist and maintain their own claims to intellectual rectitude. Observers may scoff at us for taking the stories seriously. It sounds like the usual rejoinder of policy researchers when confronted with the lack of evidence of the use of their research: "The level of discussion has gone up" (e.g., Rivlin 1971:3). But we do take it seriously. Looking at changes in the definitions of issues and the kinds of policies considered and adopted in many fields over the past two decades, we believe that the influence of the social sciences has been considerable.

The process of using research shades into what we commonly think of as "learning." There seems to be a continuum, with the direct application of specific findings to a single decision at one end and a diffuse gain (or change) in understanding at the other. Internal policy analysis, which we did *not* study, is probably better suited (in style, timing, and definition of parameters) to influencing the single decision than is outside social science research (although of course it does not always do so). Social science research formulated and carried out by external investigators seems likely to have its effects by modifying the climate of informed opinion. When it diffuses through an agency, either directly through the printed word or through the intervention of consultants, experts, professional groups, client advocates, media publicity, presidential-level advisers, influential conferences, training sessions, or any other channel or combination of channels, it can contribute to organizational learning. And in time, it may have powerful effects on which aspect of an issue the agency faces and the nature of the responses it undertakes.

Recognition that much research use involves the gradual assimilation of social science research into decision makers' understanding of issues helps to explain some of the findings in our own inquiry. The salience of Challenge to the Status Quo is the most obvious example. That decision makers find challenging studies useful, not despite their criticism of agency policy but because of it, implies that they do not expect such studies to affect today's decisions. We also found that decision makers are not good at describing their own criteria for useful research; the criteria that they report do not correspond well to the criteria that they actually apply in judging their likelihood of taking a particular study into account. But if taking a study into account is primarily a conceptual activity, then it is less surprising that they cannot specify their criteria in advance. Predicting the characteristics of studies that make a conceptual contribution is more difficult than predicting the characteristics that make a study useful for solving specific problems.

Similarly, the lack of agreement on appropriate users for a study and the indistinctness of specific functions that a study can serve are perhaps attributable in part to the amorphousness of research use. People in many positions can profit from the ideas of a study; they need not necessarily be those charged with formal responsibility for action. And many functions can be enriched by the understandings gained from a study. When research is used for enlightenment, it can permeate many phases of decision-making.

The modest levels of consensus on the usefulness of studies between decision makers and social scientists (researchers and research review committee members) may also be due to disparate definitions of use. As we have seen, social scientists' ratings of studies tend to stress the dependence of usefulness on explicit and feasible direction for action. To decision makers, this is one basis— but not the most salient—upon which usefulness depends. The nature of their utility test indicates that the characteristics associated with Challenge to the Status Quo are alternative grounds for finding a study useful. At some level of awareness, they are attuned to the conceptual, as well as the instrumental, contributions that social science research can make.

Indeterminacy of Decision-Making

If we are to deepen our understanding of research use, we have to come to terms with the phenomenon that at first seemed a technical inconvenience in the formulation of interview questions: the tendency of many "decision makers," even those in positions of considerable putative authority, to disavow that they make decisions. Combined with their descriptions of research use, it turns out that their denial of decision-making casts a rather different perspective on the whole process by which stands are taken and policies endorsed inside complex organizations. Many officials look upon the work that they do not so much as a series of discrete decisions, not even as more innocuous-sounding "choices," but as simply doing their job.

When work in authoritative positions is cast in these terms, then drawing upon appropriate knowledge becomes "part of the business of knowing one's business." The knowledge that people use is largely *tacit* knowledge. They see little opportunity for rational calculation—and little need for it. They seldom engage in explicit formulation of problems, seldom undertake directed searches for information, seldom canvass the range of alternatives available, or calculate the relative merits of each alternative. They rely on what they already know to guide their pattern of workaday activities. While they sometimes realize that their small actions will have large consequences (see, for example, the "editing" of federal guidelines cited in Davis and Salasin 1978:93–94), they work from the stock of knowledge they have already acquired. Thus, when asked to describe the conditions under which they seek out social science research, they point to the unusual case—undertaking a *new* activity, dealing with an issue that has enormous time and dollar ramifications, or to instances that require documentation and external validation—giving consultation, defending programs and budgets. Otherwise they make do with what they know.

The question can fairly be raised whether these disclaimers of decision-making represent a true perception or whether they are a bureaucratic protective device to avoid responsibility. If people don't make decisions, they cannot be held accountable for the decisions that "happen." While there may be a measure of protective coloration in the responses, they appear to be grounded in a fundamental and pervasive view of organizational life.

The acts of any one official are hemmed in not only by the history, traditions, and standard operating procedures of the agency but also by the acts of other staff members scattered across many bureaus, divisions, and departments. In fields like mental health, where authority is also dispersed across federal, state, and local levels, even more staff have a say before a "decision" is reached—not to mention the increasingly vocal (and increasingly institutionalized) participation of professional groups, client groups, and citizens. And there is the potential for intervention by politically appointed officials, legislatures, and the courts. The latitude for action by any individual is limited by the involvement of many people in many locations, people who can speak out, argue, object, or veto a course of action and people who can silently distort or undermine (by direction or indirection) the decisions made elsewhere. Even on relatively small matters, staff in large bureaucracies have to take the viewpoints of many other people into account if they want to nudge policy in a given direction. Nor does the involvement of others need to be direct or overt. Staff often engage in a kind of implicit self-censorship of policy courses that they have reason to believe "will not fly."

Even those at the top of the hierarchy sometimes aver that they do not "make" decisions. At the highest levels, the reasoning may be somewhat different. Top officials recognize that they say yes or no and that the saying is usually decisive. But they see themselves as often rubber-stamping decisions that have already been made in the maze of offices below. By the time the issue reaches them, so many separate steps have been taken, so many accommodations have been reached among interested parties, that their options are constricted. All that remains for them to do is "sign off." They have neither the time, the knowledge, nor the option for delay that would be required to review each issue from the ground up. Nor would they prosper by continually overruling their subordinates. Thus, they often feel that their "decisions" are prefabricated for them— although the many people who have participated in the fabricating process may have little sense that they were influential.

If this is a reasonably accurate account of much that goes on inside large organizations, then it suggests that many of the ways in which we think about decision-making stand in need of revision. We may need a somewhat different perspective and perhaps a different vocabulary. At the least, this view suggests that the role of policy research and analysis needs to be reconsidered. Information specifically geared to "decision points," "decision deadlines," and "decision makers" may be relevant in a surprisingly limited number of instances. When most people most of the time operate from the knowledge base that they have acquired informally and haphazardly over time, research and analysis have to become incorporated into that base if they are to be influential. Relevant research and analysis should flow to multiple audiences through multiple channels. The stream of research should match the undifferentiated, fragmented, and multilayered stream of "decisions." In fact, the amorphous and indirect absorption of research knowledge that many of our respondents report seems to match the mode of "decision-making" in which they engage.

But this is by no means to suggest that everything is peachy. It is not to say that agencies are making the best possible use of research that conditions allow. Not at all. Much of the research that officials absorb is undoubtedly incomplete, biased, or obsolete, and what they remember of it is apt to be oversimplified or distorted in recollection. Their undirected acquisition of social science research gives little protection against the faddish and the shoddy; there are no mechanisms of quality control. There are no correctives against biases in their memory or frailties in their understanding. The ways in which social science research currently influences organizational action can result in "endarkenment" as well as enlightenment.

We have shown that social science research is neither rejected nor neglected. But knowing this should not negate the quest for better means to bring its contributions to bear. The implications, however, are different from those that are usually drawn in discussions of research use. The issue, as we see it, is not necessarily to *increase* the use of research in decision-making. Rather it is to understand organizational (and political) decision-making more aptly and to devise means by which social science research can *better* contribute to the wisdom of decisions.

Contributions of Research

Bias will out. Clearly we believe that social science research can contribute to the understanding that officials bring to their work and therefore indirectly to the caliber of the actions that they take and the courses they pursue. We do not denigrate the importance of their experience and firsthand knowledge. Direct participation has taught them a great deal about their field, the organizations in which they work, the wants of clienteles and citizens, and the constraining political parameters. Experience and practical knowledge are essential components of their expertise, and even though they give officials a partial view of a complex reality, they are not lightly to be jettisoned because some social science research study suggests actions at variance with them. Nor do we believe that social science research can establish the long-term goals toward which agencies should aspire. The objectives and goals of action are beyond the purview of the social sciences. But social science research can contribute to clarifying goals, to elucidating the competition and occasional conflict among multiple goals, to predicting the un-anticipated and sometimes undesirable consequences of pursuing certain goals, and to identifying and analyzing the trade-offs that must be faced. The desirability of policy objectives are debated at least partly on empirical grounds, and social science research can improve the knowledge base upon which the debate rests.

Our investigation has suggested several particular kinds of contributions that social science research can make to organiza-tional action. By and large, officials value research not only for the specific data it provides but more importantly for its *ideas*. It is the generalizations and concepts from the social sciences that they often find most useful in helping them construct their images of their mission.

The ideas derived from social science research provide organiz-ing perspectives that help them make sense of experience. These ideas offer frameworks within which problems are interpreted and policy actions considered. They serve the vital function of helping people recognize the persisting patterns in the situations they encounter. Retrospectively, they help them understand what the agency has been doing, why they have been doing it, and what the consequences have been. Ideas like "creaming" (i.e., serving people most likely to succeed rather than those most in need), "labeling" (stigmatizing clients through the process of "serving" them), and "professional dominance" help to provide insight. Prospectively, such perspectives help raise the possibility of alternative courses of action. When agencies recognize what they have been doing, and what the incentives for such action have been, they have a chance to reconsider.

Perhaps most valuable of all, social science research can be a medium of criticism. As the respondents in our inquiry suggested, subjecting old assumptions to empirical test and introducing alternative perspectives are vital contributions. Each person individually may have twinges of doubt about the viability of certain agency policies, but in the hubbub of activity, she stills the doubts to get on with the job. When social science research demonstrates the ineffectiveness or negative side effects of policy, or the invalidity of the premises on which policy rests, it can crystallize submerged concerns. At times it identifies unsuspected failures. By showing where things are going wrong, it can provide a time and an occasion for rethinking old practices and perhaps mapping new ones. Every agency, even the most progressive, tends to settle into routine, to take its activities for granted, to grow stale and repetitive. What social science research can do is counteract the mustiness in the corridors of power with critical insights and sharp new perspectives. In its role as critic, social science may provide its most valuable, and valued, contribution. Even if it does not prevail, it offers officials a conceptual language with which to rethink accustomed practice.

Of course, the use of social science research in public organizations has its dimmer side as well. There are costs—and possible negative effects—to be entered into the ledger. Research is not a free good. It requires time and money, often substantial sums of money, and more time and money for systematic analysis by in-house staff of the implications of research for government action. Research can be pressed into service for a variety of purposes that have little to do with improvement of policy: it can be used to legitimate existing policies, to stake out turf for one agency in interagency struggles over domain, to create beachheads for further government intervention, to develop politically active constituencies of research grant recipients (e.g., in medical schools) who will support agency programs and budgets, to acquire an aura of respectability for an agency that supports research, to parry demands that something be done in an area, to delay action ("we're studying the subject"), to justify inaction ("we have to study further") (Weiss 1979). Such kinds of "uses" of research are not unknown.

Yet for all the distortions—and the waste—that beset government sponsorship and use of social science research, its consequences on balance may be benign. Even when funded by agencies for self-serving purposes, it often produces conclusions that add to understanding. Even when used as ammunition by one faction in a controversy, its results become known to other parties as well and perhaps strengthen the case of advocates of the position that the research supports. And since social science research appears to make a major contribution through the meaning it ascribes to events, its interpretive value can withstand—or outflank—efforts at self-serving application.

Toward a Sociology of Knowledge Application

We have presented a set of data, analysis, interpretation, and at the end, some biased hopes and hopeful biases. Much remains to be learned. If we are to make headway in understanding the phenomena of research use (or the use of any form of systematic information), we must recognize the complexities of the subject. Then we will have to develop a field of study to systematically investigate the many interacting elements.

Following Holzner, we have called this emerging field the sociology of knowledge application. (Perhaps it should be an interdisciplinary social science of knowledge application, since it might well have psychological, economic, and political science dimensions as well.) It is probably too early to set an agenda for its development, but we can present a preliminary prospectus, at least for that portion of "knowledge" that derives from social science research. As we see the field emerging, a sociology of knowledge application would attend to at least five main sets of questions.

The first questions have to do with the social science research enterprise. If social science research enters the policy sphere and influences the manner in which officials perceive and think about policy, the nature of the research that social scientists perform is a matter of some moment. We will want to know what kinds of research are undertaken and what conditions shape the nature of the research. How do social scientists select the research they do? What are the personal, social, and structural conditions that play a part in which topics they study and which aspects of the topic they pursue? To what extent do the traditions and fashions of the disciplines reward certain types of investigations and inhibit others? To what extent do conventional methodological practices in each discipline shape the nature of the questions that are asked and the direction of inquiry? To what extent are the political and ideological proclivities of social scientists determining factors? To what extent do the funding policies of government agencies shut off certain lines of inquiry and encourage others? How do these factors change, under what pressures, and how quickly?

To what extent do social scientists intend their work to influence action? What are the channels through which they expect this influence to flow? When they intend their research to affect government policy directly, how does the expectation affect the work they do and how they do it? When they consider themselves pure scientists, detached critics, or advocates for underrepresented causes, what kinds of research do they do and where do they publish it? What is the effect of their institutional auspices? the source of their funding? their own status?

What is the scientific quality of research done for different avowed purposes? What other dimensions of research vary by purpose, location, funding? The sociology of social science would consider a host of questions along these lines.

A second set of questions concerns the transmission of social science research. The general question is how knowledge of social science research is communicated to policy actors. What are the channels—professional, popular, and personal—through which information flows? Which audiences are reached by different channels? When research results are abstracted from disciplinary journals and books for policy audiences (by the media, consultants, newsletters, etc.), what kinds of biases and distortions are introduced? How do the biases differ by channel? Are there differences in clarity and cogency by channel? How long does it take for messages to get through, and what factors affect the time lag? Where are research results synthesized, and how are contradictions and discrepancies among studies communicated, resolved, explained, or left implicit?

Third is the reception of social science research by people in positions of influence both inside government and out. How interested and active are influentials in finding out about research? What accounts for differences in interest? How do they evaluate the research that they hear about, and what criteria govern their attention to research? What are the properties of the research they accept and what are the properties of the research they dismiss? How important for their acceptance is the source of the research? of the channel through which they hear about it?

This is the area on which our inquiry focused. Do people in other positions or other fields evidence similar patterns of behavior?

A fourth topic is the effect of social science research on action. This, as we have seen, is an exceedingly murky area and difficult to study, but the questions remain central. What are the circumstances under which policy actors draw upon social science in taking action? What do they use—data, findings, generalizations, concepts, theories? How closely does their understanding of the social science that they use approximate the meaning that social scientists intended to convey? *How* do they use their knowledge of social science? What is the relative contribution that social science makes to their actions compared with other sources of knowledge? Finally, and perhaps most difficult of all to analyze, what are the consequences of applying social science to the work they do? Are policies grounded in social science knowledge more effective or efficient in reaching their goals? Does reliance on social science tend to move policy in a particular ideological (e.g., more egalitarian) direction? Does drawing upon social science "improve" the quality of decisions? Can we ever, even in historical time, tell?

Finally, we come to the question: *cui bono*? To whose advantage does the use of social science accrue? Is it always government that uses social science, or do "out" groups who oppose the administration (or the regime) use it as well? When government uses social science, under what conditions does it benefit the groups in office and when does it support the interests of constituencies or underrepresented minorities? Under what circumstances does it buttress existing policy? support incremental change and reform? or lend support to fundamental change in the institutions and power relationships in the society?

This long-range agenda for a sociology of knowledge application represents an immodest proposal. Given the complexity of the issues and the limited methods available for their study, the development of a body of systematic knowledge on all these issues will be a long time coming. But we have the capacity to investigate at least the first three sets of issues now, and they are perhaps most salient for immediate understanding of research use.

The Process of Decision-Making

However well we come to understand the nature, flow, and response to social science research, if we are ever to discern its influence on public policy we will have to confront the realities of the decision-making process. Only with better awareness of the convoluted ways in which decisions take shape—and the complex interplay of situations, problems, opportunities, and actors—will we make headway in untangling the contributions of social science knowledge to the formation of policy.

An unanticipated insight from our inquiry was the disparity between the analytic models of decision-making that dominate the academic and professional literature and the perceptions of decision-making by participants in the process. We need to learn more about the activities that officials perform and the conditions under which they do and do not define their activities as making decisions. Since it appears likely that the manner in which they conceptualize their tasks affects whether and how they bring external knowledge to bear and the blend of knowledge that they draw upon, a better understanding of decision-making will help to sort out the role of knowledge in policy decisions.

A more realistic grasp of decision-making will not only forward the study of the uses of social science and other forms of knowledge. It is a subject eminently worth further study in its own right. Although scholars in political science and public administration have done a considerable amount of research on governmental decision-making, the cases they have selected for attention tend to be highly politicized, controversial, and visible decisions. The humdrum activities of the workaday bureaucracy have gone largely unexplored. Yet it is there that many of the most consequential acts are taken, there that the accumulation of actions (and inaction) piles up into the massive policies that affect our daily lives.

As the burgeoning literature on policy implementation has demonstrated, the adoption of a policy is only one step in a long sequence of events. *How* the policy is implemented by the operating bureaucracies—the delays, conflicts, and distortions that attend its implementation—can undo or reshape its effects (e.g., Pressman and Wildavsky 1973; Hargrove 1975; Williams and Elmore 1976; Bardach 1977). Similarly, *before* a policy is adopted, a multiplicity of actors have a hand in stirring the policy pot. Their "routine" activities inside government bureaus (and legislative staff offices) have incremental effects on the development of new policies and the modification of existing policies. The course of decisions made outside the glare of presidential action or legislative voting, issues decided at the level of "subsystem politics," tends to be opaque, screened from the view not only of observers but of most of the participants themselves. It is difficult to discern the origin of the initial idea, its nomadic course through bureaucratic warrens, its permutations, perturbations, and shifts of focus, through the eventual emergence of a full-blown policy proposal or action. Yet these are critical components in the public policy-making process. We need clearer understanding of effective participation, critical decision points, sources of influence, and levers of control. And, of course, of the mixtures of knowledge, interests, and ideology that actors bring to bear on the development of policy.

Coda

Knowledge is only one component that enters into policy, but it has a sinuous and pervasive effect. What policy actors "know" about the form and extent of need and the appropriateness and availability of interventions permeates policy discussion at every level. Social science research provides only one component of knowledge. Yet, as we have seen in this inquiry, it can carry a special authoritativeness, in part because it is presumed to have the systematic and objective hallmark of science and in part because its concepts provide a powerful vocabulary that shapes the definition of issues. The social sciences have become a language of discourse in which policy discussion is increasingly carried on.

Yet in the end it is unrealistic to think of social science solely as an independent variable that affects the dependent variable of policy. The social sciences and public policy interact in multiple and iterative ways. Often it is not until government intervenes in a policy arena with operating programs that funding for social science research becomes available and work begins. Policy stimulates research just as research stimulates policy. And both policy and social science respond to the larger currents of intellectual thought (Cohen and Weiss 1977; Aaron 1978). Both public policy and social science in their complex interconnectedness are shaped by the fads and fancies of the period and by the historical development of social ideas. They are both part of the intellectual enterprise of the time.

Appendix A
ILLUSTRATIONS OF STUDY ABSTRACTS

ABSTRACT 11

Changing Patterns of Delinquent Behavior Among Americans 13 to 16 Years Old: 1967–1972. Martin Gold and David J. Reimer, Institute for Social Research, University of Michigan, 1973.

OBJECTIVES

1. To report change in the nature and levels of delinquent behavior among American adolescents 1967 to 1972;

2. To explain changes in patterns of delinquent behavior by examining the perceptions and attitudes of adolescents.

METHOD

Sample/Site

Data from the 1967 and 1972 National Surveys of Youth were compared. For the 1967 sample, households containing a 13–16 year-old teenager were selected from previous national survey lists. The 1972 survey used a multistage sample design first to select 40 interviewing sites throughout the U.S., stratified by population size, and then within each area to randomly select 1600 dwelling units with teenagers 11–18 years old. One 13–16 year-old per household was interviewed. 847 respondents in 1967 and 661 in 1972 were interviewed.

Variables Investigated

Dependent Variables: Delinquent behavior was measured by self-report of respondents: admitting to committing one of 17 delinquent acts "once" or "more than once" in the past three years. Four indices were created: total frequency of significant (or "chargeable") incidents; total seriousness index (a summary figure for the total seriousness of all delinquent acts reported); total frequency of significant incidents, omitting drug use; frequency of marijuana and other drug use, omitting alcohol.

Independent Variables: Age; sex; SES (defined by parents' occupation using the Duncan Socioeconomic Index); area of residence (urban, suburban, town, rural); frequency of dating; autonomy from parents (measured by freedom to dress

277

and spend spare time as they pleased); perception of drug use among other teenagers.

Data Collection and Analysis

Interviews were conducted outside the respondent's home in hospitals, community centers, and libraries. Interviewers were young adults matched to the respondents by sex. Average length of the interview was an hour and fifteen minutes.

Population characteristics of age, sex, and race were compared between samples and to census data. Adjustment of the samples was necessary to equalize age and sex-race differences between samples, which proved significantly different upon analysis. Random deletions were made from the 1972 sample to match it with the 1967 proportions.

Means, crosstabulations, and correlation coefficients were used to analyze the data. Chi-square and the Mann-Whitney U-test were used to test the significance of differences between the two samples.

FINDINGS

1. The most important result of the comparison of the surveys is not that the amount of delinquency had changed from 1967 to 1972 but that the style had changed. Boys in 1972 reported significantly less delinquent behavior than their peers in 1967: less larceny, threatened assault, trespassing, forcible and non-forcible entry, and gang fighting. But they admitted to a tenfold increase in the use of illicit drugs (especially marijuana).

2. Girls in 1972 reported more delinquent behavior overall than girls in 1967, but no difference in the seriousness of crimes. The frequency of drinking doubled, and the per capita use of drugs was nine times greater, but they reported less larceny, property damage, and breaking and entering.

3. The dramatic increase in marijuana use may be explained by the low level of use reported in 1967: boys (2.1%); girls (2.4%).

4. There was little difference between blacks and whites in the changes from 1967 to 1972, although seriousness declined somewhat among white males.

5. There were no differences in the frequency of delinquency by SES: for males there was an overall drop in delinquency from 1967 to 1972 at all SES levels, but the decline was greatest in the low SES group and smallest in the high SES group. Use of marijuana and other drugs increased significantly for each SES group but the increase was much larger in the medium SES group (from 2.4% to 26.7% admitting use) than in the low SES group (from 0.7% to 7.8%).

6. Correlations between dating and drug use were higher ($r = .52$) than between dating and other delinquent behaviors ($r = .28$).

7. The amount of autonomy that parents permitted their sons increased significantly ($p < .05$) from 1967 to 1972. In 1967, autonomy was related to *less* use of drugs among boys, but in 1972 it was related to *more* use of drugs.

8. Adolescents' perceptions of how many teenagers used drugs shifted with their change in drug use from 1967 to 1972, so that the later sample, especially high-

dating boys, reported more drug use among other teenagers ($p < .01$). In 1967, both drug users and non-users perceived themselves as outside the typical adolescent behavior pattern, but in 1972 frequent drug use among socially active teens was perceived as typical behavior.

9. Adolescents in rural areas did not increase their use of drugs; this may be due to the fact that rural 15–16 year-old girls experienced only half the increase in dating frequency of their urban counterparts; rural boys did not experience greater autonomy from 1967 to 1972; rural boys did not perceive drug use as typical adolescent behavior.

CONCLUSIONS AND RECOMMENDATIONS

1. Use of drugs is more closely related to heavy involvement in adolescent social life than any other kind of delinquent behavior. Dating boys is especially important to girls' use of drugs, and greater use by girls in 1972 may be a function not only of their dates' heavier use but also of more frequent dating.

2. Newspapers and magazines continuously reported a rise in delinquency between 1967 and 1972, yet according to adolescent self-reports neither frequency nor seriousness increased. Official data on which journalistic accounts are based are tied so loosely to actual behavior that they are more sensitive to changes in measurement than they are to the object being studied. This survey's data more closely approximate the real levels and nature of juvenile delinquency and they do not provide any evidence of a juvenile crime wave.

3. While it might be assumed that youngsters would be more irresponsible when high and increase their delinquent behavior while out of control, this is not the case. Instead, marijuana use has become defined as just deviant enough to earn a reputation for deviance without inflicting extremely punishing consequences. Use of marijuana no longer requires alienation from parents, and it seems that drug use in 1967 was a symptom of rebellion while it isn't in 1972.

4. Generally, relationships with parents either provoke or restrain delinquent behavior, and probably figure more as a restraining than provoking factor. Generally, adolescents take their parents' attitudes into account in their delinquent behavior. However, delinquent behavior seems not so sensitive to changes in parent-adolescent relationships as is generally assumed. Important as this factor is, it is not the sole component in explaining delinquency.

ABSTRACT 43

Reentering the Community: A Pilot Study of Mentally Ill Patients Discharged from Napa State Hospital. Dorothy M. Place and Samuel Weiner, Stanford Research Institute, 1974.

OBJECTIVES

To describe the experiences of patients discharged from a state mental hospital in order to determine how community mental health facilities are used by ex-patients, and the outcome of their use.

METHOD

Sample/Site

(1) 160 adult patients discharged from Napa State Hospital, Napa County, California in July, 1973 who were given referrals to a Community Mental Health Center (CMHC). (The 110 other dischargees did not qualify as potential voluntary users of CMH facilities; they included patients returned to criminal justice systems or other hospitals, those who were given no referrals or left California, and adolescents.)

(2) 20 hospital patients considered by the staff likely to be discharged within 6 weeks of the initiation of the study. 18 were schizophrenic; two were manic-depressive. 16 of the sample were released on schedule and included in the study.

(3) 70 ex-patients discharged from Napa State Hospital during November, 1973, only 15 of whom could be located and would agree to be interviewed.

Variables Investigated

Dependent Variables: Patient contact with community mental health facility; rehospitalization; and for groups (2) and (3), patient satisfaction with post-hospital living and working arrangements.

Independent Variables: Hospital admission procedures, age, race, sex, marital status, length of hospitalization, type of mental illness, number of previous hospitalizations, type of community facility recommended.

Data Collection

Data for the first sample were gathered by mail questionnaire sent to the CMHCs to which the 160 patients had been referred. The requested information about participation in the facilities' programs was received for 71% of the referred patients.

Patients in the second (prospective) sample were interviewed in depth, three times while still in the hospital and once a month for four months after discharge. Hospital interviews enabled comparison to be made between the patient's capacity to operate in the hospital and, later, in the community.

For the third (retrospective) sample, ex-patients who were living in the community shortly after their discharge were interviewed only once in their homes. The retrospective sample was chosen to test whether the prospective sample had been biased by hospital interviews.

Data were analyzed by crosstabulation; no tests of statistical significance were presented.

FINDINGS

1. The mail survey revealed that almost 2/3 (63%) of those who were referred made contact with the recommended program. Not all those who made contact, however, kept their appointments. Those most likely to contact and continue treatment were those referred to a residential facility.

2. The overall readmission rate to the hospital within 6 months after discharge

differed according to original admission procedure—whether voluntary or involuntary, etc. The number of previous hospitalizations and length of stay in the hospital did not influence rehospitalization over the period of the study. Those who made contact with community programs were no less likely to be rehospitalized than those who had no contacts, indicating that the community mental health facilities contributed little to successful reentry into the community.

3. Before discharge, each patient in the prospective sample appeared anxious to leave the hospital and looked forward to returning to life outside. The 16 patients were discharged to various living arrangements: board and care homes, their own apartments, halfway houses, a family care home, and a relative's home. All types of living arrangements were found to be deficient in some respects, and only four patients were happy with their situation. None of the 16 had been able to find employment, although only two actively sought a job. All operated on the fringes of the community, relying on an agency or other people to assist them with their problems. One member of this sample appeared to be on the way to becoming a productive member of the community. The rest were marking time in day treatment programs, or desperately holding out to delay additional hospitalization.

4. The outcomes of the 15 patients in the retrospective sample paralleled those in the prospective sample. Only two patients were happy with their living arrangements, three had been rehospitalized, and none were employed. For most, the prognosis for reentry into community life as productive people was poor.

CONCLUSIONS AND RECOMMENDATIONS

1. The major problem facing the prospective and retrospective samples was not the effect of their past mental disorders, but their inability to structure their worlds after they left the hospital. Community mental health facilities contributed little to successful reentry into the community. There is a serious lack of facilities for effective aftercare, which results in high rates of rehospitalization.

2. Breakdown in former mental patients can be traced to: (a) skills learned during hospitalization were rarely transferable to the community; (b) present methods of determining client needs, either social or medical, are inadequate; (c) community programs focus on amelioration of illness through group discussion or arts and crafts, rather than on expanding the well part of the client; (d) few programs are developed to teach the patient essential social skills to help him to survive in an uncertain environment; (e) funding provided for those patients who cannot or will not cope is at maintenance level, with few opportunities for the patient to discover new activities, living arrangements, employment, or recreation; (f) few community programs use community facilities designed to meet the needs of the general population, thus strengthening the stigma attached to mental illness.

Appendix B
DISTRIBUTIONS OF KEY STUDY VARIABLES

Table B.1. Characteristics of Respondents

	Decision Makers		Researchers and Panel Members	
Profession				
Psychiatrist	19%		13%	
Physician	6		4	
Psychologist	21		47	
Social worker	18		2	
Social scientist	1		22	
Administrator	18		7	
Other health professional	6		4	
Other	12		1	
	100%	(155)	100%	(100)
Highest degree				
M.D.	23%		17%	
Ph.D.	24		70	
Other doctorate	5		5	
M.S.W.	9		2	
Other masters	27		4	
B.A., B.S.	11		1	
None	1		1	
No information	0		1	
	100%	(155)	100%	(100)
Sex				
Male	81%		72%	
Female	19		28	
	100%	(155)	100%	(100)
Political orientation				
Radical	3%		7%	
Very liberal	13		28	
Liberal	45		52	
Moderate	34		9	
Conservative	5		4	
	100%	(151)	100%	(94)

	Decision Makers		Researchers and Panel Members	
Type of position			N/A	
Policy-maker	6%			
Program manager	48%			
Administrator of support ("staff") functions	17			
Information analyst	13			
Clinical supervisor	16			
	100%	(155)		
Years in present position			N/A	
One year or less	29%			
2 to 3 years	30			
4 to 10 years	34			
11 years or more	7			
	100%	(154)		
Years in agency				
Three years or less	34%		37%	
4 to 10 years	45		30	
11 years or more	21		33	
	100%	(152)	100%	(97)
Years in government			N/A	
Three years or less	15%			
4 to 10 years	36			
11 years or more	49			
	100%	(153)		
Full-time work experience				
University teaching department	28%		76%	
University social science research institute	7		24	
Nonprofit (nonuniversity) social research institute	6		31	
For-profit social research or consulting organization	5		7	
Federal government	54		25	
State or local government	70		28	
Mental health care-giving agency	78		37	
Other direct service or private practice	44		25	
Business or industry	29	(154)	15	(99)
Best sources of research information for self				
Academic, scientific, professional journals	54%		74%	
Literature, library, papers unspecified	20		29	
Mass media, mass circulation magazines	11		7	
Intramural staff, internal colleagues	16		0	
Researchers outside own institution	7		13	
Word of mouth, people generally	22		30	
Meetings, conferences	7		17	
Other	13	(147)	9	(98)

	Decision Makers		Perceptions About Decision Makers	
Extent of use of social science research on the job				
Frequent use, integral to the job	34%		7%	
Occasional, nonregular	31		26	
Infrequent, accidental	25		64	
No use of research	11		2	
	101%	(155)	99%	(84)
Citation of specific research study used: Completeness of reference			N/A	
Complete reference (author, title, journal— at least two)	39%			
Partial reference	33			
Reference but not to research	2			
No specific reference, although has used research	16			
No reference, no use	10			
	100%	(152)		
Source of specific research study cited as used			N/A	
Done within own agency	11%			
Done outside own agency	86			
No information	3			
	100%	(113)		
Publication status of research study cited as used			N/A	
Published book or journal article	54%			
Unpublished, including agency documents	19			
No information	27			
	100%	(113)		
Frequency of seeking out research			N/A	
Often (12 or more times a year)	48%			
Sometimes (2–11 times a year)	31			
Rarely, never	21			
	100%	(152)		
Writings based on social science research: Books				
Two or more	18%		47%	
One	11		18	
None	70		34	
	99%	(88)	99%	(99)

284

	Decision Makers		Perceptions About Decision Makers	
Writings based on social science research: Articles				
Ten or more	23%		79%	
1 to 9	34		21	
None	43		0	
	100%	(155)	100%	(100)
Writings based on social science research: Unpublished reports				
Five or more	18%		66%	
1 to 4	38		34	
None	44		0	
	100%	(155)	100%	(99)

Table B.2. Characteristics of Social Research Studies Rated by Respondents

Type of research organization conducting study	
Service agency	30%
University	26
For-profit research organization	20
Nonuniversity nonprofit research organization	12
State or local government agency	8
Other	4
	100% (50)
Type of award	
Grant	74%
Contract	26
	100% (50)
Length of study (in years)	
One year	20%
Two years	14
Three years	28
Four to seven years	24
No information	14
	100% (50)
Nature of study	
Descriptive	22%
Causal analysis	28
Analysis of program process, implementation	16
Outcome evaluation	34
	100% (50)

285

Table B.2. *(Continued)*

	Decision Makers' Ratings		Researchers' and Panel Members' Ratings	
Respondent had seen or heard of study before				
Yes	14%		14%	
No	86		86	
	100%	(310)	100%	(199)
Respondent had heard of researcher				
Yes	23%		24%	
No	77		76	
	100%	(297)	100%	(190)
Respondents' judgment of researcher's reputation				
Excellent, very good	56%		35%	
Good, OK (qualified)	42		62	
Not so good, poor	2		3	
	100%	(43)	100%	(29)

Table B.3. Positions Cited by Respondents as Most Appropriate Users of Research Studies

	Decision Makers' Ratings		Researchers' and Panel Members' Ratings	
Position				
Policy-making	24%		31%	
Managerial	36		38	
Direct service professional	23		19	
Planning, program development, evaluation	13		7	
Research	*		2	
Everybody	1		1	
Other	2		2	
	100%	(271)	100%	(175)
Functional area				
Mental health, mental retardation	49%		48%	
Alcoholism	9		11	
Drug abuse	7		2	
Social work	13		14	
Education	9		11	
Criminal justice	2		2	
Legislation	1		5	
Other	10		7	
	100%	(274)	100%	(176)

286

Table B.3. (*Continued*)

	Decision Makers' Ratings	Researchers' and Panel Members' Ratings
Intergovernmental level		
Federal	15%	16%
State	15	14
City, county, town	3	6
Care-giving agency	54	55
None	6	7
Other	7	1
	100% (271)	100% (176)

*Less than 0.5%.

REFERENCES

Aaron, Henry J. 1978. *Politics and the Professors: The Great Society in Perspective.* Washington, D.C.: Brookings Institution.

Agger, Robert E., Daniel Goldrich, and Bert E. Swanson. 1964. *The Rulers and The Ruled.* New York: Wiley.

Aiken, M. and J. Hage. 1968. "The Relationship Between Organizational Factors and the Acceptance of New Rehabilitation Programs in Mental Retardation." Washington, D.C.: Social and Rehabilitation Service (report of project RD-1556-G, January 1).

Allison, Graham T. 1971. *Essence of Decision: Explaining the Cuban Missile Crisis.* Boston: Little, Brown.

Archibald, Kathleen A. 1968. *The Utilization of Social Research and Policy Analysis.* Ph.D. dissertation, Washington University. Ann Arbor, Mich.: University Microfilms (No. 68–10, 771).

Argyris, Chris. 1976. "Single-Loop and Double-Loop Models in Research on Decision-Making." *Administrative Science Quarterly* (September), 21(3):363–75.

Bardach, Eugene. 1977. *The Implementation Game: What Happens After a Bill Becomes a Law.* Cambridge, Mass.: MIT Press.

Barnard, Chester I. 1962. *The Functions of the Executive.* Cambridge, Mass.: Harvard University Press (1st ed. 1938).

Barton, Allen H. 1973. "Problems of Applied Research: Some Examples from an Applied Research Bureau." Paper presented at Conference on the Utilization of Applied Research, Greyston Conference Center, Riverdale, N.Y. (November 29–30).

Bauer, Raymond A. 1963. "Problem-Solving Behavior in Organizations: A Functional Point of View." In M.M. Hargrove, I.H. Harrison, and E.L. Swearingen, eds., *Business Policy Cases—With Behavioral Science Implications,* pp. 29–62. Homewood, Ill.: Richard D. Irwin.

Becker, Marshal H. 1970. "Factors Affecting Diffusion of Innovations Among Health Professionals." *American Journal of Public Health* 60(2):294–304.

Behavior Today. 1976. "The Small Grant Program of NIMH." *Behavior Today* (December 20), 7(49):6–8.

Bem, Daryl J. 1972. "Self-Perception Theory." In Leonard Berkowitz, ed.,

Advances in Experimental Social Psychology, 6:2–62. New York: Academic Press.

Berg, Mark R., Jeffrey L. Brudney, Theodore D. Fuller, Donald N. Michael, and Beverly K. Roth. 1978. *Factors Affecting Utilization of Technology Assessment Studies in Policy-Making*. Ann Arbor, Mich.: Center for Research on Utilization of Scientific Knowledge, University of Michigan.

Bernstein, I.N. and H.E. Freeman. 1975. *Academic and Entrepreneurial Research*. New York: Russell Sage.

Berry, Dean F. 1967. *The Politics of Personnel Research*. Ann Arbor, Mich.: Bureau of Industrial Relations, University of Michigan.

Boeckmann, Margaret E. 1976. "Policy Impacts of the New Jersey Income Maintenance Experiment." *Policy Sciences* (March), 7:53–76.

Bowen, D.C., R. Perloff, and J. Jacoby. 1972. "Improving Manuscript Evaluation Procedures." *American Psychologist,* 27:221–25.

Brewer, Garry D. 1974. "The Policy Sciences Emerge: To Nurture and Structure a Discipline." *Policy Sciences* (September), 5:239–44.

Bucuvalas, Michael J. 1978. "The General Model and the Particular Decision: Decision Makers' Awareness of Their Cue Weightings." *Organizational Behavior and Human Performance,* 22:325–49.

Burt, Marvin R., Donald M. Fisk, and Harry P. Hatry. 1972. *Factors Affecting the Impact of Urban Policy Analysis: Ten Case Histories*. Washington, D.C.: Urban Institute.

Caplan, Nathan. 1975. "The Use of Social Statistics by Federal Executives with Special Attention to Policy Decisions in Education." Paper prepared for Committee on National Statistics Panel on Methodology for Statistical Priorities, National Research Council (August).

—— 1977. "A Minimal Set of Conditions Necessary for the Utilization of Social Science Knowledge in Policy Formulation at the National Level." In C.H. Weiss, ed., *Using Social Research in Public Policy Making,* pp. 183–97. Lexington, Mass.: Lexington-Heath.

Caplan, Nathan and Eugenia Barton. 1976. *Social Indicators 1973: A Study of the Relationship Between the Power of Information and Utilization by Federal Executives*. Ann Arbor: Institute for Social Research, University of Michigan.

Caplan, Nathan, Andrea Morrison, and Russell J. Stambaugh. 1975. *The Use of Social Science Knowledge in Policy Decisions at the National Level: A Report to Respondents*. Ann Arbor, Mich.: Center for Research on Utilization of Scientific Knowledge, Institute for Social Research, University of Michigan.

Caro, Francis. 1977. "Evaluation Research: An Overview." In F. Caro, ed.,

Readings in Evaluation Research, pp. 3–38. 2nd ed. New York: Russell Sage.

Carroll, Jean. 1967. "A Note on Departmental Autonomy and Innovation in Medical Schools." *Journal of Business*, 40:531–34.

Carter, Grace M. 1974. *Peer Review, Citations, and Biomedical Research Policy: NIH Grants to Medical School Faculty*. R-1583-HEW, Santa Monica, Calif.: Rand Corporation (December).

Cherns, Albert B. 1970. "Social Research and Its Diffusion: Relations Between Research Institutions and Users of Research." *International Social Science Journal*, 23:226–42.

—— 1972. "Social Sciences and Policy." In A.B. Cherns, R. Sinclair, and W.I. Jenkins, eds., *Social Science and Government; Policies and Problems*, pp. 15–35. London: Tavistock Publications.

Chinitz, Benjamin. 1972. "The Interaction Between Research and Policy." Joint Institute of Comparative and Urban Grants Economics: University of Windsor, Canada (November).

Chu, Franklin D. and Sharland Trotter. 1974. *The Madness Establishment: Ralph Nader's Study Group Report on the National Institute of Mental Health*. New York: Grossman.

Cobb, R.W. and C.D. Elder. 1976. "Issue Creation and Agenda-Building." In J.E. Anderson, ed., *Cases in Public Policy-Making*, pp. 10–21. New York: Praeger.

Cohen, David K. 1975. "The Value of Social Experiments." In A.M. Rivlin and P.M. Timpane, eds., *Planned Variation in Education: Should We Give Up or Try Harder?* Washington, D.C.: Brookings Institution.

Cohen, David K. and Michael Garet. 1975. "Reforming Educational Policy with Applied Social Research." *Harvard Educational Review* (February), 45:17–43.

Cohen, David K. and Janet A. Weiss. 1977. "Social Science and Social Policy: Schools and Race." In C.H. Weiss, ed., *Using Social Research in Public Policy Making*, pp. 67–83. Lexington, Mass.: Lexington-Heath.

Cohen, Jacob and Patricia Cohen. 1975. *Applied Multiple Regression/ Correlation Analysis for the Behavioral Sciences*. New York: Wiley.

Cole, Stephen and Jonathan R. Cole. 1978. "Reviewing Peer Review at the National Science Foundation." Paper presented at the annual meeting of the American Association for the Advancement of Science, Washington, D.C.

Coleman, James S. 1972. *Policy Research in the Social Sciences*. Morristown, N.J.: General Learning Press.

Coleman, James S., E. Katz, and H. Menzel. 1966. *Medical Innovation: A Diffusion Study*. New York: Bobbs-Merrill.

REFERENCES

Collins, Sharon M. 1978. "The Use of Social Research in the Courts." In Laurence E. Lynn, Jr., ed., *Knowledge and Policy: The Uncertain Connection*, pp. 145–83. Washington, D.C.: National Academy of Sciences.

Cowhig, James D. 1971. "Federal Grant-Supported Research and 'Relevance': Some Reservations." *American Sociologist*, 6(supp):65–69.

Crawford, Elisabeth T. and Albert D. Biderman, eds. 1969. *Social Scientists and International Affairs*. New York: Wiley.

Croker, George W. 1969. "Some Principles Regarding the Utilization of Social Science Research Within the Military." In E.T. Crawford and A.D. Biderman, eds., *Social Scientists and International Affairs*, pp. 185–94. New York: Wiley.

Dahl, Robert A. 1965. *Modern Political Analysis*. Englewood Cliffs, N.J.: Prentice-Hall.

Davis, Howard R. 1973. "Innovation and Change." In S. Feldman, ed., *Administration in Mental Health*. Springfield, Ill.: Charles C Thomas.

Davis, Howard R. and Susan E. Salasin. 1978. "Strengthening the Contribution of Social R&D to Policy Making." In Laurence E. Lynn, ed., *Knowledge and Policy: The Uncertain Connection*, pp. 93–125. Washington, D.C.: National Academy of Sciences.

Dawes, Robyn M. 1964. "Social Selection Based on Multi-dimensional Criteria." *Journal of Abnormal and Social Psychology*, 68:104–9.

Deitchman, Seymour J. 1976. *Best-Laid Schemes: A Tale of Social Research and Bureaucracy*. Cambridge, Mass.: MIT Press.

Deutsch, Albert. 1949. *The Mentally Ill in America: A History of Their Care and Treatment from Colonial Times*. New York: Columbia University Press.

Donnison, David. 1972. "Research for Policy." *Minerva* (October), 10(4): 519–36.

Dreyfus, Daniel A. 1977. "The Limitations of Policy Research in Congressional Decision-Making." In C.H. Weiss, ed., *Using Social Research in Public Policy-Making*, pp. 99–107. Lexington, Mass.: Lexington-Heath.

Einhorn, Hillel J. 1970. "The Use of Nonlinear, Noncompensatory Models in Decision Making." *Psychological Bulletin*, 73:221–30.

—— 1971. "Use of Nonlinear, Noncompensatory Models as a Function of Task and Amount of Information." *Organizational Behavior and Human Performance*, 6:1–27.

Etzioni, Amitai. 1967. "Nonconventional Uses of Sociology as Illustrated by Peace Research." In P.F. Lazarsfeld, W.H. Sewell, and H.L. Wilensky, eds., *The Uses of Sociology*, pp. 806–838. New York: Basic Books.

Evan, W.M. and G. Black. 1967. "Innovation in Business Organizations:

Some Factors Associated with Success or Failure of Staff Proposals." *Journal of Business,* 40:519–30.

Evans, John W. 1975. "Motives for Experimentation." In R.F. Boruch and H.W. Riecken, eds., *Experimental Testing of Public Policy,* pp. 15–22. Boulder, Colo.: Westview Press.

Ferman, Lewis A. 1969. "Some Perspectives on Evaluating Social Welfare Programs." *The Annals* 385:143–56.

Foley, Henry A. 1975. *Community Mental Health Legislation.* Lexington, Mass.: Lexington-Heath.

Fulton, Oliver and Martin Trow. 1972. "Research Activity in American Higher Education." Occasional paper, Center for Research in the Educational Sciences, University of Edinburgh, Scotland (April).

Gans, Herbert J. 1971. "Social Science for Social Policy." In Irving L. Horowitz, ed., *The Use and Abuse of Social Science,* pp. 13–33. New Brunswick, N.J.: Transactionbooks.

Glaser, E.M. and H.L. Ross. 1971. *Increasing the Utilization of Applied Research Results.* Final Report to National Institute of Mental Health, grant no. 5 R12-MH-09250-02. Los Angeles, Calif.: Human Interaction Research Institute.

Glaser, E.M., H.S. Coffey, J.B. Marks, and I.B. Sarason. 1966. *Utilization of Applicable Research and Demonstration Results.* Final Report to Vocational Rehabilitation Administration, project RD-1263-G. Los Angeles: Human Interaction Research Institute.

Goode, William J. 1957. "Community within a Community: The Professions." *American Sociological Review* (April), 22:194–200.

Goodwin, Leonard. 1975. *Can Social Science Help Resolve National Problems? Welfare, A Case in Point.* New York: Free Press.

Gorden, Raymond D. 1975. *Interviewing: Strategy, Techniques and Tactics.* Rev. ed. Homewood, Ill.: Dorsey Press.

Greenblatt, Milton, Richard York, and Esther Braum. 1955. *From Custodial to Therapeutic Patient Care in Mental Hospitals.* New York: Russell Sage.

Hage, J. and M. Aiken. 1970. *Social Change in Complex Organizations.* New York: Random House.

Hall, Richard. 1972. "Professionalization and Bureaucratization." In Richard Hall, ed., *The Formal Organization,* pp. 143–63. New York: Basic Books.

Halperin, Morton H. 1974. *Bureaucratic Politics and Foreign Policy.* Washington, D.C.: Brookings Institution.

Hargrove, Erwin C. 1975. *The Missing Link: The Study of the Implementation of Social Policy.* Washington, D.C.: Urban Institute.

Havelock, Ronald G. 1969a. *Planning for Innovation Through Dissem-*

ination and Utilization of Knowledge. Ann Arbor: Center for Research on Utilization of Scientific Knowledge, Institute for Social Research, University of Michigan.

—— 1969b. "Translating Theory into Practice." *Rehabilitation Record* (November–December), pp. 24–27.

Hemphill, J., D. Griffiths, and N. Fredericken. 1962. *Administrative Performance and Personality.* New York: Columbia University Press.

Hofferbert, Richard I. 1974. *The Study of Public Policy.* Indianapolis and New York: Bobbs-Merrill.

Holzner, B. 1978. "The Sociology of Applied Knowledge." *Sociological Symposium,* 21:8–19.

Holzner, Burkart and John H. Marx. 1979. *Knowledge Application: The Knowledge System in Society.* Boston: Allyn and Bacon.

Horowitz, Irving L. 1969. "The Academy and the Polity: Interaction Between Social Scientists and Federal Administrators." *Journal of Applied Behavioral Science,* 5:309–35.

Horowitz, Irving L., ed., 1971. *The Use and Abuse of Social Science.* New Brunswick, N.J.: Transactionbooks.

Israel, Joachim. 1966. "Remarks on the Sociology of Social Scientists." *Acta Sociologica,* 9:193–99.

Janis, I.L. and L. Mann. 1977. *Decision Making.* New York: Free Press.

Janowitz, Morris. 1970. "Sociological Models and Social Policy." In Morris Janowitz, *Political Conflict: Essays in Political Sociology,* pp. 243–59. Chicago: Quadrangle.

Janowitz, Morris, Robert Lekachman, Daniel P. Moynihan, et al. 1976. "Social Science: The Public Disenchantment: A Symposium." *American Scholar* 45: 335–59.

Joint Commission on Mental Illness and Health. 1961. *Action for Mental Health.* New York: Basic Books.

Katz, Elihu. 1961. "The Social Itinerary of Technical Change: Two Studies on the Diffusion of Innovation." *Human Organization* 20:70–82.

Kirk, Stuart A. and Aaron Rosenblatt. 1977. "Barriers to Students' Utilization of Research." Paper presented at the Annual Program Meeting of the Council on Social Work Education, Phoenix, Ariz. (March).

Kissinger, Henry A. 1979. "America's Role in Cambodia." *New York Times (The Week in Review),* September 23, p. E19.

Knorr, Karin D. 1977. "Policymakers' Use of Social Science Knowledge: Symbolic or Instrumental?" In C.H. Weiss, ed., *Using Social Research in Public Policy Making,* pp. 165–82. Lexington, Mass.: Lexington-Heath.

Kornhauser, William. 1962. *Scientists in Industry: Conflict and Accomodation.* Berkeley: University of California Press.

Kuhn, Thomas S. 1970. *The Structure of Scientific Revolutions.* 2nd ed. Chicago: University of Chicago Press.

Lampman, Robert J. 1974. "What Does it do for the Poor? A New Test for National Policy." *Public Interest* (Winter), 34:66–82.

Lasswell, H.D. 1956. *The Decision Process.* College Park, Md.: Bureau of Government and Research.

Lazarsfeld, Paul F. and Jeffrey G. Reitz. 1975. *An Introduction to Applied Sociology.* Amsterdam and New York: Elsevier.

Lazarsfeld, Paul F., William H. Sewell, and Harold L. Wilensky, eds. 1967. *The Uses of Sociology.* New York: Basic Books.

Lindblom, Charles E. 1968. *The Policy-Making Process.* Englewood Cliffs, N.J.: Prentice-Hall.

Lindblom, Charles E. and David K. Cohen. 1979. *Usable Knowledge: Social Science and Social Problem Solving.* New Haven, Conn.: Yale University Press.

Lindsey, Duncan. 1978. *The Scientific Publication System in Social Science.* San Francisco: Jossey-Bass.

Lindsey, Quentin and Judith Lessler. 1976. *Utilization of RANN Research Results: The Program and Its Effects.* Research Triangle Park, N.C.: Research Triangle Institute.

Lippitt, R.O. and colleagues (staff members include: H. Barakat, M. Chesler, D. Dennerll, M. Flanders, R. Schmuck, and B. Worden). 1967. "The Teacher as Innovator, Seeker, and Sharer of New Practices." In R.E. Miller, ed., *Perspectives on Educational Change,* pp. 307–24. New York: Appleton.

Litwak, Eugene. 1961. "Models of Bureaucracy that Permit Conflict." *American Journal of Sociology* 57:173–83.

Longood, Robert and Arnold Simmel. 1972. "Organizational Resistance to Innovation Suggested by Research." In C.H. Weiss, ed., *Evaluating Action Programs: Readings in Social Action and Education,* pp. 311–17. Boston: Allyn and Bacon.

Lynd, Robert S. 1939. *Knowledge for What?* Princeton, N.J.: Princeton University Press.

Lynn, Laurence E., Jr. 1978a. "The Question of Relevance." In L.E. Lynn, Jr., ed., *Knowledge and Policy: The Uncertain Connection.* Washington, D.C.: National Academy of Sciences.

Lynn, Laurence E., Jr., ed. 1978b. *Knowledge and Policy: The Uncertain Connection.* Washington, D.C.: National Academy of Sciences.

Lyons, Gene M. 1969. *The Uneasy Partnership.* New York: Russell Sage.

McFall, David. 1978. "Peer Review of Health Sciences Research Grant Applications." *Inquiry* (September), 15:210–16.

Mackelprang, A.J. 1970. "Missing Data in Multiple Regression and Factor Analysis." *Midwest Journal of Political Science* 14: 493–505.

McLaughlin, Milbrey W. 1975. *Evaluation and Reform: The Elementary and Secondary Education Act of 1965/Title I.* Cambridge, Mass.: Ballinger.

McTavish, Donald G., Edward E. Brent, Jr., James D. Cleary, and Kjell R. Knudsen. 1975. *The Systematic Assessment and Prediction of Research Methodology.* Minneapolis, Minn.: Minnesota Systems Research.

McTavish, Donald G., J.D. Cleary, E.E. Brent, L. Perman, K.R. Knudsen. 1977. "Assessing Research Methodology: The Structure of Professional Assessments of Methodology." *Sociological Methods and Research* (August), 6(1):3–44.

Mansfield, Edwin. 1963. "The Speed of Response of Firms to New Techniques." *Quarterly Journal of Economics,* 77:290–311.

―― 1968. *Industrial Research and Technological Innovation: An Econometric Analysis.* New York: Norton.

March, James G. and Johan P. Olsen. 1976. *Ambiguity and Choice in Organizations.* Bergen-Oslo-Tromsø: Universitetforlaget.

Marcson, Simon. 1960. *The Scientist in American Industry.* New York: Harper.

Marcum, R. Laverne. 1968. *Organizational Climate and the Adoption of Educational Innovation.* Logan: Utah State University.

Marquis, D.G. and T.J. Allen. 1966. "Communication Patterns in Applied Technology." *American Psychologist,* 21: 1052–60.

Mayntz, Renate. 1977. "Sociology, Value Freedom, and the Problems of Political Counseling." In C.H. Weiss, ed., *Using Social Research in Public Policy Making,* pp. 55–65. Lexington, Mass.: Lexington-Heath.

Mechanic, David. 1969. *Mental Health and Social Policy.* Englewood Cliffs, N.J.: Prentice-Hall.

Meltsner, Arnold. 1976. Personal communication (July 27).

―― 1976b. *Policy Analysts in the Bureaucracy.* Berkeley/Los Angeles: University of California Press.

Menges, Constantine C. 1978. "Knowledge and Action: The Use of Social Science Evaluations in Decisions on Equal Educational Opportunity, 1970–73." Paper written for the National Institute of Education, Washington, D.C. (March).

Merton, Robert K. 1949. "The Role of Applied Social Science in the Formation of Policy: A Research Memorandum." *Philosophy of Science* 16(3):161–81. Reprinted as "Technical and Moral Dimensions of Policy Research," in R.K. Merton, *The Sociology of Science,* pp. 70–98. Chicago: University of Chicago Press, 1973.

—— 1961. "Social Problems and Sociological Theory." In R.K. Merton and Robert Nisbet, eds., *Contemporary Social Problems,* pp. 793–844. 3d. ed. New York: Harcourt Brace Jovanovich.

—— 1968. "Role of the Intellectual in Public Bureaucracy." In R.K. Merton, *Social Theory and Social Structure,* pp. 261–78. Enl. ed. New York: Free Press.

—— 1959. "Notes on Problem-Finding in Sociology." In R.K. Merton, Leonard Broom, and Leonard S. Cottrell, Jr., eds., *Sociology Today: Problems and Prospects,* pp. ix–xxxiv. New York: Basic Books.

Merton, Robert K. and Daniel Lerner. 1951. "Social Scientists and Research Policy." In Daniel Lerner and Harold D. Lasswell, eds., *The Policy Sciences: Recent Developments in Scope and Method,* pp. 282–307. Stanford, Calif.: Stanford University Press.

Miles, Matthew B. 1965. "Planned Change and Organizational Health: Figure and Ground." In R.O. Carlson, A. Gallaher, Jr., M.B. Miles, R.J. Pellegrin, E.M. Rogers, eds., *Change Processes in the Public Schools,* pp. 11–34. Eugene, Oreg.: Center for the Advanced Study of Education Administration, University of Oregon.

Miller, George A. 1972. "Professionals in Bureaucracy: Alienation Among Industrial Scientists and Engineers." In Richard H. Hall, ed., *The Formal Organization,* pp. 213–35. New York: Basic Books.

Millikan, Max F. 1959. "Inquiry and Policy: The Relationship of Knowledge to Action." In Daniel Lerner, ed., *The Human Meaning of the Social Sciences,* pp. 158–80. New York: World.

Moynihan, Daniel P. 1969. *Maximum Feasible Misunderstanding: Community Action in the War on Poverty.* New York: Free Press.

Nagel, Stuart and Marian Neef, eds. 1975. *The Political Science Utilization Directory.* Urbana, Ill.: Policy Studies Organization, University of Illinois.

National Academy of Sciences, Social Science Research Council. 1969. *The Behavioral and Social Sciences: Outlook and Needs.* Englewood Cliffs, N.J.: Prentice-Hall.

National Academy of Sciences. 1978. *The Federal Investment in Knowledge of Social Problems.* Washington, D.C.: National Academy of Sciences.

National Institute of Mental Health, Division of Mental Health Service Programs. 1977. "Special Report: Status of the Community Support Program." *For Your Information* (March).

National Institute of Mental Health, Research Task Force. 1975. *Research in the Service of Mental Health: Report of the Research Task Force of the National Institute of Mental Health.* Washington, D.C.: NIMH.

National Institutes of Health, Division of Research Grants. 1973. *Orientation Handbook for New Members of Study Sections.* Washington, D.C.: National Institutes of Health.

National Institutes of Health, Grants Peer Review Study Team. 1976. *Report to the Director, NIH Phase I.* Vol. 1 (December). Washington, D.C.: U.S. Government Printing Office.

National Research Council. 1968. *The Behavioral Sciences and the Federal Government.* Washington, D.C.: National Academy of Sciences.

—— 1971. *Behavioral and Social Science Research in the Department of Defense: A Framework for Management.* Advisory Committee on the Behavioral Science Research in the Department of Defense. Washington, D.C.: National Academy of Sciences.

—— 1976. *Social and Behavioral Science Programs in the National Science Foundation: Final Report.* Committee on the Social Sciences in the National Science Foundation. Assembly of Behavioral and Social Sciences. Washington, D.C.: National Academy of Sciences.

National Science Foundation. 1969. *Knowledge Into Action: Improving the Nation's Use of the Social Sciences.* Washington, D.C.: U.S. Government Printing Office.

—— 1978. *Federal Funds for Research, Development, and Other Scientific Activities, Fiscal Years 1977, 1978, and 1979.* Washington, D.C.: U.S. Government Printing Office.

Nisbett, Richard E. and Stuart Valins. 1972. "Perceiving the Causes of One's Own Behavior." In E.E. Jones, D.E. Kanaise, H.H. Kelley, R.E. Nisbett, S. Valins, and B. Weiner, eds., *Attribution: Perceiving the Causes of Behavior,* pp. 63–94. Morristown, N.J.: General Learning Press.

Nisbett, Richard E. and T.D. Wilson. 1977. "Telling More than We Can Know: Verbal Reports on Mental Processes." *Psychological Review,* 84(3):231–59.

Noble, John H., Jr. 1974. "Peer Review: Quality Control of Applied Social Research." *Science* (September 13), 184:916–21.

Orlans, Harold. 1968. "Making Social Research More Useful to Government." *Social Science Information* (December), 7(6):151–58.

—— 1972. "Comments on James Coleman's 'Principles Governing Policy Research.'" Paper presented at American Association for the Advancement of Science (December), excerpted in *Evaluation* (1973), 1(3):20.

—— 1973. *Contracting for Knowledge.* San Francisco: Jossey-Bass.

—— 1976. "The Advocacy of Social Science in Europe and America." *Minerva* (Spring), 14:6–32.

Patton, Michael Q., P.S. Grimes, K.M. Guthrie, N.J. Brennan, B. Dickey French, D.A. Blyth. 1977. "In Search of Impact: An Analysis of the Utilization of Federal Health Evaluation Research." In C.H. Weiss, ed., *Using Social Research in Public Policy Making,* pp. 141–63. Lexington, Mass.: Lexington-Heath.

Pelz, Donald C. 1978. "Some Expanded Perspectives on Use of Social Science in Public Policy." In J.M. Yinger and S.J. Cutler, eds., *Major Social Issues: A Multidisciplinary View,* pp. 346–57. New York: Free Press.

Pelz, Donald C. and Frank M. Andrews. 1966. *Scientists and Organizations.* New York: Wiley.

Pressman, Jeffrey L. and Aaron Wildavsky. 1973. *Implementation.* Berkeley, Los Angeles, and London: University of California Press.

Price, Donald K. 1954. "The Structure of Policy." In D.K. Price, ed., *Government and Science,* pp. 160–89. New York: New York University Press.

Redman, Eric. 1973. *The Dance of Legislation.* New York: Simon & Schuster.

Rein, Martin and Sheldon H. White. 1977. "Can Policy Research Help Policy?" *The Public Interest* (Fall), 49:119–36.

Reitz, Jeffrey G. 1968. "Resistances to the Utilization of Social Research in Decison-Making." New York: Bureau of Applied Social Research. Columbia University.

Rich, Robert F. 1975. "The Power of Information." Ph.D. dissertation, University of Chicago.

—— 1977. "Use of Social Science Information by Federal Bureaucrats: Knowledge for Action versus Knowledge for Understanding." In C.H. Weiss, ed., *Using Social Research in Public Policy Making,* pp. 199–233. Lexington,Mass.: Lexington-Heath.

Riecken, Henry W. 1967. "Government-Science Relations: the Physical and Social Sciences Compared." *American Psychologist* (March), 22(3):211–18

—— 1969. "Social Sciences and Social Problems." *Social Science Information* (February), 8(1):101–29.

Rivlin, Alice M. 1971. *Systematic Thinking for Social Action.* Washington, D.C.: Brookings Institution.

Roberts, M.J. 1974. "On the Nature and Condition of Social Science." *Deadalus* (Summer), 103(3):47–64.

Rogers, Everett M. 1962. *Diffusion of Innovations.* New York: Free Press.

—— 1967. "Communication of Vocational Rehabilitation Innovations."

Communication, Dissemination and Utilization of Rehabilitation Research Information, no. 5, pp. 19–32. Washington, D.C.: Joint Liaison Committee of the Council of State Administrators of Vocational Rehabilitation and the Rehabilitation Counselor Educators, Department of Health, Education, and Welfare, Studies in Rehabilitation Counselor Training.

Rogers, E.M., with F.F. Shoemaker. 1971. *Communication of Innovations: A Cross-Cultural Approach.* New York: Free Press.

Rose, Richard. 1969. "The Variability of Party Government." *Political Studies,* 17(4):413–45.

—— 1974. "Housing Objectives and Policy Indicators." In R. Rose, ed., *The Management of Urban Change in Britain and Germany,* pp. 115–37. London: Sage.

Rosen, Paul L. 1972. *The Supreme Court and Social Science.* Urbana: University of Illinois Press.

—— 1977. "Social Science and Judicial Policy Making." In C.H. Weiss, ed., *Using Social Research in Public Policy Making,* pp. 109–23. Lexington, Mass.: Lexington-Heath.

Rosenblatt A. 1968. "The Practitioner's Use and Evaluation of Research." *Social Work,* 13:53–59.

Rossi, Peter. 1969. "Practice, Method, and Theory in Evaluating Social Action Programs." In James L. Sundquist, ed., *On Fighting Poverty,* pp. 217–34. New York: Basic Books.

Rossi, Peter and Katharine C. Lyall. 1977. "The External Politics of the National Income Transfer Experiment." In F.G. Caro, ed., *Readings in Evaluation Research,* pp. 286–95, 2d ed., New York: Russell Sage.

Rossi, Peter H., James D. Wright, and Sonia R. Wright. 1978. "The Theory and Practice of Applied Social Research." *Evaluation Quarterly,* 2(2):171–92.

Rule, James B. 1971. "The Problem with Social Problems." *Politics and Society* (Fall), 2(1):47–56.

—— 1979. *Insight and Social Betterment: A Preface to Applied Social Science.* New York: Oxford University Press.

Rummel, Rudolph J. 1970. *Applied Factor Analysis.* Evanston, Ill.: Northwestern University Press.

Sabatier, Paul. 1978. "The Acquisition and Utilization of Technical Information by Administrative Agencies." *Administrative Science Quarterly* (September), 23:396–417.

Sadofsky, Stanley. 1966. "Utilization of Evaluation Results: Feedback into the Action Program." In J. Shmelzer, ed., *Learning in Action,* pp. 22–36. Washington, D.C.: Department of Health, Education, and Welfare.

Schon, D.A. 1967. *Technology and Change*. New York: Delacorte.
—— 1971. *Beyond the Stable State*. New York: Random House.
Schultze, Charles L. 1968. *The Politics and Economics of Public Spending*. Washington,D.C.: Brookings Institution.
Scott, W.A. 1974. "Interreferee Agreement on Some Characteristics of Manuscripts Submitted to the *Journal of Personality and Social Psychology*." *American Psychologist* 29(9):689–702.
Scott, W. Richard. 1965. "Reactions to Supervision in a Heteronomous Professional Organization." *Administrative Science Quarterly* (June), 10:65–81.
Shapley, Deborah. 1978. "Technology Creep and the Arms Race: Two Future Arms Control Problems." *Science* (October 20), 202:289–92.
Sharpe, L.J. 1977. "The Social Scientist and Policy-Making: Some Cautionary Thoughts and Transatlantic Reflections." In C.H. Weiss, ed., *Using Social Research in Public Policy Making*, pp. 37–53. Lexington, Mass.: Lexington-Heath.
Shaver, Kelly G. 1975. *An Introduction to Attribution Processes*. Cambridge, Mass.: Winthrop Publishers.
Sherwood, Clarence C. 1967. "Measuring Social Action Programs." *Welfare in Review* 5(7):13–18.
Shils, Edward A. 1949. "Social Science and Social Policy." *Philosophy of Science*, 16:219–42.
Shostak, Arthur B. 1966. *Sociology in Action*. Homewood, Ill.: Dorsey Press.
Siegel, Karolynn and Pamela Doty. 1979. "'Advocacy Research' versus 'Management Review': A Comparative Analysis." *Policy Analysis* 5(1):37–65.
Simon, Herbert A. 1976. *Administrative Behavior*. 3d ed. New York: Free Press.
Slovic, Paul, Baruch Fischhoff, and Sarah Lichtenstein. 1977. "Behavioral Decision Theory." *Annual Review of Psychology*, 28:1–39.
Slovic, Paul and Sarah Lichtenstein. 1971. "Comparison of Bayesian and Regression Approaches to the Study of Information Processing in Judgment." *Organizational Behavior and Human Performance*, 6:649–744.
Southwood, Kenneth E. 1978. "Substantive Theory and Statistical Interaction: Five Models." *American Journal of Sociology* (March), 81(5): 1154–1203.
Stanley, D.T., D.E. Mann, and J.W. Doig. 1967. *Men Who Govern: A Biographical Profile of Federal Political Executives*. Washington, D.C.: Brookings Institution.

Straussman, Jeffrey D. 1978. *Limits of Technocratic Politics.* New Brunswick, N.J.: Transactionbooks.

Suchman, Edward. 1967. *Evaluative Research: Principles and Practices in Public Service and Social Action Programs.* New York: Russell Sage.

Susser, Mervyn. 1968. *Community Psychiatry.* New York: Random House.

Taylor, Shelley E. and Susan Fiske. 1978. "Salience, Attention, and Attribution: Top of the Head Phenomena." In L. Berkowitz, ed., *Advances in Experimental Social Psychology,* 11: pp. 250–288. New York: Academic Press.

Truman, David. 1951. *The Governmental Process.* New York: Knopf.

Uliassi, Pio D. 1977. "Research and Foreign Policy: A View from Foggy Bottom." In C.H. Weiss, ed., *Using Social Research in Public Policy Making,* pp. 85–90. Lexington, Mass.: Lexington-Heath.

U.S. Congress, House Committee on Government Operations, Subcommittee on Research and Technical Programs. 1967. *The Use of Social Research in Federal Domestic Programs.* 90th Congress, 1st session. 4 vols. Washington, D.C.: U.S. Government Printing Office.

U.S. General Accounting Office. 1974. *Need for More Effective Management of Community Mental Health Centers.* Washington, D.C.: U.S. General Accounting Office.

—— 1977a. *Social Research and Development of Limited Use to National Policymakers.* HRD-77-34. Washington, D.C.: U.S. Government Printing Office.

—— 1977b. *Returning the Mentally Disabled to the Community: Government Needs to do More.* HRD-76-152. Washington, D.C.: U.S. General Accounting Office.

U.S. House of Representatives, Committee on Interstate and Foreign Commerce. 1975. *Report on H.R. 4925: Health Revenue Sharing and Health Services Act of 1975.* Report no. 94–192 (May 7).

Useem, Michael. 1976. "Government Patronage of Science and Art in America." *American Behavioral Scientist* (July), 19:785–804.

Useem, Michael and Paul DiMaggio. 1978. "An Example of Evaluation Research as a Cottage Industry: The Technical Quality and Impact of Arts Audience Studies." *Sociological Methods and Research* (August), 7(1):55–84.

Valdes, Donald M. and Dwight G. Dean. 1965. *Sociology in Use.* New York: Macmillan.

van de Vall, Mark. 1975. "Utilization and Methodology of Applied Social Research: Four Complementary Models." *Journal of Applied Behavioral Science* 11(1):14–38.

Ward, A.W., B.W. Hall, and C.F. Schram. 1975. "Evaluation of Published Educational Research—National Survey." *American Educational Research Journal,* 12:109–28.

Warner, W.L., P.P. Van Riper, N.H. Martin, and O.F. Collins. 1963. *The American Federal Executive.* New Haven, Conn.: Yale University Press.

Watson, G., ed. 1967. *Change in School Systems.* Washington, D.C.: Cooperative Project for Educational Development by National Training Laboratories, National Education Association.

Weiss, Carol H. 1977a. "Introduction." In C.H. Weiss, ed., *Using Social Research in Public Policy Making,* pp. 1–22. Lexington, Mass.: Lexington-Heath.

—— 1977b. "Methods for Studying the Usefulness of Sociological Research." Paper presented at American Sociological Association, Chicago, Ill.

—— 1979. "The Many Meanings of Research Utilization." *Public Administration Review* (September/October), 39(5):426–31.

Weiss, Janet A. 1976. "Using Social Science for Social Policy." *Policy Studies Journal* (Spring), 4(3):234–38.

—— 1979. "Access to Influence: Some Effects of Policy Sector on the Use of Social Science." *American Behavioral Scientist,* 22(3):437–58.

Weiss, Robert and Martin Rein. 1969. "The Evaluation of Broad-Aim Programs: A Cautionary Case and a Moral." *The Annals,* 385:133–42.

Wildavsky, Aaron. 1979. *Speaking Truth to Power: The Art and Craft of Policy Analysis.* Boston and London: Little, Brown.

Wilensky, Harold L. 1956. *Intellectuals in Labor Unions: Organizational Pressures on Professional Roles.* Glencoe, Ill.: Free Press.

Williams, Walter. 1971. *Social Policy Research and Analysis: The Experience in the Federal Social Agencies.* New York: Elsevier.

Williams, Walter and Richard F. Elmore. 1976. *Social Program Implementation.* New York, San Francisco, and London: Academic Press.

Wilson, James Q. 1978. "Social Sciences and Public Policy: A Personal Note." In L.E. Lynn, ed., *Knowledge and Policy: The Uncertain Connection,* pp. 82–92. Washington, D.C.: National Academy of Sciences.

Wirt, John G., Arnold J. Lieberman, and Roger E. Levien. 1974. *R&D Management: Methods Used by Federal Agencies.* R-1156-HEW. Santa Monica, Calif.: Rand Corporation.

Wolanin, Thomas R. 1976. "Congress, Information and Policy Making for Post-Secondary Education: Don't Trouble Me with the Facts." *Policy Studies Journal* (Summer), 4:382–94.

Young, Pauline V., Calvin F. Schmid, and Stuart A. Rice. 1939. *Scientific Social Surveys and Research.* New York: Prentice-Hall.

FURTHER READING

As a guide to readers who wish to pursue the issues discussed here further, we have compiled a selective list of further reading. This section, together with the references, provides a comprehensive assortment of perspectives on the relationship of social science and policy.

Abrams, Mark. 1974. "Social Surveys, Social Theory and Social Policy." [British] *SSRC Newsletter* (July 24), pp. 11–14.

Abramson, Mark. 1978. *Funding of Social Knowledge Production and Application.* Vol. 2 of NAS Study Project on Social R&D. Washington, D.C.: National Academy of Sciences.

Adams, Walter. 1978. "The Contributions of Economics to Public Policy Formulation." In J.M. Yinger and S.J. Cutler, eds., *Major Social Issues: A Multidisciplinary View,* pp. 358–69. New York: Free Press.

Alexander, Tom. 1972. "The Social Engineers Retreat Under Fire." *Fortune* (October), 86(4):132–48.

Alkin, Marvin C., Richard Daillak, and Peter White. 1979. *Using Evaluations: Does Evaluation Make A Difference?* Beverly Hills, Calif.: Sage.

Alkin, Marvin C., Jacqueline Kosecoff, Carol Fitz-Gibbon, and Richard Seligman. 1974. *Evaluation and Decision Making: The Title VII Experience.* Center for the Study of Evaluation, UCLA Graduate School of Education, Los Angeles: CSE Monograph Series in Evaluation.

Anderson, James E. 1976. *Cases in Public Policy-Making.* New York: Praeger.

Anderson, Odin W. 1966. "Health Services Research: Influence of Social and Economic Research on Public Policy in the Health Field." *Milbank Memorial Fund Quarterly* (July), 44(3):11–51.

Arad, Uzi B., William I. Bacchus, Edward Gonzalez, and Harvey Starr. 1975. "Developing the Relevance Potentialities of National Security and Foreign Policy Research: Some Proposed Criteria." *Policy Sciences,* 6:161–73.

Archibald, Kathleen A. 1970a. "Alternative Orientations to Social Science Utilization." *Social Science Information* 9(2):7–34.

—— 1970b. "Three Views of the Expert's Role in Policymaking: Systems Analysis, Incrementalism, and the Clinical Approach." *Policy Sciences,* 1:73–86.

Argyris, Chris. 1972. *The Applicability of Organizational Sociology.* London/New York: Cambridge University Press.

Averch, Harvey. 1975. "Notes on Improving Research Utility." *Inquiry* (September), 13(3):231–34.

Banfield, Edward C. 1968. "Why Government Cannot Solve the Urban Problem." *Daedalus* (Fall), 97(4):1231–41.

Bauer, Raymond A. and Kenneth J. Gergen. 1968. *The Study of Policy Formation.* New York: Free Press.

Beals, Ralph L. 1969. *Politics of Social Research: An Inquiry into the Ethics and Responsibilities of Social Scientists.* Chicago: Aldine.

Bem, Daryl J. 1967. "Self-perception: An Alternative Interpretation of Cognitive Dissonance Phenomena." *Psychological Review,* 74:183–200.

Ben-David, Joseph. 1973. "How to Organize Research in the Social Sciences." *Daedalus* (September), 102(2):39–49.

Bennis, Warren. 1956. "Some Problems to Teamwork in Social Research." *Social Problems,* 3(4):223–35.

—— 1965. "Theory and Method in Applying Behavioral Science to Planned Organization Change." *Journal of Applied Behavioral Science,* 1(4):337–60.

—— 1970. "The Failure and Promise of the Social Sciences." *Technology Review* (October/November), 73(1):39–43.

Bennis, Warren G., K.D. Benne, and R. Chin, eds. 1964. *The Planning of Change: Readings in Applied Behavioral Sciences.* 2d ed. New York: Holt, Rinehart and Winston.

Benson, Oliver. 1971. "The Policy Sciences and Problem Solving." *Social Science Quarterly* 52(1):157–69.

Benveniste, Guy. 1972. *The Politics of Expertise.* Berkeley, Calif: Glendessary Press.

Berlin, I.N. 1969. "Resistance to Change in Mental Health Professionals." *American Journal of Orthopsychiatry,* 39:109–15.

Biderman, Albert D. 1970a. "Information, Intelligence, Enlightened Public Policy: Functions and Organization of Societal Feedback." *Policy Sciences* 1(2):217–30.

—— 1970b. "Self-Portrayal." *Science* (September), 169:1064–67.

Biderman, Albert D. and Elisabeth T. Crawford. 1970. "Paper Money:

Trends of Research Sponsorship in American Sociology Journals."
Social Science Information (February), 9(1):51–77.

Biderman, Albert D. and Laure M. Sharp. 1972. *The Competitive Evaluation Research Industry.* Washington, D.C.: Bureau of Social Science Research.

—— 1974. *An Analysis of 36 Competitive Procurements of Social Program Evaluation Studies.* Washington, D.C.: Bureau of Social Science Research.

Blanchard, Robert O. 1975. "The Use of Political Science: The Journalists' View." *Policy Sciences* (Fall), 8(4):382–85.

Blum, Richard H. and Mary Lou Funkhouser. 1965. "Legislators on Social Scientists and a Social Issue: A Report and Commentary on Some Discussions with Lawmakers about Drug Abuse." *Journal of Applied Behavioral Science* 1(1):84–112.

Blume, Stuart S. 1974. *Toward a Political Sociology of Science.* New York: Free Press.

—— 1975. "Toward a Science Policy for the Social Welfare Field." *Zeitschrift für Soziologie* (October), 4(4):301–15.

Boruch, Robert F. and Henry W. Riecken, eds. 1975. *Experimental Testing of Public Policy* (The Proceedings of the 1974 Social Science Research Council Conference on Social Experiments). Boulder, Colo.: Westview Press.

Botein, Bernard. 1965. "The Manhattan Bail Project: Its Impact on Criminology and the Criminal Law Processes." *Texas Law Review* (February), 43(3):319–31.

Boulding, Kenneth. 1966. *The Impact of the Social Sciences.* New Brunswick, N.J.: Rutgers University Press.

Brewer, Garry D. 1973. *Politicians, Bureaucrats and the Consultant: A Critique of Urban Problem Solving.* New York: Basic Books.

Brigham, John. 1977. *Making Public Policy: Studies in American Politics.* Lexington, Mass.: Heath.

Bryson, Lyman. 1951. "Notes on a Theory of Advice." *Political Science Quarterly* (November), 66(3):321–39.

Bulmer, Martin, ed. 1978. *Social Policy Research.* London and Basingstoke: Macmillan.

Bunker, Douglas R. 1978. "Organizing to Link Social Science With Public Policy Making." *Public Administration Review* (May–June), 38(3): 223–32.

Burger, R.M. 1975. *RANN Utilization Experience.* Final report to the National Science Foundation, prepared by Research Triangle Institute. Washington, D.C.: National Science Foundation (June 16).

Caldwell, Catherine. 1970. "Social Science as Ammunition." *Psychology Today* (September), 4(4)38–41, 72–73.

Caplan, Nathan. 1974. "Science is Seldom Put to Good Use by U.S. Officials." *ISR Newsletter* (Spring), 2(1):2, 8.

—— 1977. "Sandcastles in the Rain." *American Psychological Association Monitor* (December), 8(12):2.

Caplan, Nathan and Eugenia Barton. 1978. "The Potential of Social Indicators: Minimum Conditions for Impact at the National Level as Suggested by a Study of the Use of 'Social Indicators '73'." *Social Indicators Research*, 5:427–56.

Caplan, Nathan and Stephen D. Nelson. 1973. "On Being Useful: the Nature and Consequences of Psychological Research on Social Problems." *American Psychologist*, 28:199–211.

Carter, Luther J. 1966. "Social Sciences: Where do they Fit in the Politics of Science?" *Science* (October 28), 154:488–91.

Carter, Reginald K. 1971. "Clients' Resistance to Negative Findings and the Latent Conservative Function of Evaluation Studies." *The American Sociologist* (May), 6:118–24.

Charlesworth, James C., ed. 1972. *Integration of the Social Sciences Through Policy Analysis*. Philadelphia: American Academy of Political and Social Science.

Cherns, Albert. 1968. "The Use of the Social Sciences." *Human Relations* (November), 21(4)313–25.

—— 1969. "Social Research and its Diffusion." *Human Relations* (June), 3(3):209–18.

—— 1970a. "Relations Between Research Institutions and Users of Research." *International Social Science Journal* 22(2):226–42.

—— 1970b. "Social Sciences and Policy." *The Sociological Review Monograph* (September), 16:53–75.

Cherns, Albert, ed. 1976. *Sociotechnics*. London: Malaby Press.

Cherns, Albert B., R. Sinclair, and W.I. Jenkins, eds. 1972. *Social Science and Government: Policies and Problems*. London: Tavistock Publications.

Chesler, Mark and Mary Flanders. 1967. "Resistance to Research and Research Utilization: The Death and Life of a Feedback Attempt." *Applied Behavioral Science*, 3(4):469–87.

Chinitz, Benjamin. 1971. "The Management of Federal Expenditures for Research on Social Problems." In Irving Louis Horowitz, ed., *The Use and Abuse of Social Science*, pp. 71–85. New Brunswick, N.J.: Transactionbooks.

Clark, Terry Nichols. 1978. "Policy Research and Urban Public Policy." *Policy Analysis* (Winter), 4(1):67–90.

Clinard, Marshall B. 1966. "The Sociologist's Quest for Respectability." *Sociological Quarterly* (Fall), 7:399–412.

Consolidated Analysis Centers Inc. 1972. *The Utilization of ARPA-Supported Research for International Security Planning: A Conference Summary.* Arlington, Va.: CACI.

Costello, Timothy W. 1970. "Psychological Aspects: The Soft Side of Policy Formulation." *Policy Sciences,* 1(2):161–68.

Coulam, Robert F. 1977. *Illusions of Choice: The F-111 Decision and the Problems of Weapons Reform.* Princeton, N.J.: Princeton University Press.

Crawford, Elisabeth and Stein Rokkan. 1976. *Sociological Praxis: Current Roles and Settings.* Beverly Hills, Calif.: Sage Publications (Sage Studies in International Sociology 3).

Cronbach, Lee J. and Patrick Suppes, eds. 1969. *Research for Tomorrow's Schools: Disciplined Inquiry for Education.* Report of the Committee on Educational Research of the National Academy of Education, London: Collier-Macmillan.

Cronin, Thomas E. and Norman C. Thomas. 1970. "Educational Policy Advisors and the Great Society." *Public Policy* (Fall), 18(5):659–86.

—— 1971. "Federal Advisory Processes: Advice and Discontent."*Science* (February 26), 171:771–79.

Dahl, Robert A. and Charles E. Lindblom. 1953. *Politics, Economics, and Welfare.* New York: Harper & Row.

Dallmayr, Fred R. and Thomas A. McCarthy, eds. 1977. *Understanding and Social Inquiry.* Notre Dame and London: University of Notre Dame Press.

Danhof, Clarence H. 1968. *Government Contracting and Technological Change.* Washington, D.C.: Brookings Institution.

Datta, Lois-ellin. 1976. "The Impact of the Westinghouse/Ohio Evaluation of the Development of Project Head Start: An Examination of the Immediate and Longer-Term Effects and How They Came About." In Clark C. Abt, ed., *The Evaluation of Social Programs.* Beverly Hills and London: Sage.

Davis, Howard R. 1971. "A Checklist for Change." In National Institute of Mental Health, *A Manual for Research Utilization.* Washington, D.C.: U.S. Government Printing Office.

Davis, James. A. 1975. "On the Remarkable Absence of Nonacademic Implications in Academic Research: An Example from Ethnic Studies." In N.J. Demerath III, Otto Larsen, and Karl J. Schuessler, eds., *Social Policy and Sociology,* pp. 233–42. New York: Academic Press.

Davis, Jerome. 1940. "The Sociologist and Social Action." *American Sociological Review* (April), 5:171–76.

Dawis, Rene V., G.W. England, L.H. Lofquist, with the assistance of V. Myers-Schletzer and C.I. Stein. 1959. "The Application of Research Results." *Minnesota Studies in Vocational Rehabilitation,* Bulletin 29 (November), pp. 1–21.

Demerath, N.J. III, Otto Larsen, and Karl F. Schuessler, eds. 1975. *Social Policy and Sociology.* New York: Academic Press.

Denzin, Norman K., ed. 1973. *The Values of Social Science.* 2d ed. New Brunswick, N.J.: Transactionbooks.

Deutsch, Karl W., John Platt, and Dieter Senghaas. 1971. "Conditions Favoring Major Advances in Social Science." *Science* (February), 171:450–59.

Dexter, Lewis Anthony. 1958. "A Note on Selective Inattention in Social Science." *Social Problems* (Fall), 6(2):176–82.

—— 1965. "On the Use and Abuse of Social Science by Practitioners." *American Behavioral Scientist* (November), 9(3):25–29.

—— 1966. "Impressions About Utility and Wastefulness in Applied Social Science Studies." *American Behavioral Scientist* (February), 9(6):9–10.

Dickson, Paul. 1971. *Think Tanks.* New York: Atheneum.

Downs, Anthony. 1965. "Some Thoughts on Giving People Economic Advice." *American Behavioral Scientist* (September), 9(1):30–33.

—— 1967. *Inside Bureaucracy.* Boston: Little, Brown.

Dror, Yehezkel. 1968. *Public Policy Reexamined.* Scranton, Pa.: Chandler.

—— 1969. *A General Systems Approach to Uses of Behavioral Sciences for Better Policymaking.* Santa Monica, Calif.: Rand Corporation.

—— 1971. *Design for Policy Sciences.* New York: Elsevier.

Duncan, Otis Dudley. 1969. "Social Forecasting: The State of the Art." *The Public Interest* (Fall), no. 17, pp. 88–119.

Eaton, Joseph W. 1962. "Symbolic and Substantive Evaluation Research." *Administrative Science Quarterly* (March), 6(4):421–42.

Edelman, Murray. 1977. *Political Language: Words that Succeed and Policies that Fail.* New York: Academic Press.

Eiduson, Bernice T. 1966. "Scientists as Advisors and Consultants in Washington." *Bulletin of the Atomic Scientists* (October), 22(8):26–31.

Einhorn, Hillel J. 1974. "Expert Judgment: Some Necessary Conditions and an Example." *Journal of Applied Psychology* 59(5):562–71.

Elmore, Richard F. 1978. "Organizational Models of Social Program Implementation." *Public Policy* (Spring), 26(2)185–228.

Empey, LaMar T. 1973. "Open Forum: Reactions to Coleman on Policy Research." *ASA Footnotes* (August), p. 4.

Enthoven, Alain C. and K. Wayne Smith. 1971. *How Much is Enough? Shaping the Defense Program 1961–1969.* New York: Harper & Row.

Etzioni, Amitai. 1966. "Social Analysis as a Sociological Vocation." In Arthur B. Shostak, ed., *Sociology in Action*, pp. 317–23. Homewood, Ill.: Dorsey Press.

—— 1968a. "How May Congress Learn?" *Science* (January), 159:170–72.

—— 1968b. *The Active Society: A Theory of Societal and Political Processes.* London: Collier-Macmillan; New York: Free Press.

—— 1971. "Policy Research." *American Sociologist* (June), 6:8–12.

Fairweather, George W. 1967. *Methods for Experimental Social Innovation.* New York: Wiley.

Fairweather, George W., D.H. Sanders, H. Maynard, and D.L. Cressler. 1969. *Community Life for the Mentally Ill: An Alternative to Institutional Care.* Chicago: Aldine.

Fairweather, George W., David H. Sanders, and Louis G. Tornatzky. 1974. *Creating Change in Mental Health Organizations.* New York: Pergamon Press.

Fairweather, George W. and Louis G. Tornatzky. 1977. *Experimental Methods for Social Policy Research.* Oxford/New York/Toronto: Pergamon Press.

Falkson, Joseph L. 1976. "Minor Skirmish in a Monumental Struggle: HEW's Analysis of Mental Health Services." *Policy Analysis* 2:93–119.

Fantini, Mario D. and Gerald Weinstein. 1966. "Strategies for Initiating Educational Change in Large Bureaucratic School Systems." In Arthur B. Shostak, ed., *Sociology in Action*, pp. 22–32. Homewood, Ill.: Dorsey Press.

Farley, Reynolds. 1971. "Social Science and Social Policy—A Review of Some Recent Books." *The American Sociologist* 6(supp.):75–76.

Fennessey, James. 1972. "Some Problems and Possibilities in Policy-Related Social Research." *Social Science Research,* 1(4):359–83.

Flash, Edward S. 1971. "Macro-Economics for Macro-Policy." *The Annals* (March), 384:46–56.

Flook, E. Evelyn and Paul J. Sanazaro, eds. 1973. *Health Services Research and R & D in Perspective.* Ann Arbor, Mich.: Health Administration Press, University of Michigan.

Frankel, Charles, ed. 1976. *Controversies and Decisions: The Social Sciences and Public Policy.* New York: Russell Sage.

Freeman, Howard E., ed. 1978. *Policy Studies Review Annual.* vol. 2. Beverly Hills and London: Sage.

Friedman, Robert S. 1971. *Professionalism: Expertise and Policy Making.* New York: General Learning Press.

Furstenberg, Frank F., Jr. 1971. "Political Intrusion and Governmental Confusion: The Case of the National Institute of Law Enforcement and Criminal Justice." *The American Sociologist* 6(supp.):59–62.

Gelb, Joyce and Marian Lief Palley. 1971. *The Politics of Social Change: A Reader for the Seventies.* New York: Holt, Rinehart and Winston.

George, Alexander. 1975. "Towards a More Soundly Based Foreign Policy: Making Better Use of Information." In *Appendices: Commission on the Organization of the Government for the Conduct of Foreign Policy,* vol. 2. Washington, D.C.: U.S. Government Printing Office (June).

Gerver, Israel and Joseph Bensman. 1954. "Towards a Sociology of Expertness." *Social Forces* (November), 32(3):226–35.

Gifford, Bernard R. 1973. "Analysis and Urban Government: Experience of the New York City-Rand Institute." New York City Rand Institute, New York (January).

Gilpin, Robert and Christopher Wright, eds. 1964. *Scientists and National Policy-Making.* New York: Columbia University Press.

Glaser, E.M. 1973. "Knowledge Transfer and Institutional Change." *Professional Psychology,* 4:434–44.

Glaser, E.M. and S.H. Taylor. 1969. *Factors Influencing the Success of Applied Research: A Study of Ten NIMH-Funded Projects.* Los Angeles: Human Interaction Research Institute.

Glock, Charles Y., R. Lippitt, J.C. Flanagan, E.C. Wilson, C.L. Shartle, M.L. Wilson, G.W. Croker, H.E. Page. 1961. *Case Studies in Bringing Behavioral Sciences into Use.* Stanford, Calif.: Institute for Communications Research, Stanford University.

Goodwin, Leonard. 1966. "Conceptualizing the Action Process." *Sociology and Social Research,* 50:377–92.

—— 1971. "On Making Social Research Relevant to Public Policy and National Problem Solving." *American Psychologist* (May),26(5):431–42.

—— 1975. "The Relation of Social Research to Practical Affairs." *The Journal of Applied Behavioral Science,* 11(1):7–13.

Gouldner, A.W. 1961. "Engineering and Clinical Approaches to Consulting." In W.G. Bennis, K.D. Benne, and R. Chin, eds., *The Planning of Change: Readings in Applied Behavioral Sciences.* New York: Holt, Rinehart and Winston.

—— 1970. *The Coming Crisis of Western Sociology.* New York: Basic Books.

—— 1956. "Exploration in Applied Social Science." *Social Problems* (January), 3:169–81.

Gouldner, Alvin and S.M. Miller. 1965. *Applied Sociology.* New York: Free Press.

Green, Philip. 1971. "The Obligations of American Social Scientists." *The Annals* (March), 384:13–27.

Greenberg, Daniel S. 1967. *The Politics of Pure Science.* New York: New American Library.

Greenberger, Martin, Matthew A. Crenson, and Brian L. Crissey. 1976. *Models in the Policy Process.* New York: Russell Sage.

Gregg, Phillip M. 1976. *Problems of Theory in Policy Analysis.* Lexington, Mass.: Lexington Books, D.C. Heath.

Gross, Neal. 1977. "Theoretical and Policy Implications of Case Study Findings About Federal Efforts to Improve Public Schools." *The Annals* (November), 434:71–87.

Gusfield, Joseph. 1975. The [F]Utility of Knowledge?: The Relation of Social Science to Public Policy Toward Drugs." *The Annals* (January), 417:1–15.

—— 1976. "The Literary Rhetoric of Science: Comedy and Pathos in Drinking Driver Research." *American Sociological Review* (February), 41:16–34.

Hage, Jerald and J. Rogers Hollingsworth. 1977. "The First Steps Toward the Integration of Social Theory and Social Policy." *The Annals* (November), 434:1–23.

Hagstrom, Warren O. 1965. *The Scientific Community.* Carbondale, Ill.: Southern Illinois University Press, Arcturus Books.

Hall, Harry S. 1962. "Scientists and Politicians." In Bernard Barber and Walter Hirsch, eds., *The Sociology of Science,* pp. 269–87. New York: Glencoe Press.

Halperin, Morton H. 1971. "Why Bureaucrats Play Games." *Foreign Policy* (Spring), (2):70–90.

Halpert, H.P. 1966. "Communications as a Basic Tool in Promoting Utilization of Research Findings." *Community Mental Health Journal,* 2:231–36.

Harris, Fred, ed. 1970. *Social Science and National Policy.* New Brunswick, N.J.: Transactionbooks.

Hauser, Philip. 1949. "Social Science and Social Engineering." *Philosophy of Science,* 16(3):209–18.

Haworth, L. 1960. "The Experimenting Society: Dewey and Jordan." *Ethics* (October), 71(1):27–40.

Heclo, H. Hugh. 1972. "Review Article: Policy Analysis." *British Journal of Political Science,* 2:83–108.

Heiskanen, Veronica Stolte. 1969. "Uses of Sociology: A Case Study of Commissioned Research in Finland." *Social Science Information* (June), 8(3):87–98.

Heiss, F. William. 1974. *Urban Research and Urban Policy-Making: An Observatory Perspective.* Boulder, Colo.: Bureau of Governmental Research and Service, University of Colorado.

Hilgard, Ernest R. and Daniel Lerner. 1951. "The Person: Subject and Object of Science and Policy." In D. Lerner and H.D. Lasswell, eds., *The Policy Sciences: Recent Developments in Scope and Method*, pp. 16–43. Stanford, Calif.: Stanford University Press.

Hobbs, Daryl. 1969. "A Comment on Applied Sociological Research." *Rural Sociology* (June), 14(2):241–45.

Holton, Gerald. 1974. *Thematic Origins of Scientific Thought: Kepler to Einstein*. Cambridge, Mass.: Harvard University Press.

Horowitz, Irving Louis. 1969. "Engineering and Sociological Perspectives on Development: Interdisciplinary Constraints in Social Forecasting." *International Social Science Journal*, 21(4):545–56.

—— 1970. "Social Science Mandarins: Policymaking as a Political Formula." *Policy Sciences*, 1:339–60.

Horowitz, Irving Louis, ed. 1974. *The Rise and Fall of Project Camelot: Studies in the Relationship Between Social Science and Practical Policies*. Cambridge, Mass.: MIT Press.

Horowitz, Irving Louis and James Katz. 1975. *Social Science and Public Policy in the United States*. New York: Praeger.

Huitt, Ralph K. 1969. "Rationalizing the Policy Process." *Social Science Quarterly* (December), 50(3):480–86.

Human Interaction Research Institute. *Putting Knowledge to Use: A Distillation of the Literature Regarding Knowledge Transfer and Change*. Los Angeles: Human Interaction Research Institute in collaboration with the National Institute of Mental Health.

Ikenberry, Stanley O. and Renee C. Friedman. 1972. *Beyond Academic Departments: The Story of Institutes and Centers*. San Francisco: Jossey-Bass.

Janowitz, Morris. 1971. "Sociological Research on Arms Control." *The American Sociologist*, 6(supp.):23–30.

Jenkins, William I. and Irving Velody. 1970. "The Social Sciences and Government: Do the Natural Sciences Show the Prescribed Path?" *Social Science Information*, 9(5):91–118.

Jones, Charles O. 1970. *An Introduction to the Study of Public Policy*. Belmont, Calif.: Wadsworth.

Jones, Charles O. and Robert D. Thomas, eds. 1976. *Public Policy Making In a Federal System*. Beverly Hills, Calif. and London: Sage.

Jung, Charles and Ronald Lippitt. 1966. "The Study of Change as a Concept in Research Utilization." *Theory into Practice*, 5(2):25–29.

Kaysen, Carl. 1968. "Model-Makers and Decision-Makers: Economists and the Policy Process." *The Public Interest* (Summer), no. 12. pp. 80–95.

Kelly, George A. 1963. "The Expert as Historical Actor." *Daedalus* (Summer), 92(3):529–49.

Kelman, Herbert C. 1965. "The Social Consequences of Social Research: A New Social Issue." *Journal of Social Issues,* 21(3):21–40.

—— 1970. "The Relevance of Social Research to Social Issues: Promises and Pitfalls." *The Sociological Review Monograph* (September), no. 16, pp. 77–99.

Killian, Lewis M. 1966. "The Social Scientist's Role in the Preparation of the Florida Desegregation Brief." In Arthur B. Shostak, ed., *Sociology in Action,* pp. 129–34. Homewood, Ill.: Dorsey Press.

King, Lauriston R. and Phillip H. Melanson. 1972. "Knowledge and Politics: Some Experiences from the 1960s." *Public Policy* (Winter), 20:83–101.

Klonglan, Gerald E. and E. Walter Coward, Jr. 1970. "The Concept of Symbolic Adoption: A Suggested Interpretation." *Rural Sociology* (March), 35(1):77–83.

Knezo, Genevieve. 1970. *Interdisciplinary Research—An Exploration of Public Policy Issues.* Legislative Reference Service, Library of Congress (October 30).

Kochen, Manfred. 1975. *Information for Action: From Knowledge to Wisdom.* New York: Academic Press.

Kogan, Leonard S. 1963. "The Utilization of Social Work Research." *Social Casework,* 44:569–74.

Komarovsky, Mirra, ed. 1975. *Sociology and Public Policy.* New York: Elsevier.

Lakoff, Sanford A. 1971. "Knowledge, Power, and Democracy." *The Annals* (March), 384:4–12.

Lane, Robert E. 1966. "The Decline of Politics and Ideology in a Knowledgeable Society." *American Sociological Review* (October), 31:649–62.

Lasswell, Harold D. and Abraham Kaplan. 1950. *Power and Society: A Framework for Political Inquiry.* New Haven, Conn.: Yale University Press.

Lazarsfeld, Paul F., Lawrence R. Klein, and Ralph W. Tyler. 1964. *The Behavioral Sciences: Problems and Prospects.* Boulder, Colo.: Institute of Behavioral Science (August).

Lazarsfeld, Paul F. and Sam D. Sieber. 1964. *Organizing Educational Research.* Englewood Cliffs, N.J.: Prentice-Hall.

Lerner, Allan W. 1976. *The Politics of Decision-Making: Strategy, Cooperation, and Conflict.* Beverly Hills, Calif.: Sage.

Lerner, Daniel. 1959. *The Human Meaning of the Social Sciences.* Cleveland, Ohio: Meridian.

Lerner, Daniel and Harold D. Lasswell, eds. 1951. *The Policy Sciences: Recent Developments in Scope and Method.* Stanford, Calif.: Stanford University Press.

Levien, R.E. 1969. *Independent Public Policy Analysis Organizations—A Major Social Invention.* Santa Monica, Calif.: Rand Corporation.

Light, Richard J. 1968. "Report Analysis: National Advisory Commission on Civil Disorders." *Harvard Educational Review,* 38:756–67.

Likert, Rensis and Samuel P. Hayes, Jr., eds. 1967. *Some Applications of Behavioral Research.* Paris: UNESCO.

Likert, Rensis and Ronald Lippitt, 1953. "The Utilization of Social Science." In L. Festinger and D. Katz, eds., *Research Methods in the Behavioral Sciences,* pp. 581–646, New York: Dryden Press.

Lippitt, Ronald. 1965. "The Use of Social Research to Improve Social Practice." *American Journal of Orthopsychiatry* (July), 35(4):663–69.

—— 1966. "The Process of Utilization of Social Research to Improve Social Practice." In Arthur B. Shostak, ed., *Sociology in Action.* Homewood, Ill.: Dorsey Press.

Lipsky, Michael. 1971. "Social Scientists and the Riot Commission." *The Annals* (March), 384:72–83.

Lompe, Klaus. 1968. "The Role of the Social Scientist in the Processes of Policy-Making." *Social Science Information,* 7(6):159–75.

Lucas, Henry C., Jr. 1975. *Why Information Systems Fail.* New York: Columbia University Press.

Lundberg, Craig C. 1966. "Middlemen in Science Utilization: Some Notes Toward Clarifying Conversion Roles." *American Behavioral Scientist* (February), 9(6):11–14.

Lynch, Thomas D. 1975. *Policy Analysis in Public Policymaking.* Lexington, Mass.: Heath.

Lyons, Gene M., special ed. 1971a. "Social Science and the Federal Government." *The Annals* (March), vol. 394.

—— 1971a. "The President and His Experts." *The Annals* (March), 394:36–45.

Lyons, Gene M., ed. 1975. *Social Research and Public Policies.* The Dartmouth/OECD Conference. The Public Affairs Center, Dartmouth College, Hanover, N.H.

McCrone, John D. and Margery E. Hoppin. 1973. "Requests for Proposals and Universities." *Science* (March 9), 179:975–77.

Mackie, Robert. 1974. "Viewpoint: Chuckholes in the Bumpy Road from Research to Application." *Behavior Today* (November 11), 5(41):295–96.

Mackie, Robert R. and P.R. Christensen. 1967. *Translation and Applica-*

tion of Psychological Research. Human Factors Research, Inc. (Technical report to ONR).

MacRae, Duncan, Jr. 1971. "A Dilemma of Sociology: Science versus Policy." *The American Sociologist* 6(supp.):2–7.

—— 1973. "Science and the Formation of Policy in a Democracy." *Minerva,* 11(2):228–42.

—— 1975. "Policy Analysis as an Applied Social Science Discipline." *Administration and Society,* 6(4):363–88.

—— 1976. *The Social Function of Social Science.* New Haven, Conn.: Yale University Press.

March, James G. 1978. "Bounded Rationality, Ambiguity, and the Engineering of Choice." *Bell Journal of Economics* (Autumn), 9(2):587–608.

March, James G. and Herbert A. Simon. 1958. *Organizations.* New York: Wiley.

Marris, Peter and Martin Rein. 1969. *Dilemmas of Social Reform.* New York: Atherton Press.

Martin, Ben L. 1973. "Experts in Policy Processes: A Contemporary Perspective." *Policy* (Winter), 6(2):149–73.

May, Judith V. and Aaron B. Wildavsky. 1978. *The Policy Cycle.* Beverly Hills, Calif.: Sage.

Mayntz, Renate. 1976. "Environmental Policy Conflicts: The Case of the German Federal Republic." *Policy Analysis,* 2(4):577–88.

Mazur, Allan. 1973. "Disputes Between Experts." *Minerva* (April), 11(2): 243–62.

Melanson, Philip H. 1971. "The Political Science Profession, Political Knowledge and Public Policy." *Politics and Society,* 2(4):489–501.

Meltsner, Arnold J. 1972. "Political Feasibility and Policy Analysis." *Public Administration Review* (November/December), 32:859–67.

Merton, Robert K. 1973. *The Sociology of Science.* Chicago and London: The University of Chicago Press.

Merton, Robert K., and Edward C. Devereux, Jr. 1964. "Practical Problems and the Use of Social Science." *Trans-action,* 1(4):18–21.

Miles, M.B. 1964. "Innovation in Education: Some Generalizations." In M.B. Miles, ed., *Innovation in Education.* New York: Bureau of Publication, Teachers College, Columbia University.

Moynihan, Daniel P. 1967. "A Crisis of Confidence." *The Public Interest* (Spring), no. 7, pp. 3–10.

—— 1970. "Eliteland." *Psychology Today* (September), 4(4):35–37, 66–70.

—— 1973. *Coping: On the Practice of Government.* New York: Random House.

Nagel, Stuart S. 1975a. *Policy Studies and the Social Sciences.* Lexington, Mass.: Lexington-Heath.

—— 1975b. *Policy Studies in America and Elsewhere.* Lexington, Mass.: Lexington-Heath.

Nagel, Stuart S. and Marian Neef. 1975. "The Use of Political Science." *Policy Sciences* (Fall), 8(4):376–80.

Nagi, S.Z. 1965. "The Practitioner as a Partner in Research." *Rehabilitation Record* (July/August), 6(4):1–4.

Nagi, S.Z. and Ronald G. Corwin. 1972. *The Social Contexts of Research.* New York: Wiley-Interscience.

National Academy of Sciences. 1968. *The Behavioral Sciences and the Federal Government.* Washington, D.C.: National Academy of Sciences.

—— 1971. *Policy and Program Research in a University Setting.* Washington, D.C.: National Academy of Sciences.

National Advisory Committee on Criminal Justice Standards and Goals. 1976. *Criminal Justice Research and Development.* Report of the Task Force on Criminal Justice Research and Development. Washington, D.C.: U.S. Government Printing Office (0-219-286).

Nelson, Richard R. 1974. "Intellectualizing about the Moon-Ghetto Metaphor: A Study of the Current Malaise of Rational Analysis of Social Problems." *Policy Sciences* (December), 5:375–414.

—— 1977. *The Moon and the Ghetto: An Essay on Public Policy Analysis.* New York: Norton.

Nettler, Gwynn. 1972. "Knowing and Doing." *The American Sociologist* (February), 7(2):1–6.

Nisbet, Robert A. 1969. "Project Camelot: An Autopsy." In Philip Rieff, ed., *On Intellectuals*, pp. 283–313. Garden City, N.Y.: Doubleday.

Office of Management and Budget. 1973. "NIH and NIMH Peer Review System." *Drug Research Reports* 16(22):4–9.

Orlans, Harold. 1967. "Ethical Problems in the Relations of Research Sponsors and Investigators." Washington, D.C.: Brookings Institution.

—— 1971a. "Science and the Polity, or How Much Knowledge Does a Nation Need?" *Proceedings of the American Philosophical Society* (February), 115(1):4–9.

—— 1971b. "The Political Uses of Social Research." *The Annals* (March), 384:28–35.

—— 1972. *The Non-Profit Research Institute: Its Origin, Operations, Problems, and Prospects.* New York: McGraw-Hill.

—— 1976. "On Social Order and Orderly Knowledge." In E. Crawford and N. Perry, eds., *Demands for Social Knowledge*, pp. 35–58. London and Los Angeles: Sage.

Packenham, Robert A. 1978. "Social Science and Public Policy." In S. Verba and L. Pye, eds., *The Citizen and Politics: A Comparative Perspective*, pp. 237–57. Stamford, Conn.: Greylock.

Patton, Michael Q. 1978. *Utilization-Focused Evaluation*. Beverly Hills, Calif.: Sage.

Perl, Martin L. 1971. "The Scientific Advisory System: Some Observations." *Science* (September 24), 173:1211–15.

Peterson, Paul E. 1976. *School Politics Chicago Style*. Chicago and London: University of Chicago Press.

Pettigrew, Thomas F. 1971. "Sociological Consulting in Race Relations." *The American Sociologist*, 6(supp.):44–47.

Philips, Derek L. 1971. "Sociologists and Their Knowledge." *American Behavioral Scientist* (March/April), 14(4):563–82.

Pierce, J.R. 1968. "When Is Research the Answer?" *Science* (March), 159:1079–80.

President's Commission on Mental Health. 1978. *Report to the President from the President's Commission on Mental Health*, vol. 1. Washington, D.C.: U.S. Government Printing Office.

Quade, Edward. 1975. *Analysis for Public Decisions*. Amsterdam and New York: Elsevier.

Rainwater, Lee. 1974. *Social Problems and Public Policy: Inequality and Justice*. Chicago: Aldine.

Rainwater, Lee and William L. Yancey. 1967. *The Moynihan Report and the Politics of Controversy*. Cambridge, Mass.: MIT Press.

Rein, Martin. 1970. *Social Policy: Issues of Choice and Change*. New York: Random House.

—— 1976. *Social Science and Public Policy*. New York: Penguin.

Reiss, Albert J. 1970. "Putting Sociology into Policy." *Social Problems* (Winter), 17(3):289–94.

Reissman, Leonard. 1972. "The Solution Cycle of Social Problems." *The American Sociologist* (February), 7:7–9.

Reitz, Jeffrey G. 1973. *Social Interaction Between Policy-makers and Social Scientists*. New York: Bureau of Applied Social Research.

—— 1975. "Use of Social Research in Population Programs: A Case Study of a Policy Debate Among Social Science Experts." In S.R. Inginan and A.E. Thomas, eds., *Topias and Utopias in Health: Policy Studies*, pp. 478–505. The Hague: Mouton.

Rettig, Richard A. 1967. *Federal Support of Scientific Research: A Comparative Study*. Ph.D. dissertation, Department of Political Science, MIT (August).

—— 1977. *Cancer Crusade: The Story of the National Cancer Act of 1971*. Princeton, N.J.: Princeton University Press.

Rich, Robert F. 1975. "Selective Utilization of Social Science Related Information by Federal Policy-Makers." *Inquiry* (September), 8(3): 239–45.

—— Forthcoming. *Translating Evaluation into Policy.* Beverly Hills, Calif.: Sage.

Riecken, Henry W. 1971. "The Federal Government and Social Science Policy." *The Annals* (March), 384:100–13.

Riecken, Henry W. and Robert F. Boruch. 1974. *Social Experimentation: A Method for Planning and Evaluating Social Intervention.* New York: Academic Press.

Ritchie, Ronald S. 1971. *An Institute for Research on Public Policy.* Ottawa: Information Canada.

Rivlin, Alice M. 1974. "How Can Experiments Be More Useful?" Washington, D.C.: Brookings Institution, General Series Reprint.

Rivlin, Alice M. and P. Michael Timpane, eds. 1975. *Planned Variation in Education: Should We Give Up or Try Harder?* Washington, D.C.: Brookings Institution.

Roberts, A. Oscar H. and Judith K. Larsen. 1971. *Effective Use of Mental Health Research Information.* Final Report. Palo Alto, Calif.: American Institutes for Research.

Rock, Vincent P. 1965. "The Policy-Maker and the Social Sciences." In A.W. Gouldner and S.M. Miller, eds., *Applied Sociology: Opportunities and Problems,* pp. 358–66. New York: Free Press.

Rodman, H. and R. Kolodny. 1965. "Organizational Strains in the Researcher-Practitioner Relationship." In A.W. Gouldner and S.M. Miller, eds., *Applied Sociology: Opportunities and Problems,* pp. 93–113. New York: Free Press.

Rose, Arnold M. 1965. "The Social Responsibility of the Social Scientist." In Donald M. Valdes and Dwight G. Dean, eds., *Sociology in Use.* New York: Macmillan.

Rose, Richard. 1977. "Disciplined Research and Undisciplined Problems." In C.H. Weiss, ed. *Using Social Research in Public Policy Making,* pp. 23–35. Lexington, Mass.: Lexington-Heath.

Rossi, Peter. 1969. "No Good Idea Goes Unpunished: Moynihan's Misunderstanding and the Proper Role of Social Science in Policy Making." *Social Science Quarterly* (December), 50:469–79.

—— 1975. "Field Experiments in Social Programs: Problems and Prospects." In Gene M. Lyons, ed. *Social Research and Public Policies: The Dartmouth/OECD Conference,* pp. 117–30. The Public Affairs Center, Dartmouth College, Hanover, N.H.

Rothman, Jack, John Erlich, and Joseph Teresa. 1976. *Promoting In-*

novation and Change in Organizations and Communities. New York: Wiley.

Rubin, L.J. 1968. "Installing an Innovation." In R.R. Goulet, ed., *Educational Change: The Reality and the Promise*, pp. 154–65. New York: Citation Press.

Samuelson, Paul A. 1959. "What Economists Know." In Daniel Lerner, ed., *The Human Meaning of the Social Sciences*, pp. 183–213. Cleveland and New York: World.

Sanford, Nevitt. 1965. "Social Science and Social Reform." *Journal of Social Issues* (April), 21(2):154–70.

Schick, Allen. 1971. "From Analysis to Evaluation." *The Annals* (March), 384:57–71.

—— 1976. "Evaluating Evaluation: A Congressional Perspective." In *Legislative Oversight and Program Evaluation*, prepared for U.S. Senate, Committee on Government Operations by Congressional Research Service, Library of Congress, pp. 334–54. Washington, D.C.: U.S. Government Printing Office.

Schilling, Warner R. 1964. "Scientists, Foreign Policy, and Politics." In Robert Gilpin and Christopher Wright, eds., *Scientists and National Policy-Making*, pp. 144–73. New York: Columbia University Press.

Schooler, Dean Jr. 1971. *Science, Scientists, and Public Policy.* London: Collier-Macmillan, and New York: Free Press.

Scott, Robert A. and Arnold Shore. 1974a. "Sociology and Policy Analysis." *The American Sociologist* (May), 9(2):51–59.

—— 1974b. *Sociology and Social Experimentation: Observations on the Application of Sociology to Applied Problems.* Mathematica Policy Analysis Series: Comments and Papers on Current Research, no. 4. Princeton, N.J. (August).

—— 1979. *Why Sociology Does Not Apply: A Study of the Use of Sociology in Public Policy.* New York: Elsevier.

Selvin, Hanan C. and David Nasatir. 1963. "The Use of Social Research by College Administrators." *Journal of the National Association of Women Deans and Counselors* (April), 26(3):3–10.

Semas, Philip W. 1977. "How Influential is Sociology?" *Chronicle of Higher Education* (September 19), 15(3):4.

Sharkansky, Ira, ed. 1970. *Policy Analysis in Political Science.* Chicago: Markham Publishing.

Smith, Bruce. 1966. *The RAND Corporation.* Cambridge, Mass.: Harvard University Press.

Smith, Charles. 1967. "Knowledge for Sale: Private Knowledge for Public Purposes." Santa Monica, Calif.: System Development Corp.

Sproull, Lee, Stephen Weiner, and David Wolf. 1978. *Organizing an Anarchy: Belief, Bureaucracy, and Politics in the National Institute of Education.* Chicago: University of Chicago Press.

Steinbruner, John D. 1974. *The Cybernetic Theory of Decision: New Dimensions of Political Analysis.* Princeton, N.J.: Princeton University Press.

Stokey, Edith and Richard Zeckhauser. 1978. *A Primer for Policy Analysis.* New York: Norton.

Street, David P. and Eugene A. Weinstein. 1975. "Problems and Prospects of Applied Sociology." *The American Sociologist* (May), 10:65–72.

Stufflebeam, Daniel L., Walter J. Foley, William J. Gephart, Egon G. Guba, Robert L. Hammond, Howard O. Merriman, and Malcolm M. Provus. 1971. *Educational Evaluation and Decision Making.* Itasca, Ill.: Peacock.

Tavistock Institute. 1964. *Social Research and a National Policy for Science* (A paper of the Council of the Tavistock Institute of Human Relations). London: Tavistock.

Teitz, Michael B. 1971. "Some Observations on Policy Analysis in New York." *Papers of the Regional Science Association,* 27:247–56.

Thompson, James D. 1967. *Organizations in Action.* New York: McGraw-Hill.

Thurley, Keith. 1972. "The Organization and Sponsorship of Action Research." [British] *Social Science Research Council Newsletter* (March 14), pp. 18–21.

Tribe, Laurence H. 1972. "Policy Science: Analysis or Ideology?" *Philosophy and Public Affairs,* 2(1):66–110.

Trist, Eric. 1970. "Social Research Institutions: Types, Structures, Scale." *International Social Science Journal,* 22(2):301–24.

Uliassi, Pio D. 1971. "The Prince's Counselors: Notes on Government Sponsored Research on International and Foreign Affairs." In Irving Louis Horowitz, ed., *The Use and Abuse of Social Science,* pp. 309–342. New Brunswick, N.J.: Transactionbooks.

Ulmer, S. Sidney. 1970. "Introduction." In S. Sidney Ulmer, ed., *Political Decision Making,* pp. 3–13. New York: Van Nostrand.

Unger, Roberto Mangabeira. 1975. *Knowledge and Politics.* New York: Free Press.

U.S. Commission on Government Procurement. 1972a. *Report of the Commission on Government Procurement.* 4 vols. Washington, D.C.: U.S. Government Printing Office.

—— 1972b. *Summary of the Report of the Commission on Government Procurement.* Washington, D.C.: U.S. Government Printing Office (December).

U.S. Congress. 1974. *Congressional Research Support and Information Services.* Hearings before the Joint Committee on Congressional Operations, 93rd Congress, 2nd session (May 16–July 31). Washington, D.C.: U.S. Government Printing Office.

U.S. Department of Health, Education, and Welfare. 1969. *Toward a Social Report.* Washington, D.C.: U.S. Department of Health, Education, and Welfare (January).

U.S. General Accounting Office. 1976. *Long-Range Analysis Activities in Seven Federal Agencies.* Report to the Congress by the Comptroller General. Washington, D.C.: U.S. General Accounting Office (December 3).

van de Vall, Mark. 1973. "A Theoretical Framework for Applied Social Research." *International Journal of Mental Health,* 2(2):6–25.

Vollmer, Howard M. 1969. "Toward a Sociology of Applied Science." *The American Sociologist* (August), 4(3):244–48.

—— 1970. "Basic Roles for Applying Social Science to Urban and Social Problems." *Urban and Social Change Review* (Spring), 3(2):32–33.

Voss, Harwin L. 1966. "Pitfalls in Social Research: A Case Study." *American Sociologist* (May), 1(3):136–40.

Walker, Jack L. 1977. "Setting the Agenda in the U.S. Senate: A Theory of Problem Selection." *British Journal of Political Science,* 7:423–45.

Warner, Kenneth E. 1974. "The Need for Some Innovative Concepts of Innovation: An Examination of Research on the Diffusion of Innovations." *Policy Sciences* (December), 5(4):433–51.

Watson, Goodwin, and Edward M. Glaser. 1965. "What we Have Learned About Planning for Change." *Management Review* (November), 54(1): 44–46.

Weber, Max. 1946. "Politics as a Vocation" and "Science as a Vocation." In H.H. Gerth and C.W. Mills, eds., *From Max Weber,* pp. 77–156. New York: Oxford University Press.

Weiss, Carol H. 1972. "Utilization of Evaluation: Toward Comparative Study." In C.H. Weiss, ed., *Evaluating Action Programs: Readings in Social Action and Education.* Boston: Allyn and Bacon.

—— 1973. "The Politics of Impact Measurement." *Policy Studies Journal,* 1:179–83.

—— 1975. "Evaluation Research in the Political Context." In E. Struening and M. Guttentag, eds., *Handbook of Evaluation Research,* pp. 13–26. Beverly Hills, Calif.: Sage.

—— 1976. "Policy Research: Practical Aid or Academic Exercise?" *Policy Studies Journal,* 4(3):224–28.

—— 1977. "Research for Policy's Sake: The Enlightenment Function of Social Research." *Policy Analysis* (Fall), 3(4):521–45.

—— 1978. "Improving the Linkage between Social Research and Public Policy." In Laurence E. Lynn, ed., *Knowledge and Policy: The Uncertain Connection,* pp. 23–81. Washington, D.C.: National Academy of Sciences.

Weiss, Carol H., ed., 1977. *Using Social Research in Public Policy Making.* Lexington, Mass.: Lexington-Heath.

Weiss, Carol H. and Michael J. Bucuvalas. 1977. "The Challenge of Social Research to Decision-Making." In C.H. Weiss, ed., *Using Social Research in Public Policy Making,* pp. 213–30. Lexington, Mass.: Lexington-Heath.

White, Bayla F. 1975. "The Atlanta Project: How One Large School System Responded to Performance Information." *Policy Analysis,* 1(4):659–91.

Wholey, Joseph S. 1970. *Federal Evaluation Policy.* Washington, D.C.: Urban Institute.

Wholey, Joseph S., Joe N. Nay, John W. Scanlon, and Richard E. Schmidt. 1974. "If You Don't Care Where You Get To, Then it Doesn't Matter Which Way You Go." In Gene M. Lyons, ed., *Social Research and Public Policies: The Dartmouth/OECD Conference,* pp. 175–97. Hanover, New Hampshire: The Public Affairs Center, Dartmouth College.

Wildavsky, Aaron. 1962. "The Analysis of Issue-Contexts in the Study of Decision-Making." *The Journal of Politics,* 24:717–32.

—— 1964. *The Politics of the Budgetary Process.* Boston: Little, Brown.

—— 1966. "The Political Economy of Efficiency: Cost-Benefit Analysis, Systems Analysis, and Program Budgeting." *Public Administration Review* (December), 26(4):292–310.

—— 1971. *The Revolt Against the Masses and Other Essays on Politics and Public Policy.* New York: Basic Books.

Wilensky, Harold L. 1967. *Organizational Intelligence: Knowledge and Policy in Government and Industry.* New York: Basic Books.

Williams, Sherman R. and Jere A. Wysong. 1974. "The Uses of Research in National Health Policy: An Assessment and Agenda." *Health Politics* (Winter), 5(2):8–14.

—— 1977. "Health Services Research and Health Policy Formulation: An Empirical Analysis and a Structural Solution." *Journal of Health Politics, Policy and Law* (Fall), 2:362–87.

Wilson, Logan 1964. *The Academic Man.* New York: Octagon Books.

Wood, Robert C. 1964. "Scientists and Politics: The Rise of an Apolitical Elite." In Robert Gilpin and Christopher Wright, eds., *Scientists and National Policy Making,* pp. 41–72. New York: Columbia University Press.

Yarmolinsky, Adam. 1963. "Confessions of a Non-User." *Public Opinion Quarterly* (Winter), 27(4):543–48.

—— 1971. "The Policy Researcher: His Habitat, Care and Feeding." In Irving Louis Horowitz, ed., *The Use and Abuse of Social Science*, pp. 196–211. New Brunswick, N.J.: Transactionbooks.

Yin, Robert K. 1979. *Changing Urban Bureaucracies.* Lexington, Mass.: Lexington Books.

Zaltman, Gerald and Robert Duncan. 1977. *Strategies for Planned Change.* New York: Wiley.

Zaltman, Gerald, Robert Duncan, and J. Holbek. 1973. *Innovations and Organizations.* New York: Wiley.

Zaltman, Gerald, David Florio, and Linda Sikorski. 1977. *Dynamic Educational Change: Models, Strategies, Tactics, and Management.* New York: Free Press.

Znaniecki, Florian. 1940. *The Social Role of the Man of Knowledge.* New York: Columbia University Press.

Zurcher, Louis A. Jr. and Charles M. Bonjean. 1970. *Planned Social Intervention.* Scranton/London/Toronto: Chandler Publishing.

INDEX